Community Work and Social Action

Community Work and Social Action

Pradeep Kotwal

ADHYAYAN

ADHYAYAN PUBLISHERS & DISTRIBUTORS
NEW DELHI (INDIA)

Published by
ADHYAYAN PUBLISHERS & DISTRIBUTORS
4378/4B, 105, J.M.D. House, Murari Lal Street
Ansari Road Darya Ganj, New Delhi - 110002
Ph.: 011-23263018, 011-23277156, Fax: 011-23280028
Email: adhyayanpublishers@yahoo.com

Community Work and Social Action

Edition 2011
ISBN 978-81-8435-237-5

Printed in India

Published by Harish Chandra Yadav for Adhyayan Publishers & Distributors, Laser Typeseting at A.V. Rao and Printed at Tarun Offset Printers, Delhi

Preface

Community work involves work done by community based, non-profit or not-for-profit associations, whether they are incorporated or unincorporated. It occurs across a range of services including information and advice, counselling, advocacy and support—targeting an equally diverse range of people and areas of interest.

Community organisations are formal or informal groups of people based in or around a "community" and are organised in some way, usually having some structure, rules or legal entity but sometimes being just an informal association. Community workers are those who provide direct or indirect services to or for the benefit of members of the community. Some are paid, some are unpaid. We don't discriminate between paid and unpaid community workers other than where a necessary distinction needs to be made because of differences in law or policy.

Complexity in community sector systems presents a significant barrier to accessing services. It is important to ensure that you do not contribute to this complexity and make your service as accessible as possible. Community workers need to be aware of the need to remain client-focused and to ensure they are always talking to the client rather than third parties except where they might be taking instructions from a third party on behalf of the client, or by necessity talking to a third party about the client.

The dynamic field of community work continues to grow and become more complex. So it is essential to be familiar with the practices and trends in this field. Everyone who is associated with community work—from professor to student, from novice to experienced professional—should own this book for understanding the practices of community work and related disciplines.

Pradeep Kotwal

Contents

1

Introduction to Community Work

Community work can mean a range of things:

1. Being involved in local or neighbourhood groups or associations
2. Being a volunteer or unpaid worker
3. Being involved in a non-profit, not-for-profit, or charitable organisation or association
4. Doing public interest or public benefit work
5. Doing work for a "cause" or a "calling".

For the purposes of this book, community work involves work done by community based, non-profit or not-for-profit associations, whether they are incorporated or unincorporated.It is important to note that both employed staff and unpaid volunteers do community work. Community work occurs across a range of services including information and advice, counselling, advocacy and support — targeting an equally diverse range of people and areas of interest.

1.1. Emergence of Community Work

The term community work has a relatively short history in the United Kingdom. Nonetheless, the number of full-time practitioners who were described as being engaged in community work by the early 1980s was roughly equivalent to youth work or adult education. Then there appeared to be some 5,365 community workers, 60 per cent of which were employed in the voluntary sector. Since then there has been no substantial survey of community workers—and there have also been fundamental changes in the economic and institutional context in which they operate.

In this piece we explore: the emergence of community work in the UK; the impact of anti-poverty initiatives such as the Community Development Project in the late 1960s and early 1970s; the shape of work in the 1980s—here focusing upon the categorisation and definition of community work advanced by David Thomas in his book *The Making of Community Work*; and the state of practice in the 1990s and at the turn of the century.

In the late 1950s and early 1960s accounts of practice and theoretical explorations began to appear that viewed community workers as a distinct occupation. Prior to this there were separate groups of workers such as community centre wardens, secretaries of councils of social services and development workers on new housing estates, who did not possess a common occupational identity. The main orientation was to the educational. Not unexpectedly—given the process-focus of many of the key figures, and the institutional location of much of the funding and work. The *Younghusband Report* on social work was a significant turning point. It specifically drew on the North American division of social work into casework, group work and community organization, describing the latter as: primarily aimed at helping people within a local community to identify social needs, to consider the most effective ways of meeting these and to set about doing so, in so far as their available resources permit.

The first major collection of material took up the notion of 'community organization', but it was the terms 'community development' and 'community work' that became popular—and tended to merge. The term 'community development' was adopted by many U.K. workers and projects for work that focused on work with local neighbourhood groups to set and meet their own needs. The changes were symbolized in two initiatives—the setting up a study group by the Gulbenkian Foundation in 1966 to look at the nature and future of community work in the UK; and the development of the Community Development Projects by the Home Office as part of an anti-poverty strategy. We will look at both in turn.

The Gulbenkian Report was actually focused around training but inevitably spread its net much wider. Community work was taken to include:

— helping local people to decide, plan and take action to meet their own needs with the help of available outside resources;

— helping local services to become more effective, usable and accessible to those whose needs they are trying to meet;
— taking account of the interrelation between different services in planning for people;
— forecasting necessary adaptions to meet new social needs in constantly changing circumstances.

From this the committee concluded that community work had in it aspects of direct neighbourhood work, closer relations between services and people, inter-agency coordination, and planning and policy formulation. In a crucial section they argued:

> This community work function should be a recognised part of the professional practice of teachers, social workers, the clergy, health workers, architects, planners, administrators and others. In the modern conditions of social change it is also a necessary full time professional task.

The educationalists on the committee had argued for the conceptualization of community work as part of education—especially adult education. Their case rested on a belief that as an intervention it was fundamentally an educational or learning process, in fulfilment of which the use of specialist community workers was only one strategy Thus, the advancement of specialist workers—and the emphasis on the role of workers in making services more effective, and in planning, signalled a significant movement away from the educational position. Further, this report needs to be considered in conjunction with other shifts, especially in social work with the move to generic workers recommended by the Seebohm Report. There did appear to be a possibility that community work might become a key element of social work (mirroring the three strands of practice in the North American literature—casework, groupwork and community organization). Thomas argues that:

> The most profound effect of the demise of the educational influence was that the process goals of community work were not developed beyond the rudimentary expression they were given in the texts of the 1950s and 1960s... The educational aspects of intervention... have remained rooted in two narrow orthodoxies... The first... was that process goals became associated in the minds of the new practitioners of the 1970s only with changes in individual or personal

> development. The second orthodoxy was to identify process goals with the rhetoric of 'raising political consciousness'... The educational goals of community work embrace both these... but they are also much wider.

The opportunity was also lost of developing community work within community centres and the definition of community work continued to be tied to the particular issues of the day.

In Scotland, the position was a little different. Following the Alexander Repor and the establishment of a new local government structure community education services were formed in most regions. While a considerable amount of community work remained in social service departments in a number of regions, there has been a significant lobby for community development within community education. Significantly, bearing in mind our earlier comments concerning community associations, the linking of adult education with youth and community work, has meant that the educative core of community development has been asserted.

The process is educational. It is about people in communities creating opportunities for growth and change and deliberate movement towards the ends which they determine and in process of doing so increase their critical awareness, knowledge, skills and attitudes.

1.1.1. Community Development Projects

During the 1960s and early 1970s there was a growing recognition of the extent to which poverty remained a major feature of UK society. There had also been a fairly substantial series of debates around the significance and importance of people's participation in various aspects of government activity—perhaps the best known being the Skeffington Report on planning. Following the efforts of the Democratic administration in the United States of America to wage a 'War on Poverty', the UK government sought a similar, but cheaper, initiative. Self-help and resident participation were seen to be possibilities for the improvement of inner city situations.

The result, in 1969, was the launch of the Community Development Projects programme. It was the largest action-research project ever funded by government. The avowed intention was to gather information about the impact of existing social policies and services and to encourage innovation and co-ordination. The projects had a strong and explicit research focus and an emphasis on social action 'as a means of creating more responsive local services and of encouraging self help'. The projects were initially based in 12 areas of social deprivation. These were neighbourhoods of 3,000 to 15,000 people. Each project involved a small group of professional workers and researchers. The emphasis in CDPs on research meant that they produced a range of important material both about the nature of community work and about the social, political and economic condition of particular areas.

Workers in many of the projects came to reject the analysis and strategies of the original project proposals. They sought to organise and research around larger questions of inequality and deindustrialisation rather than more localized concerns around community organization. There was often a desire to bring about a much stronger link between the struggles of the workplace and those of the neighbourhood and community; and to develop means by which groups can join together in things like federations to better influence decision making on a city-wide, regional and national basis.

In some respects, the optimism and enthusiasm with which community work and 'participation' were greeted in the early 1970s and late 1960s waned with the realisation that many of the issues the work sought to confront were not resolvable at the local level—a realisation that was underlined by the widespread public expenditure cuts after the oil crisis of 1974. There was a considerable growth in the political awareness of community workers in the mid to late 1970s and this has been reflected in the adoption by workers of very different ideological stances. This is sometimes represented by the contrasting of so called social work or community development traditions of practice, with political action traditions:

> The former focused on the community as a social unit or organism, and was concerned with so called 'soft' issues such as social disorganisation and the need to build up networks and resources. The 'political action tradition' identified the community as a political unit, and emphasised 'hard' issues such as oppression and

> powerlessness. People associated themselves with each tradition, and each was thought to have its own particular organising styles and methods ('consensual' and 'conflict').

Three further dynamics were also at work: a more general movement away from associational and community group activity (perhaps best articulated in more recent years in the work of Robert Putnam); the rise of managerialism; and the coming to power of politicians who stressed market solutions. All can be seen in developments during the 1980s.

1.2. Community Work in 1980s

In the early 1980s another report sponsored by the Calouste Gulbenkian Foundation suggested that community work had three major aspects:

— First, to help people take action on specific issues of importance to them. These issues will almost invariably involve the influence of resources, either those held, for example, by local authorities, or to be found within communities themselves.

— Secondly, the development of political responsibility; and

— Thirdly, that of communal coherence.

1.2.1. Approaches in Community Work

David Thomas isolated five main strands or approaches in his study of community work in the early 1980s:Community Action focuses on the organisation of those adversely affected by the decisions, or non-decisions, of public and private bodies and by more general structural characteristics of society. The strategy aims to promote collective action to challenge existing socio-political and economic structures and processes, to explore and explain the power realities of people's situations and, through this twin pronged approach, develop both critical perspectives of the status quo and alternative bases of power and action.

Community development emphasises self-help, mutual support, the building up of neighbourhood integration, the development of neighbourhood capacities for problem-solving and self-representation, and the promotion of collective action to bring a community's preferences to the attention of political decision-makers.Social Planning is concerned with the assessment of community needs and problems and the systematic planning of strategies for meeting them. Social planning comprises the analysis of social conditions, social policies and agency services; the setting of goals and priorities; the design of service programmes and the mobilisation of appropriate resources; and the implementation and evaluation of services and programmes.Community Organisation involves the collaboration of separate community or welfare agencies with or without the additional participation of statutory authorities, in the promotion of joint initiatives.Service Extension is a strategy which seeks to extend agency operations and services by making them more relevant and accessible. This includes extending services into the community, giving these services and the staff who are responsible for them a physical presence in a neighbourhood.

In a sense these five approaches are far broader than 'community work'—especially the last, service extension. As David Thomas argues:

> The correct relationship is that community work is a contribution to each of these approaches and, perhaps more importantly, we need to be aware of the range of other contributions that are possible and desirable, and whose value may have been obscured by the attention given to community work.

The nature of community work had shifted. While some workers still had the freedom, and were disposed, to encourage opposition to the social and economic policies of the Conservative government in Britain—and their impact on local communities (especially with regard to the closure of heavy industries, engineering works and mines upon local communities); the context in which many were employed had changed. The language of managerialism had spread through many local authorities recasting much of the work in terms of meeting organizational objectives rather than local community needs. Most particularly, the focus was upon the more effective use of resources and the efficiency of services—especially with regard to housing and care. There was a significant shift away from locating workers in local neighbourhoods in order to sustain and develop local groups and associational life.

In many respects we have a clearer picture of local activity in Scotland than in England from this time. This is largely due to Alan Barr's (detailed account of practice in Strathclyde. He brought out a number of significant elements. However, two things in particular stand out. The first is the emphasis on community development and process that the workers studied still had (in contrast with the context in which they were working). This may flow, in part, from the particular cultural, political and social situation in Scotland and the focus that community education provides. That said, the work was located in a social work department; and it is likely that a number of community workers in other parts of the UK would have assented to these concerns at this time. The second, and endearing, feature of this research is that it brings out a great deal of the routine day-to-day activities that go to make up jobs such as ours. One of the significant features here is the relatively low amount of face-to-face work undertaken by senior workers as compared to their assistants.

1.3. Community Work in 1990s

By the early 1990s the position of community development work had become a little battered and activity was reduced The squeeze on public expenditure; moves to curtail the activities of local authorities (and even to abolish some—such as the Greater London Council); continued high levels of unemployment and poverty; and movements into community care had all acted to alter the face of the work. As Butcher argued at the beginning of the decade, 'community work' was going through considerable change and redefinition.

By the mid-1990s it was clear that community work approaches were being further harnessed to the development of centrally planned initiatives such as community care; and have become less the province of the traditional concerns of community organization and development. Where people have been able to hang on to some of these concerns—as perhaps has been the case in a number of the rural community initiatives—the emphasis was arguably less on fostering democracy than on facilitating enterprise, holding onto local services such as post offices and pubs, and on developing social provision such as housing. There has also been a flurry of interest in rural work and in children's work.

Instead of looking to community work as an organizing idea, a number of people started to talk of community practice. In other words, various areas of work can be seen to have a 'community dimension' and that we need to do is look at the ways in which ideas of 'community' permeate public and social policies and can be used to create alternatives.

A further shift in the rhetoric of community development emerged in the mid-1990's with the turn to 'capacity building'. Skinner defines capacity building as follows:

> Development work that strengthens the ability of community organizations and groups to build their structures, systems, people and skills so that they are better able to define and achieve their objectives and engage in consultation and planning, manage community projects and take part in partnerships and community enterprises.

It includes aspects of training, organizational and personal development and resource building, organized in a planned and self-conscious manner, reflecting the principles of empowerment and equality.

The language and direction of 'capacity-building' fitted in with moves toward a greater concern with economic development and planning—although a number of those interested in promoting are aware of some of its limitations. It was deeply inscribed with a technicist orientation—and was a long way from the more radical concerns of community workers in the early 1970s.

The radical tradition has kept alive (in the literature at least—see the material on community participation in particular). Cooke and Shaw argued for the re-etablishment of the value of and direction of radical community work—but freedom of movement remained limited for many practitioners—and much of the writing remained caught up in the theoretical concerns of the early 1970s.

1.4. Community Work Today

State-sponsored community work remains largely locked into the mix of care, economic development and service delivery improvement work that developed during the 1980s and 1990s. However, three particular areas of state-sponsored work did, to some limited extent, bring a stronger emphasis upon community-based organization and group-functioning in England. First, the emergence and growth of tenant management organizations has led to some attention being given to the cultivation of local groups and the deepening of their capacity to develop and run their own organizations. However, this has not been without tensions. In particular local authorities have tended to see tenant management organizations as extensions of their management activity whilst those involved are more likely to see themselves as community activists. They have also tended to see them as rivals. The result was that those employed to facilitate the development of tenant's management organizations and cooperatives often slipped into either representing the view or policies of the local authority to the group or advising them on the technicalities of housing finance funding. The enhancement of local group life was commonly sidelined into a series of courses on 'how to chair a committee' and such like.

Second, the *New Deal for Communities* Programme in England—part of the government's strategy to 'tackle multiple disadvantage in the most deprived neighbourhoods'—has involved an emphasis upon local community involvement. However, results from the interim evaluation of the initiative indicate that there is only patchy evidence of increased participation in local networks, neighbourliness and involvement in local groups. In contrast, there does appear to have been a significant increase in the trust invested by local residents in local institutions. As the evaluators stressed, community involvement and engagement takes time.

Third, the *Sure Start* programme, originally announced in 1998 and aimed at increasing the quality and availability of child care in selected areas in England, improving the health and well-being of children, and providing support for parents initially involved a significant emphasis upon community development and involvement. Some interesting and apparently successful locally-based work emerged. A strong case was made for this by Norman Glass and others involved in the development of the programme on the grounds that:

> ... it was necessary, in the case of early years at any rate, to involve local people fully in the development and management of the

> programme if it was to take root and not simply be seen as another quick fix by middle-class social engineers. "What works" is important, but "how it works", at least in this policy area, is equally, if not more, important.

If people 'owned' programmes it was argued, then they would both be more likely to address relevant needs and to engage people. However, the community development orientation also contributed to the effective abolition of the programme.

Community development takes time. Disadvantaged communities have to be persuaded to participate, and their natural suspicion leads them to hang back until there is something to show. So the "local" Sure Start programmes have always been behind schedule, and—a mortal sin under New Labour—underspent.

The governments desire to rapidly extend the programme as part of a larger strategy around child care and parenting involved the establishment of large numbers of children's centres within what was termed a 'children's trust approach' and the development of interdisciplinary professional teams. The patient, and it was argued, ultimately rewarding business of community development and full participation did not fit in with such a model.

The main carrier of a concern to cultivate community coherence and local group life in England and Wales at least, were churches and religious groups. The numbers of youth workers employed by local churches had increased significantly during the 1990s and alongside it there had also been a noticeable emphasis placed upon community development. In part this was linked to the need to encourage better use of church buildings and facilities—but there was also a strong theological argument for attention to community life beyond that of the church. A number of Methodist churches, for example, used a community centre model around which to base their activities. Within, and associated with, mosques there developed a significant range of welfare and other networks and services.

In Scotland, the picture was a little different. The community education tradition remained reasonable strong and vocal—adopting, in significant part, the language of community learning. In a Scottish Executive paper this was defined as 'informal learning and social development work with individuals and groups in their communities.

The aim of this work is to strengthen communities by improving people's knowledge, skills and confidence, organisational ability and resources'. The paper continued, 'Community learning and development makes an important contribution towards promoting lifelong learning, social inclusion and active citizenship'. There is a real sense in which the educational role of community development had not been lost.

One further important element came into play in terms of debates about policy—social capital. Significant press attention was given to Putnam's arguments around the diminution of social capital in the USA (and the impact this had upon people's health, education and happiness). It also encouraged some important debates within academic and policy circles (see lifelong learning and social capital). While there has been some exploration of what a concern with deepening social capital might mean in terms of work in communities it has been, on the whole, rather disappointing. Part of the problem is that it entails policymakers and practitioners entertaining and making sense of issues within a markedly different frame of reference than that which dominates discussion and policy today.

References

Jones, D. and Mayo, M. eds. 1974. *Community Work One*, London: Routledge and Kegan Paul.

Kelly, T. 1970. *A History of Adult Education in Great Britain. From the Middle Ages to the Twentieth Century*, Liverpool: Liverpool University Press.

Kuenstler, P. ed. 1961. *Community Organization in Great Britain*, London: Faber and Faber.

Leaper, R. A. B. 1968. *Community Work. Common ground explored in an experimental course*, London: National Council of Social Service.

Loney, M. 1983. *Community Against Government. The British Community Development Project 1968-78: a study of government incompetence*. Heinemann.

Lupton, R. D. 2005. *Renewing the City: Reflections on Community Development and Urban Renewal*, London: InterVarsity Press. 240 pages.

2

Community Workers and Clients

Community workers are those who provide direct or indirect services to or for the benefit of members of the community. Some are paid, some are unpaid. We don't discriminate between paid and unpaid community workers other than where a necessary distinction needs to be made because of differences in law or policy. For example, the issue surrounding legal liability for actions of paid community workers differs for those engaged in purely unpaid or volunteer work.As an example, community legal centres provide direct client services through a mixed model of employed staff (lawyers, social workers and paralegals), volunteer lawyers (usually at evening advice sessions) and other volunteers (committee members, students). Therefore, the volunteer at an evening advice session is engaging in community work even though they are employed elsewhere, perhaps in private legal practice. Likewise, individuals who voluntarily staff telephone-counselling lines are engaging in community work.

Characteristics which help to define community workers or the way they work or practise may include a combination of one or more of the following:

— qualifications (formal or informal)
— position or job descriptions or duty statements
— experience
— membership (professional or otherwise)
— whether they are a volunteer or not.

2.1. Qualifications of Community Workers

Community workers have many and varied qualifications. Qualifications includes all relevant qualifications from secondary and tertiary education providers, including:

— secondary schools and colleges
— colleges
— universities
— private education providers
— registered training organisations (RTOs).

Community workers carry a range of qualifications, not necessarily related to the work they do. Some obvious examples include individuals with tertiary (university or other) qualifications in:

— social work
— social sciences
— community welfare
— counselling
— psychology
— occupational therapy
— physiotherapy
— nursing.

These areas are often called the caring professions. Community workers may hold other types of qualifications such as in law, teaching or child-care, or even music, art and science.

Organisations may not be readily recognisable as being community based. For example community legal centres and other community based legal services are often perceived as being closer to private for profit businesses than non-profit associations simply because of the work they do. Community legal centres employ lawyers who are admitted to legal practise and who engage in community legal work. Though not perhaps immediately recognisable as community workers, these lawyers undertake similar work to people in counselling and support roles. They call themselves "community lawyers" and their work "community law".

2.2. Experience of Community Workers

Community workers are often defined by their experience in a particular field, regardless of whether they have formal qualifications. Experience counts for a lot in most areas of community work and some examples include work with:

— people with disability in provision of care or lifestyle support

— young people in residential care

— relationships, couples

— victims of crime, family or domestic violence.

Community workers who engage in "para-legal" work are good examples of this:

— organisations who provide services to victims of domestic violence employ staff who have experience in providing a range of services but who do not have formal qualifications.

— community legal centres employ non legally qualified staff who act as para-legals to provide legal information and assistance. These staff work alongside qualified staff to provide services to the target client group.

2.3. Employment Conditions

Community workers are often described by their position or job description, for example:

— community development officers

— welfare officers

— disability support workers

— community resource workers

— caseworkers.

Organisations often employ a range of staff to provide the services that are offered. Some organisations use generic terms, whereas others will use their own terms, titles or descriptions. The position descriptions and titles can also be influenced by the nature of the organisation. For example, one organisation might call a worker a counsellor, whereas another might use support worker or advocate even though the workers may do the same work, or even be funded under the same or similar program.

Community legal centres often employ non-legal staff to assist clients with information, advice, counselling and advocacy services. These positions include community development workers, financial counsellors, caseworkers etc.

Like the range of position descriptions that exist, community workers are employed in a range of ways, including:

— Under an employment contract: at the simplest level, community workers are employed under a contract with their employer which sets out the terms and conditions of their employment
— Under awards: the most common awards are: Social and Community Services Award (SACS Award)
— Under agreements: the most common agreements are: Enterprise Bargain Agreements (EBAs) and Certified Agreements (CAs) filed with the Queensland Industrial Relations Commission.

2.4. Membership of Community Workers

Community workers can sometimes be described to some extent by their membership of a particular organisation. These organisations range from unions, professional associations, societies, trades associations etc.There are important distinctions between the role played by the various organisations. Some of these bodies such as unions play a support and advocacy role whereas as others such as professional associations can be involved in regulatory and disciplinary actions. Sometimes membership is compulsory, at other times membership may be voluntary.

2.5. Clients

Clients are members of the public who seek services from community organisations. Clients may also be referred to as:

— customers
— consumers
— patients

— service users.

The name given within each service or organisation can be influenced by a range of factors including adoption of political, corporate or academic language, historical changes in language or terminology, political correctness, funding agreements or professional or other relevant practice frameworks.

Clients come from all over the place, including:

— referrals
— word of mouth
— advertising
— service directories.

Mistakes in referral are easily made. For example, financial counsellors regularly get referrals from people seeking financial advice or financial planning when they actually offer financial counselling. There is a considerable distinction here. Firstly, those who seek advice or planning often have money to invest whereas as those who seek counselling do not.Inappropriate referrals are problematic for a number of reasons:

— the client cannot obtain the services they seek, want or need
— the client's expectations cannot be met
— the client may be angry about the referral roundabout
— the client may make a complaint
— the referral is wasteful of the organisation's time and resources.

For all of these reasons, it is important to have a referral policy. At its simplest a referral policy includes the following points:

— what types of services are offered?
— what is the extent of those services?
— what services are not offered?
— whether the services are targeted at a particular group (e.g. a particular group within victims of crime is women who are victims of domestic violence)
— the requirements of any referral (e.g. does it need to be in writing or by telephone? what information needs to be included?)

2.6. Cost Service

If an organisation is receiving large numbers of inappropriate referrals, it may be wise to keep records on these referrals so action can be taken to remedy the problem. Policies on a range of issues that make clear to prospective clients and referring agencies what services are offered and what they can expect from your organisation may include but are not limited to:

— General information such as location, contact details, business hours etc

— Client Referral policy

— Casework guidelines

— Fees and charges guidelines

— Grievance and dispute policies

— Any codes of conduct or ethics that are relevant.

It's worth considering that clients don't always come because they want assistance. They may be referred because they need assistance despite their unwillingeness to get help. They may be subject of a mandatory referral from the Courts or another agency. Clients who access Job Network agencies may do so because they are required to do so in order to continue to receive social security payments.

Clients who access counselling services sometimes do so because it has been ordered by a judge.Some clients who do self-refer may not have a commitment to the service and may see accessing the service as a means to an end. For example, clients within the family law system sometimes access mediation services as a step in the process simply because they have to show they have taken that dispute resolution step.

Complexity in community sector systems presents a significant barrier to accessing services. It is important to ensure that you do not contribute to this complexity and make your service as accessible as possible.Community workers need to be aware of the need to remain client-focused and to ensure they are always talking to the client rather than third parties except where they might be taking instructions from a third party on behalf of the client, or by necessity talking to a third party about the client.

2.7. Community Worker-Client Relationship

The community worker client relationship is a complex one, often subject to legislative rules, ethical or conduct regimes and other considerations. In this section we look at the separate components that make up the client relationship.

2.7.1. Retainer

A retainer is a term given to describe a contract for services between a professional and their client. Retainers are known by a range of terms:

— client retainer

— client agreement

— service contract.

Regardless of what term is used to describe the agreement between client and community organisation, the law would most likely recognise it as a retainer. Services offered by community organisations are probably no different from any other services such as hairdressers, plumbers, carpenters etc.The significance of a retainer is that it describes what services are going to be provided by the professional to the client. The fact that no money passes hands for the services may not affect the existence of a retainer. The scope of the retainer is significant because it sets up the expectation that the client takes away with them after they leave the office. The scope of the retainer is important for a number of reasons:

— it establishes the terms of the contract for services between the worker and client

— it establishes the extent of any duty of care owed by the worker to the client

— it establishes whether a community worker has breached relevant codes, policies, rules or laws

— it may be relevant to professional regulatory or disciplinary proceedings

— it may be relevant to internal industrial disputes.

Although few community workers are sued for negligence or breach of contract, it does happen from time to time. Duty of care has become something of a bogeyman for community workers, rarely encountered but frightening nonetheless. The retainer, when utilised, may assist to clarify some points of potential future contention, including:

— how personal records are dealt with including relevance of privacy laws
— the relevance of mandatory reporting laws
— the circumstances in which confidence can be breached.

For example, if a community worker agrees to undertake a certain piece of work for a client, say the drafting of a letter on their behalf, and they fail to do that work they have breached the contract between themselves and the client. Additionally, they may have breached their duty of care to the client and may be found to have been be negligent as well. When considering the use of a retainer or similar client agreement, ask yourself:

— Is there a standard form of client agreement used?
— What does the client agreement contain?
— Do client agreements need to differ in specific cases, and if so, how?
— Does the client agreement mention issues such as privacy, mandatory reporting, and has the client been made aware what happens to their records, including storage and data transmission to funding bodies?

Importantly, the retainer establishes the expectations of the parties about what is going to be done and thereby achieved.

2.7.2. Limiting the Scope

The confines of the retainer are the most important part in establishing expectations and limiting liability. There is clearly a huge amount of variation between what community organisations do for their clients so therefore the range of retainers between community workers and their clients varies greatly.

For example community organisations that offer counselling and support services to people with relationship issues may each provide a different combination of one or more of the following:

- information to clients
- non-professional support for clients
- ongoing professional counselling or therapy for clients
- primary dispute resolution services for clients
- crisis counselling for clients
- advice for clients.

Each of the services offered by an organisation usually sets up a different retainer with a client in that it sets up different terms of service between community organisation (and worker) and client, in particular being different:

- types of assistance
- durations of assistance
- methods of service delivery
- requirements for qualification, accreditation
- professional, ethical and conduct obligations.

Being clear about what work is going to be done is the key to managing expectations between community workers and clients. This includes clients expectations before, during and after your work with them. Issues that need to be discussed with a client are varied and may include:

- the nature of the services to be provided
- whether the contract is time-restricted or open- ended
- whether the services are contingent on other happenings
- whether information or documentation is required to ensure the services can be delivered
- whether the services are offered under a service agreement or for another party
- whether there are any fees associated with the services
- whether there are any relevant legislative standards.

2.7.3. Conflicts of Interest

A conflict of interest may occur when a person allows a personal interest to clash with a public duty. Acting in conflict of interest is to act unethically and sometimes unlawfully. In a general way, acting in conflict of interest calls into question the trust and confidence that the public needs to put in service providers, particularly those who suggest they are independent, unbiased and non-partisan.Examples of unethical and unlawful acts in conflict of interest might be where a city councillor takes a monetary payment in exchange for confidential information, or where a community worker takes a substantial gift in exchange for provision of services not normally available.When considering conflicts of interests for your organisation and its community workers, ask yourselves:

— does your organisation have a policy on conflicts of interest?
— does your organisation have particular policies on conflict situations?
— has a risk assessment been carried out to identify possible areas of conflict?
— has the outcomes of the risk assessment been addressed and implemented?
— is risk assessment undertaken in an ongoing way?
— do you have policies on misuse of confidential client information?
— do you have policies on non-declaration of relevant personal interests?
— do you have policies on unsanctioned acceptance of gifts and/or monetary payments?
— do you have policies on misuse of business property?

2.7.3.1. Specific conflicts

Specific conflicts might include:

— misuse of confidential client information
— non-declaration of relevant personal interests
— unsanctioned acceptance of gifts and/or monetary payments
— misuse of business property.

A checklist of things to do to help ensure against conflicts of interest would include:

- identifying relevant codes, rules, and by-laws
- ensuring that workplace policies accord with relevant codes
- ensuring that your organisation has a process to assess client conflicts
- identifying who is responsible for assessment and reporting
- identifying if there are professional supports or advisers available
- do you need to advise in writing.
- how can you advise without breaching confidence

2.7.4. Capacity Issues

Capacity issues can arise because of a number of issues, including cases where clients who have impaired capacity for reasons such as intellectual disability, psychiatric disability or lack decision-making capacity for reasons of their young age, such as children. Capacity issues can affect a client's ability to enter contracts, to understand advice and information or to provide instructions and information. When faced with a person with capacity issues, ask yourselves:

- has the impaired capacity been assessed properly?
- do you adequately understand the principles that apply to those with impaired capacity?
- are there any relevant powers of attorney in place, including general powers of attorney, enduring powers of attorney, statutory health attorneys? If so, can the appropriate documentation be produced
- is the power of attorney (if any) properly made?
- is the Guardianship and Administration Tribunal involved?
- is the Public Trustee involved?
- is the Adult Guardian involved?

2.7.5. Liability

Liability can arise in a range of ways, including:

- liability under statute

— liability in contract
— liability in tort
— liability in equity
— criminal liability
— vicarious liability

Liability can also arise for a range of losses including personal injuries and economic loss. Generally speaking, where one of the parties fails to keep their end of the agreement issues of liability for breach of contract can arise.In the case of professionals, the test for liability applied depends on whether a claim is under common law or statute.

A professional does not breach a duty arising from the provision of a professional service if it is established that the professional acted in a way that (at the time the service was provided) was widely accepted by peer professional opinion by a significant number of respected practitioners in the field as competent professional practice.

References

Van Rees, W. *et al.* 1991. *A Survey of Contemporary Community Development in Europe*, The Hague: 7 Opbouwteksten. Alinsky, S. D. 1946. *Reveille for Radicals*. 1969 edn.), New York: Random House.

Willmott, P. 1963. *The Evolution of a Community. A study of Dagenham after forty years*, London: Routledge & Kegan Paul.

Willmott, P. 1989. *Community Initiatives. Patterns and prospects*, London: Policy Studies Institute.

Young, A. F. and Ashton, E. T.(1956. *British Social Work in the Nineteenth Century*, London: Routledge and Kegan Paul.

Younghusband, E. L. 1959. *Report of the Working Party on Social Workers in the Local Authority Health and Welfare Services*, London: HMSO.

3

Social Work and Volunteerism

The historical relationship between social work and volunteerism can be divided into three discernable periods. Before we discuss the three periods, it's important to begin with a brief review of the underlying importance of volunteerism to society.

Volunteerism is crucial to society. More specifically, having the freedom to organize and participate in volunteer associations is vital to a functioning democracy. The more citizens involve themselves as volunteers, the closer they come to making the ideals of democracy a reality. In 1835, when Alex de Tocqueville visited the United States to study American democracy, he observed that the key that enabled the Americans to make democracy work was their disposition toward forming volunteer associations. Tocqueville commented on this unique aspect of American society: "Americans of all ages, all stations in life and all types of dispositions are forever forming [volunteer] associations. They are not only commercial and industrial associations in which they take part, but others of a thousand types—religion, moral, serious, futile, very general and very limited, immensely large and very minute". The propensity for forming volunteer associations in America began as an effort for survival.

In the seventeenth century, cooperative farm ventures were formed to assist with building construction, collective cattle herding, and labor sharing. Groups of volunteers would also work together to erect churches that would function both as places of worship and as meeting places for all types of community functions. Government took the form of voluntary town meetings where unpaid officials were selected to fulfill numerous roles such as clerks of the market, town criers, and surveyors of the highways. Although at first volunteer efforts did not formally address organized charity, as the population increased, benevolent societies formed to provide relief to the poor when families were unavailable to assist them. As these benevolent societies failed to meet the growing needs of the poor, they eventually began to regard the entire community as ultimately responsible for the care of the unfortunate. It was through the formation of volunteer associations, therefore, that the need for community social welfare was recognized.

During the eighteenth and nineteenth centuries, nearly every advance in society came about as a result of volunteerism. Volunteer societies formed to improve transportation, sanitation, communication, fire prevention, public safety, and education. Volunteer associations also advocated fair labor practices, especially concerning children; women's rights;

African Americans' rights; better medical practices; and humane treatment of the mentally ill and brought attention to the debilitating effects of. Ellis and Noyes even go so far as to suggest that nearly every social need recognized and addressed by the government was first recognized and advocated for by some volunteer effort. Even the social reform advances of the Progressive Era depended upon the volunteer collaboration between the lower and middle classes. Whereas their efforts had once been fueled by a need for survival, now the common thread of their collaboration was humanitarianism. During the Progressive Era, volunteer efforts worked toward encouraging the government to act "upon the public's civic alertness and will" and to temper the zealousness for economic prosperity with the protection of human rights.

3.1. Volunteerism and Origin of Social Work

The profession of social work owes its existence to volunteerism. Volunteers founded relief societies, children's homes, day care programs, recreation services, family and child welfare associations, and mental health associations. In other words, volunteers preceded social work in almost every field of practice. Many introductory texts on social work and social welfare recognize the profession's origin in volunteerism.

For example, Morales and Sheafor describe the beginning of social work as being "found in the extensive volunteer movement during the formative years of the United States". Most notably, the contributions of volunteers are recognized as essential to the development of the Charity Organization Society (COS) movement and the settlement house movement. It is in these two movements that the role of volunteerism is linked to the emergence of the social work profession. As a volunteer movement, the COS movement emerged to become a significant precursor to social work, representing the first efforts to serve poor people in a systematic way. Essentially the movement consisted of volunteers who assisted families in meeting their physical, economic, emotional, and spiritual needs.

In 1877 the Reverend S. Humphrey Gurteen established the first COS in Buffalo, New York, to provide an alternative method to indiscriminate giving for helping the poor. The proponents of COS worked to make philanthropic practices more systematic and efficient. The principle method to improve efficiency was volunteer cooperation. COS organizations usually consisted of an executive council of volunteer leaders who were already actively engaged in providing services to the poor. Moreover, the council trained direct service volunteers, commonly referred to as "family visitors," to screen applicants, conduct family histories, and manage cases to make informed choices about the best ways to provide support. The settlement house movement also emerged from the efforts of volunteers. As a volunteer member of the Woman's City Club of Chicago, Jane Addams turned an old and battered building into Hull-House.

The Hull-House Woman's Club would become one of the largest women's volunteer clubs in the city of Chicago. Addams acknowledged the value of the women's volunteer clubs, saying, "The entire organization of the social life at Hull House, while it has been fostered and directed by residents and others, has been largely pushed and vitalized from within by the club members themselves". More specifically, it was within the context of her membership in these clubs that Addams was able to encourage fellowship among women of different ethnicities, connect residents of Hull-House with better housing, and advocate improved conditions within Chicago's city jails.

The COS and settlement house movements characterized the shift away from individual and volunteer philanthropy toward scientific charity. As people such as Mary Richmond, Josephine Shaw Lowell, Robert Hunter, and Edward Devine recognized the importance of comprehensive assessments, clear record keeping, and effective coordination of services, there was a growing recognition of the need for people to be professionally trained to work with the poor and needy. Professional training, however, was never intended to replace individual concerns and volunteer efforts. In fact, Mary Richmond believed that social workers could never completely stand in as the social servants of the community. She believed instead that a basic responsibility of the social work profession was to guide and support the efforts of volunteers.

As the delivery of services became more systematic, however, Richmond's reminder and Addams's example of the importance of reciprocal partnerships between professional helpers and volunteers were quickly forgotten. By the time President Roosevelt's administration enacted the New Deal, the government had become primarily responsible for social welfare services, and social work became the primary profession in the provision of these services. Trattner summarizes the shift in the relationship this way:

The devaluation of volunteers did not take the form of outright rejection, largely because of the long tradition of volunteerism in social welfare and because professional social workers needed the power, influence, and financial help of volunteers. What occurred, then, was a reversal of roles. Whereas earlier what was considered the real work of the agency, friendly visiting, was conducted by volunteers and the menial labor by paid staff members, by the turn of the century, the opposite was beginning to occur; volunteers did the office work or, by serving as trustees helped shape policy and raise funds, while the work in the field, casework, was in the hands of paid professional agents. Viewed earlier as a civic duty, volunteerism became, instead, a privilege granted by agencies to those who accepted their authority and discipline.

Of course, the social work profession did not abandon ties with volunteerism altogether. Instead, as Trattner points out, the relationship shifted. Cnaan accurately depicts the relationship as one in which social workers develop and deliver systematic and professional services while volunteers provide a hidden safety net. Indeed, during certain critical periods, social workers have enlisted the help of volunteers. During the Great Depressicn and World War II, social workers turned to volunteers as necessary personnel for addressing social needs. In the 1950s, vclunteers were partners in auxiliary social work services, helping as fundraisers, educators, office assistants, and drivers. In the 1960s, some volunteers moved into direct service roles, offering lay therapy in child abuse and neglect programs, counseling on telephone crisis lines, advocating in domestic violence programs, and participating in self-help and mutual aid groups.

More recently, in response to the shortage of professionals available, social work is again turning to volunteers, this time asking them to fill many traditional social work jobs. The idea is that if properly trained and supervised, volunteers can fill in and allow professional social workers to focus on the more complex aspects of practices.

Reviewing the three periods in the relationship between social work and volunteerism only illustrates the shift that occurred. They do not explain what caused the shift in the relationship. At some point, however, something must have happened to make social work want to separate and distinguish itself from volunteerism. The answer is found in the 1915 proceedings of the forty-second annual session of the National Conference of Charities and Corrections—a precursor to the National Association of Social Workers.

3.2. Flexner's Analysis of Social Work

At the 1915 NCCC conference, Abraham Flexner, an accepted authority on the study of professions, was invited to present an analysis of whether social work was a profession. Apparently, the organizers assumed that Flexner's presentation would offer them assurance that social work was, or was about to become, a full-fledged profession similar to medicine, law, and engineering. They were not prepared for the possibility that he would draw the opposite conclusion.

At the beginning of his presentation, Flexner distinguished between the relative use of the term "professional" and the absolute use of the term "profession." To Flexner, the term "professional" loosely denotes a person who devotes his or her time to a specific activity, be it baseball, basketball, dancing, acting, bartending, or truck driving. In contrast, Flexner defined the term "profession" as a limited group of activities that meet a certain predetermined set of objective criteria. He spelled out six criteria that separate a profession from all other occupations. He then used the criteria to assess whether social work was a profession.

1. Professions involve activities that are essentially intellectual—the thinking process is the main instrument applied to address problems. Individuals who use their intelligence in their professional capacity are often held accountable for outcomes. To Flexner the activities of a social worker were definitely intellectual: "The worker must possess fine powers of analysis and discrimination, breadth and flexibility of sympathy, sound judgment, skill in utilizing whatever resources available, facility in devising new combinations. These operations are assuredly of intellectual quality".
2. Professions derive their own raw material from science and learning—the thinking process uses information specifically learned for the given field instead of drawing upon knowledge and experience that is easily accessible from general sources of information. Flexner indicated that social workers perform a mediating function with material developed by other fields instead of using raw material that they developed themselves. He questioned whether the social worker was a professional or the person who brought professional activity into action. He stated, "The very variety of the situations [a social worker] encounters compels him to be not a professional agent so much as the mediator invoking this or that professional agency".
3. Professions apply learning in a way that is practical—the thinking process and the development of raw knowledge have a clear-cut end that is recognized and sanctioned by society. To Flexner social work did not have definitive ends that distinguished it from other professions. He viewed social work as being in touch with many professions rather than a profession in and of itself. "It

appears not so much a definite field as an aspect of work in many fields".

4. Professions use a transmittable technique that requires education—there are specific objectives a practitioner must master before gaining entry into the profession. In addition, there is an agreed-upon standard for the admission requirements and the content and length of education. Flexner viewed the fields of social work as too numerous and diverse to constitute a single educational discipline. Although he determined schools of social work to be important, he posited that the content was not technically professional. Instead, he characterized the education of social workers as supplemental and "broadly cultural in a variety of realms of civic and social interest".
5. Professions are self-organized—the activities of a profession are so definitive, so absorbing in interest, so richly engaging in duties and responsibilities that individuals and their families tend to organize around a strong nucleus. As Flexner pointed out in his presentation, the annual conferences testified to the development of professional self-identity leading to selforganization.
6. Professions become increasingly altruistic in motivation—as time goes on, devotion to the common well-being of society becomes more and more an accepted mark of professional activities. Eventually the interests of individual practitioners of a given profession yield to the increasing realization of responsibility to the larger social environment. To Flexner, this was the one criterion in which social work exceeds most other occupations. Although he would not officially call social work a profession, he did acknowledge that social work's professional spirit, in many ways, was what mattered most. According to Flexner, "The unselfish devotion of those who have chosen to give themselves to making the world a fitter place to live in can fill social work with the professional spirit and thus to some extent lift it above all the distinctions which I have been at pains to make".

3.2.1. Sustained Impact of Flexner's Presentation

Flexner described social workers as intelligent, kindhearted, and resourceful people who perform an important mediating function. In his opinion, however, social work was not a profession. What happened thereafter, and still continues to occur, was an all-out attempt to demonstrate to colleagues, clients, society, and most importantly ourselves that social work was and is a profession. And if social work was to be considered a profession, there would have to be separation between the field of social work and the efforts of volunteerism. Social work thus abandoned its roots in its quest for professional status.

In the decades following Flexner's presentation, the focus of social work was dominated by its search for a knowledge base and practice methods. In its search, social work became infatuated with psychiatry and Freudian psychology, which conveniently offered two advantages in terms of achieving professional status. First, the use of psychiatry and Freudian psychology allowed social work to claim adherence to a specific knowledge base that would satisfy the gap pointed out by Flexner. Within a few years of his presentation, several leading social workers began promoting their new knowledge base. Eventually psychiatric social work emerged as a distinct field of practice, and Freudian psychology emerged as the primary theory in most areas of practice. Second, psychiatry and Freudian psychology offered social work the opportunity to associate its practice methods with the medical model of practice, thus elevating the status of social workers to that of trained experts providing treatment. Instead of emphasizing the larger environmental causes of poverty and other community problems, the scope of social work practice narrowed to more definable ends—providing services and treatment to enhance the well-being of individuals. Under the medical model, social workers essentially study the problems of their clients, diagnose the problems (or strengths, in the current perspective), and prescribe action steps to produce the desired outcome. Whether working in child and family services, foster care, mental health, substance abuse, or gerontology, the social worker today commonly equates practice with working directly with individual clients to enhance their well-being.

The prominence of the medical model remains evident in the NASW Code of Ethics. The code states, "Social workers' primary responsibility is to promote the well-being of clients". Furthermore, of the term "clients" is narrowly defined as individuals receiving treatment or services from trained social workers.

While the field's use of psychiatry and Freudian psychology helped to legitimize social work as a profession, Richmond's and Addams's belief that social workers could never completely stand in as the social servants of the community was forgotten.

On one hand, the profession blossomed during the twentieth century as social work secured its place as the primary profession in the development and provision of social services. On the other hand, several scholars suggest that social work has tended to focus primarily on individual needs while neglecting to pay adequate attention to the social and environmental factors that contribute to people's vulnerability, oppression, and poverty. For example, Brueggemann asserts that current social service organizations (the main employers of social workers) do not promote compassion, empathy, reciprocity, or asset building. Instead, the emphasis on social work licensing and systematic and efficiently run organizations has actually perpetuated social and economic injustice.

McKnight argues that the growth and professionalization of social work has become dependent upon there being enough people in need of services to validate the need for more social workers. For instance, he states that "We may have reached that point where there are more people in Chicago who derive income from serving the poor than there are poor people". He then raises the question, "Do [social workers] need the welfare clients more than the clients need their service?".

In the same vein, Specht and Courtney wonder if social work has abandoned its mission altogether. They point out that at a time when social problems have become more difficult and complex, too many social workers are practicing psychotherapy, and too many of them are in private practice. Meanwhile, instead of partnering with volunteers to define and address social problems, social work continues spending too much time and energy staking its claim as the profession that should be called upon to work with an ever-expanding list of populations. As we shall now discuss, there are two reasons why social work is wary of partnering with volunteers.

3.2.2. Insecurity

Almost a century after the 1915 NCCC annual convention, there are several outward signs that the profession of social work is undeniably secure. Foremost, the job outlook for trained social workers is more optimistic than that for all other human service professions. Social workers are the main providers of social welfare and mental health services in the United States and are represented in growing numbers in other fields, such as substance abuse, aging, schools, health, and employment assistance. Schools of social work have also increased in number. In 2003, there were over 450 BSW programs, almost 160 MSW programs, and 72 social work doctoral programs in North America. Moreover, state social work licensure laws and the work of large national membership associations such as the National Association of Social Work and the Council on Social Work Education have earned the publics recognition of social work as a profession. Despite these accomplishments, however, social workers continue to allow Flexner's presentation to raise doubts about our professional standing. As a result, the profession remains preoccupied with its ability to develop discipline-specific knowledge.

Social work simply does not have its own theoretical knowledge base. For example, systems theory emerged from the field of biology; the ecological perspective is derived from anthropology, sociology, and psychology; life course theory is rooted in psychology and sociology; and social exchange theory evolved from psychology, anthropology, and economics. Therefore, in this regard, Flexner was and is still correct in his assessment: the fields of professional social work are too numerous and diverse to identify or rely upon a single discipline-specific knowledge base. With this in mind, there are three important questions to consider concerning social work's relationship with volunteers: Should social workers continue searching for discipline-specific knowledge? Does social work need its own theoretical knowledge base to qualify as a profession? And how has social work's relationship with volunteers been affected by the profession's search for its own body of knowledge?

While social work has gained professional status by developing a unified code of ethics, establishing social work licensure and credentials, and implementing an agreed-upon criteria for social work education, it has been unable to develop a specialized body of knowledge. The inability to develop knowledge that is unique to social work is not the result of a lack of effort. In fact, many social workers remain preoccupied with the search. In some cases, social workers have attempted to claim different theories to be primary to social work practice. For example, Robinson advocated the psychoanalytic contributions to social work practice, Hollis the psychosocial approach, Smalley the functional approach, Thomas behavioral modification, and Saleebey the strengths perspective. Nevertheless, each theoretical framework is ultimately rooted in knowledge developed by another field. Other social workers have attempted to develop a unique social work knowledge base through scientific research. For example, Thyer candidly admits having spent his entire career searching for social work's unique knowledge base. After twenty-five years, he has reluctantly come to the conclusion that it is impossible to identify unique social work contributions in any given area of practice research.

The fact that social work cannot claim a unique theoretical knowledge base doesn't necessarily mean social work is not a profession. What it does mean is that the profession must decide how much credence it will continue to give to Flexner's presentation. The time has come for social work to leave Flexner behind. By all other indicators, social work is seen by society as a profession. There is no need for social work to continue evaluating its status other than for self-serving purposes. Yet at various points over the past three decades, major social work journals have published articles and entire issues dedicated to assessing social work's professional status. In each case there is usually some mention of Flexner's influence on the profession and in some cases his presentation is the focal point.

Flexner himself questioned his own ability to assess social work. He admitted that his knowledge was too limited, and he doubted his competency in drawing a valid conclusion. Moreover, his six criteria represent only one approach to assessing professional status—an approach based upon a medical model of practice that emphasizes specialization. Social work will never meet this criteria because its focus is the antithesis of specialization. Instead, social work is a profession that applies theories derived from other fields to enhance the well-being of individuals and advocate socially and economically just societies. Social work needs to abandon its preoccupation with identifying a discipline-specific body of knowledge, accept its position as an applied profession, and begin steering all its attention toward interdisciplinary efforts to develop knowledge that will help address specific social problems. The lack of a unified knowledge base and the preoccupation with finding or claiming one have left social work insecure about its professional status.

Gambrill suggests the profession's insecurity is evident in its reliance on information that is authority based rather than evidence based. As a result, social work remains apprehensive about expanding its relationship with volunteers because it fears it could jeopardize its professional status in society. In the same way, the social work profession has attempted to define itself as separate from its volunteer origins. Partnering with volunteers to deliver services and address social problems gives volunteers access to the social welfare turf that the profession has worked so hard to establish for itself and threatens the profession's perceived authority over that turf.

Gambrill explains that social work has been "bamboozling the public and those who fund service programs into believing that professionals offer unique services that require specialized training and experience". The reality is that social work interventions steeped in psychotherapeutic strategies and a medicalmodel approach, while serving to protect social work's professional status, are of limited use when it comes to addressing social problems that affect the most vulnerable and oppressed groups of people—the stated emphasis of the work of the profession. Partnering with volunteers is an alternative way for social workers to develop and deliver services. Social workers need to see volunteers as partners in their quest to bring about social change. Instead of practicing as experts providing care or as agents representing large social service bureaucracies, social workers can work side by side with volunteers, helping to support and direct them in the promotion of social and economic justice. Expanding practice with volunteers, however, will require social work to gain a level of confidence that will allow it to abandon its obsession with its professional status.

3.2.3. Avoidance

As a result of social work's professional insecurity, the profession has tended to avoid practice with volunteers. A decade after Flexner's presentation, Jane Addams recognized social work's fascination with psychiatry, psychotherapy, and the medical-model approach to practice. While acknowledging their professional benefits, she tried reminding her colleagues of the importance of working with volunteers. Speaking to her colleagues, she posited the following request: "I should like now to ask a favor of the psychiatric social workers. They are the newest and most popular group among us. They are taking great care of the individual who is brought to them, whether he comes as a free nursery child, or whether he comes from the courts. Perhaps we can ask them that they go outside of this individual analysis and give us a little social psychiatric work". She then reminded them that, from a clearly ethical point of view, social work must always involve partnering with people in the community who are closest to the poor and are living as best they can.

It appears very few social workers listened to Addams. In fact, a few years later, in a famous address to the 1929 National Conference of Social Work, Porter Lee, director of the New York School of Philanthropy, declared that training volunteers to lead and participate in social movements was no longer a function of social work. Instead, he suggested that social work's primary function was serving individuals through the use of primarily methods based on psychiatric and other psychotherapeutic interventions. His views represented the dominant position in the field. A quick glance at current employment trends indicate that his views are held by the majority of social workers today. Social workers are most likely to work in direct clinical roles that generally do not involve work with volunteers.

The profession as a whole continues to avoid social work practice with volunteers and to ignore both calls for more practice with volunteers and scholarship demonstrating the value of volunteers to the social work profession. Theilen and Poole have argued that volunteer associations are one of the most effective yet frequently overlooked avenues that social workers have to achieve social change. They suggest that social work educators need to cover content on volunteerism throughout the entire curriculum. Other scholars have suggested that the profession's emphasis on facilitating transactions between the person and the environment makes social workers well suited to educate, support, and partner with volunteers to develop and implement effective services. Moreover, a few social work scholars, such as Ram Cnaan and Robert Wineburg, have spent their careers teaching students to practice with volunteers. Both have published numerous articles and books imploring the social work community to appreciate the possibilities of working with volunteers. Considering the concerted bipartisan efforts to encourage more volunteerism and localize social welfare services, Wineburg laments that the social work community has "virtually ignored one of the most important changes to hit local human services systems in many years".

3.3. Duties of Volunteers

A volunteer is most commonly defined as someone who undertakes community service work of his or her own free will, without receiving a salary or wage in return. Both elements of this definition are important: individual *choice* and the fact that *no salary or wage is paid.*

What motivates people to volunteer has been the subject of many articles and books. Each identifies a variety of motives that lead people to volunteer, and emphasizes their importance. *Why* people volunteer is intimately and directly related to the kind of volunteer activity they undertake, its conditions and duration, their commitment to it, and the success or failure of the volunteer placement. It used to be awkward and, in some cases, unacceptable to talk about the numerous and often complex motives that draw people into volunteer activity. Many people felt — and some still feel — that 'real' or 'pure' volunteer work is done without any expectation or hope of any return or benefit, and that the only motive behind 'real' volunteer work is altruism — 'the unselfish regard for or devotion to the welfare of others'.

Today, more and more people agree that volunteers act out of many motives, that volunteer activity undertaken for other motives than altruism can be fruitful and meaningful, and that *all* volunteer effort involves some kind of exchange, even that which is based on altruism. Many Canadians volunteer because they believe it is the right thing to do. Their moral values, religious beliefs, or understanding of the nature of a community motivate them to assist others. The return or benefit they receive is the satisfaction of having fulfilled their moral, religious, civic, or altruistic responsibilities. This is a tangible benefit and should not be ignored or denied. But many Canadians volunteer for other reasons. In fact, most people volunteer for a mixture of reasons, *including* a belief that it is the right thing to do.

People volunteer because they understand that it is important for citizens to participate in the life of their communities, and that this work benefits *all* citizens, not just the 'poor and unfortunate'. Many volunteer to 'give something back', helping others in order to express their gratitude for help given to them or someone they love. Other people volunteer as a way to integrate into a new community or find their way back from tragedy by reaching out to others. Still others volunteer to meet people and build new relationships. A large and growing group of youngsters is turning to volunteer work for yet another reason: as part of their search for paid employment. Some individuals find their own way to volunteering; some are encouraged by other people, including employment counsellors, outplacement firms, therapists, friends, family members, and volunteers. The rest of this paper will examine what volunteer work has to offer those who are seeking a job, and how volunteer centres and agencies that engage volunteers can respond to this phenomenon.

What does volunteering have to do with employment at all? Though few in the voluntary sector would ask this question, others sometimes do. And what is really being asked is 'what has volunteering to do with *work*'? That the question is still asked underlines the fact that misunderstandings persist about the real nature, scope, and import of the work of volunteers.

Anyone who is a volunteer or works with volunteers knows that volunteer activity is real work —volunteers 'exert their strength and their faculties to accomplish something, to perform something, or to produce something'. We sometimes find it difficult to call this activity 'work' because the word *work* has become synonymous with *paid employment.*

In addition, professionals who deal with volunteers are deliberately careful about the use of the word 'work' when it is associated with volunteer activity, because volunteerism should never be promoted as a way to supplant or displace paid workers.

However, the negative effect of upholding this principle is the widespread misconception that volunteer work is peripheral, a frill, and of no real consequence to agencies, their clients, or to the community at large. This misunderstanding needs to be corrected.

Volunteers accomplish real work through their efforts. Sometimes the work supports, complements, and extends the work of paid staff, but often it is central to the purposes of the organizations they serve. For example, volunteers in hospitals support the work of the paid staff: doctors, nurses, and technicians. volunteers provide ancillary services and spend the kind of time with individuals that paid staff often cannot. On the other hand, volunteer Big Sisters and Big Brothers and telephone distress line volunteers provide the core services of their organizations, and are supported by paid staff. Volunteer activity for the most part is, and should be, real work. It should be activity that accomplishes something, performs something, or produces something; it should never be activity done without a purpose, to simply fill time. Volunteer work must be significant to the organization and its clients, and meaningful to the volunteer performing it. This is as true for people who volunteer as a means of enhancing their search for paid employment as it is for any other volunteer.

3.4. Volunteer Work and Health

About 10 years ago, the World Health Organization introduced a new definition of health, which is gradually gaining acceptance in our society. 'Health' no longer refers only to physical well-being and freedom from illness or disease. The new understanding of health is that it encompasses physical, social, emotional, mental, psychological, and spiritual well-being. The promotion of a holistic healthy lifestyle is widespread and growing, and includes encouraging people to stop doing things which harm health as well as promoting activities and lifestyle choices that improve health in all its aspects. Volunteering is one of these health-promoting activities, and its value to people who are looking for employment is significant.

The link between volunteering and health is real and tangible. Volunteers and those who work with them have always known this. The link has now been established in scientific research. It has been and is being documented and explored in studies. It is demonstrated daily in the life and work of volunteers. "Volunteering can generate a heightened sense of self-esteem, self-worth and confidence, reduce heart rate and blood pressure, increase endorphin production, resulting in greater feelings of well-being and calm, boost immune system and nervous system functioning, reduce life's stresses, and overcome social isolation." Looking for a job today can be a brutal experience. Individuals face a struggle that can crush self-esteem and erode self-confidence. Young people, regardless of their academic qualifications, often face a long drawn out search for a job that will allow them to use and develop their newly acquired skills and knowledge. People who have lost a job and are searching for new employment face that same market with an additional burden: many have been very badly hurt and shaken by losing a job in the first place. One of the most significant rewards that volunteering has to offer people — those seeking employment among them — is its health-enhancing properties, in particular the opportunity to build or rebuild confidence and self-esteem, to help restore perspective and change attitudes, and to reduce isolation by enlarging the volunteer's circle of acquaintances, contacts, and friends.

People who are unemployed often feel that they are not needed, that their skills are not wanted, that their contribution is irrelevant. Volunteer work — whether visiting a person who is shut in, running a special event, or writing copy for an agency newsletter — can change that. It can help establish or restore an individual's belief that he or she has something to offer, and that what they offer makes a difference — to other people, to organizations, and to themselves.

Calling on an individual's expertise, be it newly developed in school or seasoned by years of experience, can be a great boost to self-confidence and self-esteem. Putting their skills, knowledge, talents, and experience to work for your organization offers people an opportunity to exercise those skills, to feel that they are valuable and valued, and to test those skills in new ways. As a result, confidence in their own skills and expertise can grow. This confidence can enhance their job search in obvious ways; it may also enable and encourage them to explore other career paths.

One of the most difficult — indeed frightening — aspects of unemployment, especially long-term unemployment, can be the sense of a loss of control over one's own life, and over the future. Many people who are unemployed feel that they have few real choices, and little or no control. In addition, they are often left without the routines and discipline imposed by regular employment, routines and discipline that generally help people accomplish their goals. The absence of these can be frightening and debilitating. Volunteer work can help in several ways. Generally, people can determine what they want to do, how often, where, and under what circumstances. Having these choices offers them a measure of control and choice. Being responsible for a job, with goals, objectives, and deadlines can help them re-establish routines and selfdiscipline in their lives.

Volunteers often take on freestanding projects for agencies, seeing them through from planning through execution to evaluation. These opportunities can provide individuals with a significant sense of power and control: "There is work to be done, which I can do. I can make choices about whether or not to do it, and how to do it". This sense that one *has* choices and some measure of control over planning, strategy, and outcomes can enormously enhance an individual's self-esteem and sense of accomplishment.

Volunteers constantly say that 'they get more than they give through their volunteer work'. Often, they talk about coming away from the experience feeling great — physically, emotionally, intellectually, and socially recharged. This "helper's high", as it has been called, can be equally strong for those who come to volunteer work as part of their effort to find paid employment. The most important common characteristics of the work that produces this 'high' are that the work is freely chosen and not done as a result of coercion or pressure, and that it involves working with other people, rather than in isolation.

3.4.1. Physical Health

Opportunities to improve physical health through volunteering should be mentioned as well. Many volunteer placements include or focus on physical activity, for example, coaching baseball, taking kids swimming, running, walking, biking, or wheelchairing in fundraising events. These volunteer activities can enhance health in all the ways described above, and can help improve volunteer's physical fitness besides. The mind-body connection is well established: being physically fit helps people feel better about themselves.

Likewise, those who feel good about themselves are more likely to be physically active. The helper's high can affect physical as well as emotional health. "When the experiences of over 1,700 women who were involved regularly in helping others were analyzed at the Institute for the Advancement of Health in New York City, they revealed relief of actual physical ailments in the wake of the helping. Disorders such as headaches, loss of voice, pain due to lupus and multiple sclerosis, and depression improved." In short, volunteering provides opportunities for people to exercise body, brain and heart, and to significantly improve their health in all its facets.

3.5. Volunteer Work and Skills

Richard Bolles places volunteer skills into three categories: self-management skills, work-content skills, and functional or transferable, skills. Volunteering can help people gain, maintain, and enhance skills in each of these areas.

3.5.1. Self-Management Skills

Self-management skills are those which relate to the way we get along with others, deal with authority, govern our own behaviour, and accomplish things. Examples of self-management skills are resourcefulness, ingenuity, initiative, perseverance, loyalty, and dependability.

Clearly volunteer work can provide individuals with opportunities to test and develop these skills, since the work they are involved in often demands a search for ingenious ways to solve problems, and the taking of initiative when opportunities present themselves. Volunteers are integral members of the staff of organizations and are depended on to complete the tasks assigned to them

3.5.2. Work-Content or Specific-Content Skills

Work-content or specific-content skills are those which we use to "master a *particular* vocabulary, or procedure, or subject-matter." Examples of work-content skills are knowing a particular language.

being able to build or repair a computer, or knowing the rules of baseball. Many volunteers become involved in agencies whose work is unlike anything they are familiar with. In order to carry out their work, volunteers often must learn skills specific to their agency's work. A volunteer baseball coach must learn the rules of baseball; a volunteer on a distress line must learn the techniques and skills that will allow him or her to listen effectively and help someone in crisis. Volunteers in information centres must become familiar with the database systems that they will be accessing to provide information to the public. These skills are very specific to the job that is being done by the volunteer.

3.5.3. Functional Skills

Functional skills are those we use to work with "...the basic tangibles of the everyday world, namely: data (or information), people and things." Functional skills describe how people act upon, or work with, information, people, and things, irrespective of the setting in which we are working, and include skills such as supervision, negotiation, analysis, computation, consultation, mentoring, precision working, operating, handling, and exchanging information. For example, an individual may be a skilled supervisor. That skill, supervision, can be used in any number of settings. Likewise, analytical skills can be brought to bear on a wide variety of data in many settings.

3.5.4. Transferable Skills

Breaking down people's skills into categories like these and separating them from their association with a particular job allows individuals to look at the basic skills, which may be transferred from one job context to another, and from one field of work to another. This kind of analysis can identify what volunteer opportunities someone might be good at and which activities would engage and develop particular skills or skill sets, and can also help people identify different potential fields of employment. Voluntary sector organizations seek volunteers to expand their capacity as they strive to become more and more efficient and effective, to respond to growing demands, and to anticipate and plan for the future. Volunteers with specialized skills can complement this work while practising, developing, and maintaining their skills as they provide the organization's services to its clients. While we who work in the voluntary sector may take this fact for granted, many people are surprised by the range of volunteer jobs available, and by the types and levels of skill needed to accomplish those jobs. Indeed, the skills important in paid employment are often the same kind as are valued and sought for in volunteers. A few examples will illustrate the point.

3.5.4.1. Marketing

Voluntary sector agencies are concerned with enhancing and improving the marketing of their programs and services to their clients, government, and the public at large. People with newly acquired or seasoned skills in marketing can help agencies review their history, identify goals, audit their resources, and develop and help carry out a marketing plan.

3.5.4.2. Computerization/Electronic Exchange of Information

Most voluntary-sector agencies are either computerized or heading towards it, and are faced with a bewildering, often overwhelming array of choices and decisions.

People with expertise in the field of computers can help agencies decide what equipment and software they really need for present needs, where their organization is headed over the next five years, and what the most cost-effective decisions on acquisitions and training are likely to be over that time. In addition, volunteers with those skills can help set up the systems and train staff.

3.5.4.3. Administration/Management/Evaluation

A stereotype of the voluntary sector portrays non-profits and charities as entirely different from private sector companies. In fact, most agencies employ trained managers and are run in a business-like fashion according to accepted accounting principles. Nevertheless, many agencies could benefit from the expertise and knowledge of people trained in management, administration, and evaluation.

3.5.4.4. Library Organization/Research

Information is a critical component of the work of any organization.

Access to meaningful, comprehensive and easily understood information can greatly improve an agency's ability to provide service. Trained librarians and researchers can assist agencies in developing appropriate databases of information that can support, enhance, and even shape the way the agency does business. These four are rather obvious examples of the way volunteers can develop their skills while providing service to agencies and their clients. Other possibilities are not as obvious, but can be identified with a little effort.

An example: The purchasing manager of a manufacturing company is laid off. Few voluntary sector agencies need purchasing managers as such. However, his or her skills could be used by an organization to help rationalize and consolidate its purchasing practices for equipment and supplies. This volunteer could help a number of agencies develop a group purchasing mechanism, thereby improving efficiency and reducing costs. Or, he or she could help agencies that operate businesses to improve their purchasing decisions and inventory control. A completely different way to engage this person's skills would be to have the volunteer work with individual agency clients in preparing personal or family budgets. By identifying the various skills that the prospective volunteer possesses, he or she and the volunteer centre and the agencies involved can develop new and different ways to use those skills in volunteer work. The range of possible employment fields, and therefore of opportunities for the volunteer to explore, expands as well.

3.5.5. Skills Transferable from Volunteer to Paid Work

An American research project conducted in 1985 investigated job skill development in volunteer work through surveys and interviews with close to 1000 individuals. Respondents identified the following list of skills which they had developed or enhanced through their volunteer work:

— Arts and Crafts Skills
— Child Care Skills
— Clerical/Secretarial Skills
— Education Skills
— Financial Skills

— Health Care skills
— Household Skills
— Managerial Skills
— Mechanical Skills
— Public Policy Skills
— Public Relations Skills
— Research Skills
— Technical/Professional Skills

The 1987 National Survey on Voluntary Activity in Canada echoed these results, clearly identifying that "...learning new skills was an important feature of volunteer work for 3.4 million volunteers, or 70% of volunteers. These skills included technical and office skills, management and organizational skills, communications, interpersonal skills, fundraising, and increased knowledge of certain subjects and issues.

Many of the volunteers (353,000) could transfer the skills learned in their volunteer work directly to their paid jobs. As well, 44% of volunteers said it was important to them that volunteer work offered them an opportunity for improving their job possibilities."

3.6. Work Experience and Training

People looking for paid work, especially young people, are often frustrated in their search because employers are looking for people with experience. Of course, in order to gain experience, they must find work.

Volunteer activity listed on a résumé was once regarded only as an indication of good citizenship, not as a record of work experience, reflecting the stereotype that volunteer work was peripheral, a frill, nonessential. As volunteer work changes, involving people in more varied and complex activities, that view is changing as well. Both the public and the private sectors now recognize that volunteer work should be factored into the evaluation of a job candidate's skills, training, and experience. More and more often, employment application forms ask explicitly about volunteer experience. Many of them list it directly alongside paid work experience. Indeed, volunteer work on someone's résumé can often be a determining factor in college and university applications as well as in job competitions, especially if the qualifications of candidates are otherwise very similar.

Work experience in a volunteer placement can be every bit as rigorous and demanding as in the private sector. Volunteer work can provide real job experience, good, solid training, and opportunities for workers to innovate and experiment in ways that often aren't allowable in the regular job market. The transferable skills that individuals bring to their volunteer work can often be applied to a different work-context in the voluntary sector, in such a way that the agency, its clients, and the volunteer can all benefit. But this doesn't happen just by chance.

In order for volunteer work to provide meaningful work experience and training, placements must have the following characteristics:

— Volunteer placements must be well thought out and well designed;

— Volunteer job descriptions must be clear: the respective expectations, rights and responsibilities of volunteer and agency must be clear and agreed upon;

— Volunteers must be properly interviewed and matched with a placement, and they must be given an orientation on the organization;

— Volunteers must be given the training needed to accomplish the job they are doing, and should receive appropriate supervision and support from a trained volunteer manager, including regular feedback and evaluation;

— Where possible, volunteers should be offered opportunities to expand or modify their volunteer roles to develop new skills and expand their horizons.

Investing in training for volunteers is a sign that an agency truly values the contribution its volunteers are making. By offering training, or making it available to volunteers, agencies help ensure that their work is done well. It is also a way for agencies to recognize and thank volunteers for their efforts, and assist individuals in attaining their career goals.

3.6.1. Volunteer Work and Career Changing

As the world changes, so too do the skills, trades, and professions that employers are seeking. Consequently, many people who have lost a job and are looking for work face an added difficulty as they contemplate entirely different career and work options. This is also true of many people who are still employed, but want to change their line of work, as well as of those who are re-entering the job market after a period of absence. Volunteer work provides opportunities for all three groups. Volunteering has always given people a chance to do something entirely different from what they do at the 'office' all day (or all night). Accountants by day are volunteer drivers on the weekend; truck drivers teach swimming; law clerks design newsletters; factory workers are board members. What has changed is the number of people who are not just looking for something different to do with their leisure time, but for something different to do with their lives, during their remaining years of paid employment.

Volunteer work provides an opportunity for people to test their interests, to experiment, to discover whether or not they are really suited for or called to a particular field of work before they commit years of study and significant expenditures to making that kind of change. A bookkeeper can volunteer on a distress line to see if he or she has the aptitude and attitudes necessary to become a counsellor or social worker. A nurse can volunteer at a daycare centre to test his or her interest in early childhood education, and so on. Volunteering also has much to offer those who take early retirement, whether chosen or imposed. Some may not need the salary or wages of paid employment, but would still like to keep working for a time. These individuals can provide vast expertise and skill to voluntary sector agencies through their own efforts, and may be available to act as mentors for others in the organization.

3.6.2. Volunteer Work and Networking

While no one who volunteers can be *guaranteed* a paid job as a direct result of their volunteer work, it is nevertheless a fact that many people *do* find paid employment because of the connections they have made in the course of their volunteer work. If it is true that 80% of the jobs available are never advertised, then networking assumes great significance in a job search.

People unfamiliar with the voluntary sector may not realize the large web of connections that tie agencies to one another, to government, to the private sector, and to the public at large. Volunteers often have the opportunity to meet people from many walks of life and various sectors of the community in the course of their volunteer assignments, at organization meetings, or at special events. This contact offers them opportunities to establish relationships with people they might not otherwise have met, thus expanding their network of contacts, and the range of paid job opportunities they come to learn about. Their volunteer work itself is often the basis on which someone from the agency or organization might recommend them for a paid job.

3.7. Role and Responsibility of Volunteer Centres

Increasingly complex demands coupled with inadequate resources — the voluntary sector labours under this strain now as perhaps never before. The need for ever more participation in communities and community agencies is tremendous.

In consequence, the growing number of people looking for volunteer work as a way to enhance their chances of finding paid employment can be seen as a gold mine: with relative suddenness, the sector is receiving unprecedented offers of assistance from people with outstanding skills and talents. Voluntarysector agencies must work carefully with these individuals, recognizing the particular character of volunteer work done primarily for this purpose, and the special needs of those who do it.

3.7.1. Volunteer Bureaux and Centres

Local volunteer bureaux and centres serve two client groups: agencies seeking volunteers, and individuals seeking volunteer opportunities. The role of volunteer centres with respect to this group of potential volunteers is twofold. They recruit and refer volunteers to organizations that will benefit from their assistance, skills, and experience. At the same time, volunteer centres must respect the motivation of these volunteers, and refer them to placements that will help them achieve their own goals. In addition, centres will have an opportunity to encourage them to continue volunteering even after they find paid employment.

The volunteer centre's role should be to:

— Help the volunteer identify opportunities that match his or her skills, interests and available time, and respect the motivation that has brought him or her to volunteering;

— Refer the volunteer to an appropriate, well managed, well organized volunteer program. The program should have clearly defined volunteer jobs, and offer an opportunity for work in an area identified by and agreed to by the volunteer;

— Seek to ensure that the volunteers referred to agencies meet the needs and requirements of those agencies;

— Work with agencies to develop, design, or redesign volunteer placements *where and when possible* so that they can be filled by members of this new group of volunteers.

3.7.2. Agencies Engaging Volunteers

Agencies that engage volunteers have a complex role to play. The first priority of the agency must be to meet the needs of its clients. Its volunteer program, policies, and placements should be designed to meet that goal. It is within this framework that individual volunteers are engaged to support and extend its work. What this means in practical terms is that agencies have to be particularly careful in ensuring that they are engaging volunteers to meet the clients' needs first, and not placing the needs of the client second to the needs of the volunteer.

It can be very tempting to see the range of skills and expertise which volunteers bring to the sector, and to create volunteer opportunities to engage them. There are often creative ways to shape and redesign volunteer jobs to take advantage of the particular circumstances and skills of a volunteer. It is, however, ultimately detrimental to all concerned to create a volunteer job around the skills of a volunteer if that job does not meet the needs of clients or fulfil the goals of the agency.

In addition, volunteer centres and agencies must recognize that for these volunteers the search for paid employment must come first.

Therefore, the best volunteer placements for them will generally be flexible, relatively short-term, and focused on specific goals or tasks.

These placements should offer the volunteer the kind of experience, training, feedback and practice he or she is looking for. At the same time, the placements must be designed so that the work of the agency is not jeopardized if the volunteer is called away to interviews, or finds a paid job. Agencies must also understand, and be prepared to work with, people who may be feeling very fragile because of their unemployed status and difficult job search.

3.8. Volunteer Work and Well-Being

Although volunteer work is widely believed to be beneficial not only for the community but for the individuals who perform it, surprisingly little attention has been paid to the actual consequences of volunteer service for individuals' physical and/or psychological well-being. Most studies of well-being outcomes examine the benefits of voluntary group *membership* rather than volunteer *work* per se. Because membership in voluntary associations is consistently found to be beneficia, these findings are often assumed to apply to volunteer work as well. Moreover, those studies that demonstrate positive physical or mental health consequences of membership *or* community service are usually cross-sectional in design; researchers rarely assess the possibility that individuals who are selected (or select themselves) into community associations or service already possess more physical and psychological resources than non-volunteers.

Finally, when longitudinal studies do control for prior levels of well-being, researchers almost always emphasize the "social causation" implications of their findings, pleased that they can rule out "selection" effects. That is, they are eager to demonstrate that social involvements benefit individuals net of the physical or emotional factors that might have selected those individuals into volunteer work in the first place. This is perhaps an understandable impulse for sociologists who must struggle to convince other disciplines that social forces indeed shape individuals' lives and psyches. However, by focusing on social causation processes, investigators inadvertently de-emphasize the antecedents and role of human agency. This is especially ironic, given that the topic is *volunteer* work, where agency must be involved for it to occur! We will argue that individuals' personal resources and well-being both facilitate their involvement in volunteer work and are subsequently enhanced by such work. In short, the purposes of this paper are to reexamine general well-being as an antecedent *and* a consequence of volunteer *work* in the community and to focus attention on the neglected topic of *agency*.

Volunteering is the voluntary giving of time and talents to deliver services or perform tasks with no direct financial compensation expected. Volunteering includes the participation of citizens in the direct delivery of service to others; citizen action groups; advocacy for causes, groups, or individuals; participation in the governance of both private and public agencies; self-help and mutual aid endeavors; and a broad range of informal helping activities.

In other words, volunteer work includes not only the unpaid provision of services directly to others in need, but also political activism and community representation on boards of various agencies. We adopt the above definition with one exception: We exclude "informal helping activities" such as caregiving for family members or friends and isolated altruistic acts such as intervening in emergencies. Our focus is on what Wilson and Musick call "formal volunteering," i.e., volunteer *work* in or for the *community*, where time and effort are given for the betterment of the community in general or for specified subsets of community members who are in need (e.g., elderly shut-ins, poor residents of a housing unit, children with unfilled leisure time). Belonging to religious or secular organizations and attending services or group meetings, although clearly voluntary acts, are not sufficient to indicate volunteer *work* or *service* (which we use here as interchangeable terms).

3.8.1. Sociodemographic Characteristics of Volunteers

The literature on volunteers (both members and workers) has been and continues to be dominated by studies of their sociodemographic characteristics, motivations, attitudes, and values. Researchers have attempted to identify the "prototypical volunteer. According to some studies, the person most likely to volunteer is a middle-aged, middle class, married woman with more than high school education and with dependent schoolage children. However, many studies are based on samples of volunteers only, rather than samples that allow comparisons between volunteers and non-volunteers. Moreover, as mentioned earlier, studies often operationalize volunteerism as belonging to organizations or attending organization meetings rather than giving community service per se. Studies that explicitly compare volunteer to non-volunteer workers yield mixed findings regarding the social characteristics of the typical community volunteer. Patterns by gender, race, or age are unclear; some studies suggest that any differences by gender, race/ethnicity, or age disappear when differences in socioeconomic status are controlled. More consistently across studies, individuals with higher education and income and married persons are more likely to participate in voluntary organizations *and* to do volunteer work. Having children at home also fosters group participation and volunteer service, especially for women.

3.8.2. Determinants of Volunteer Work

Beyond sociodemographic characteristics, a number of other factors have been considered as determinants of volunteerism, although their effects have not been thoroughly or consistently documented. These factors can be summarized through four theoretical models of volunteer work that presently guide the literature. What might be called the "volunteer motivations model" emphasizes individuals' motivations for or goals in volunteering. Research indicates that people give service for a variety of reasons, for example, to learn new skills, to develop the self, to enhance self-esteem, to prepare for a career, to express personal values and community commitment, and even to reduce ego-conflicts or identity threats. Motivation researchers suggest that volunteering can serve different functions (i.e., motivations) for different people and sometimes multiple functions for a single individual. Thus, selection into volunteer service may not be broadly socially patterned or systematic, an implication which is at odds with other empirical literature discussed below.

A second model, what might be termed the "values and attitudes model," focuses on the connection between volunteering and individuals' beliefs about the importance of civic participation or charitable responsibility. Not surprisingly, civic-oriented values and attitudes do positively influence volunteerism. Researchers typically note the weakness of the empirical relationships found; other factors seem more strongly associated with volunteer work. A third model, the "role-identity model," posits and shows that past volunteer service leads to the development of a "volunteer role identity," which in turn motivates future volunteer activity. This model is especially appropriate for examining processes that sustain volunteerism once it has begun. A related model, what might be termed the "group-identity model", suggests that individuals are motivated to help others with whom they are collectively identified (for example, gays who are identified with the gay community will be more likely to aid those with HIV/AIDS). In this variation, prior identification with a needy or disadvantaged group may become a motivating factor for giving or continuing service.

The fourth model, what might be called "the volunteer personality model," suggests that personality or dispositional variables motivate volunteer work. Penner and his colleagues have demonstrated that a prosocial personality orientation, including traits of "other-oriented empathy" and "helpfulness," were related to length of service and time spent in volunteer activities. Interestingly, helpfulness was associated with other positive personality characteristics such as dominance, self-efficacy, confidence, and feelings of competence. Relatedly, in a literature review of the personality characteristics of community mental health volunteers, Allen and Rushton concluded that volunteer participation was higher for individuals with an internal locus of control, with higher selfesteem, and with greater emotional stability. Such results hint that people who generally have greater personal coping resources (e.g., high self-esteem or an internal locus of control) and who are in better mental health might be more likely to volunteer.

The personal well-being model. These findings suggest a fifth potential model which has not often been examined in the literature and upon which we focus in this paper. We might call our guiding model the "personal wellbeing model." We examine personality characteristics and physical and mental health as resources necessary for seeking out and becoming involved in community service. In the stress literature, "internal or personal resources" refer to aspects of personality upon which people draw when dealing with challenges and difficulties in their lives. They include confidence, control, and selfworth, and they allow individuals not only to meet problems head-on but to initiate and pursue desired lines of action. Not surprisingly, people who are confident, feel in control of their lives, and have high self-esteem have good physical and mental health as well. We hypothesize that individuals who volunteer—for whatever reason, motivation, or goal—are more likely to possess such personal resources, enabling them to pursue their values or goals more easily or effectively. Just as people are selected into achieved statuses such as marriage and employment partly on the basis of their personality characteristics, interpersonal skills, and physical and mental health, so they may be selected into or select themselves into volunteer associations and volunteer work by similar factors.

3.8.3. Consequences of Volunteer Work

With respect to the *consequences* of volunteering, as mentioned earlier, a large literature documents positive physical and mental health consequences of voluntary association *membership or frequency of organizational attendance.* For example, voluntary association membership contributes to decreased psychological distress and buffers the negative consequences of stressors; it increases life satisfaction and decreases depression; and it is associated with better physical health and lower mortality as much as 30 years later. These findings for voluntary group membership and attendance (which are robust and frequently reported) are consistent with the idea that volunteer work (which is less often studied) is beneficial to well-being, even net of prior levels of wellbeing that might have prompted or facilitated the work in the first place.

Indeed, that is what cross-sectional studies suggest for volunteer workers. For example, Hunter and Linn compared elderly volunteers and non-volunteers and found that those who did volunteer *work* had significantly higher life satisfaction, a stronger will to live, greater feelings of self-respect, and fewer symptoms of depression and anxiety compared to nonvolunteers.

Similar positive effects of volunteer work on psychological well-being have been found repeatedly in studies of elders, who are often the focus of research on volunteer involvement, presumably because community service becomes a substitute for employment when individuals retire. Additionally, Oman, Thoresen, and McMahon reported a 63 percent lower mortality rate among older adults who gave volunteer service for two or more organizations compared to non-volunteers, net of other factors known to affect mortality.

In sum, studies suggest that people with greater personal well-being (i.e., greater psychosocial resources and physical and mental health) may volunteer more often, and people who are involved in community service may have greater life satisfaction, self-esteem, sense of purpose in life, physical health, and mental health, among other consequences. It should be noted again that much of the empirical literature producing these sets of findings rely on cross-sectional data, leaving open the question of the direction of effects. Those few studies that involve longitudinal data do not explicitly examine the reciprocal effects of personal well-being and volunteer service. There are good reasons to expect bi-directionality in the relationship between various aspects of personal well-being and volunteer work. Persons who are in superior physical and mental health are not only physically able to engage in volunteer work but are likely to be equipped with the kinds of internal coping resources that expedite seeking out volunteer opportunities, becoming involved, and staying involved (e.g., high selfesteem, a strong sense of mastery or control over life). Volunteer work in turn is likely to require or maintain certain minimal levels of physical activity, and the intrinsic and extrinsic gratifications of the work may generate feelings of self-worth, self-efficacy, happiness, and satisfaction-aspects of positive mental health.

References

Batten, T. R. and Batten M. 1967. *The Non-Directive Approach in Group and Community Work*, London: Oxford University Press.

Cannan, C., Berry, L. and Lyons, K. 1992. *Social Work and Europe*, London: Macmillan.

Curno, P. ed. 1978. *Political Issues and Community Work. Community Work 4,* London: Routledge and Kegan Paul.

David N. Thomas. 1983. *The Making of Community Work*, London: George Allen and Unwin. 3

Hardcastle, D. A. and Powers, P. R. 2004. *Community Practice: Theories and Skills for Social Workers* 2e, New York: Oxford University Press.

Popple, K. 1995. *Analysing Community Work. Its theory and practice*, Buckingham: Open University Press.

Smith, J. 1991. *Community Development and Tenant Action*, London: Community Development Foundation. 42 + x pages.

Twelvetrees, A. 1982; 1991; 2001. *Community Work*, London: Palgrave Macmillan.

4

Community Work for Development

The notion of community development owes a great deal to the efforts of colonial administrators. After the Second World War the British Colonial Office became concerned with 'community development'. Mayo suggests that administrators 'concocted' the term out of their attempts to develop 'basic education' and social welfare in the UK colonies. For example, a 1944 report, *Mass education in the colonies*, placed an emphasis on literacy training and advocated the promotion of agriculture, health and other social services through local self help. This was a set of concerns similar to those surrounding the interest in rural development and educational 'extension' in North America in the first two decades of the century. Community development was defined in one UK government publication as: active participation, and if possible on the initiative of the community, but if this initiative is not forthcoming spontaneously, by the use of techniques for arousing and stimulating it in order to achieve its active and enthusiastic response to the movement.

The concern with community development was, in part, a response to the growth of nationalism, and, in part an outcome of a desire to increase the rate of industrial and economic development. The notion began to feature strongly in United Nations documents during the 1950s - and these drew extensively on the British literature and experiences in Africa and India. Three important elements were identified:

— a concern with social and economic development.

— the fostering and capacity of local co-operation and self-help.

— the use of expertise and methods drawn from outside the local community.

Within this there does appear to be a certain contradiction. Community development emphasizes participation, initiative and self help by local communities but is usually sponsored by national governments as part of a national plan. While from one side it can be seen as the encouragement of local initiative and decision making, from the other it is a means of implementing and expediting national policies at the local level and is a substitute for, or the beginning of, local government.

The focus on the social and economic, local and global, also helps to situate debates about community development - and the disillusionment with its achievements that was widespread in many Southern countries by the 1970s. Many governments, particularly in Africa, failed to provide adequate financial support but nevertheless extolled the virtues of self-help. Community development was soon recognized by the people to amount to little more than a slogan which brought few tangible benefits.

However, we should not forget in this process is that community development had also spawned a growing literature. Workers were not only able to draw on the extensive American literature of community organization- there were now various guides and discussions arising specifically out of the experience of 'developing' countries, for example, Batten's classic textbook *Communities and their Development.*

It is not without significance that while the community organization literature became broadly located in social work, the community development literature had far more an 'educational' hue. Yet, we do need to take some care here - just because a discourse found expression in North American social work does not mean that it was not informed by educational thinkers. However, the institutional location of the work, combined with the orientation of its proponents is important. Batten, for example, who wrote a string of influential books was based at the University of London Institute of Education.

To make sense of the notion of community development it is helpful to situate it alongside other strands of community work practice. Here it is useful to consider David Thomas' discussion of the five main strands or approaches that characterized community work in the early 1980s. He talked about:

— *Community Action.* Community action was seen as focusing on the organisation of those adversely affected by the decisions, or non-decisions, of public and private bodies and by more general structural characteristics of society. The strategy aims to promote collective action to challenge existing socio-political and economic structures and processes, to explore and explain the power realities of people's situations and, through this twin pronged approach, develop both critical perspectives of the status quo and alternative bases of power and action.

— *Community Organisation.* Community organization, according to Thomas, involves the collaboration of separate community or welfare agencies with or without the additional participation of statutory authorities, in the promotion of joint initiatives.

— *Community Development.* Community development was seen as emphasizing self-help, mutual support, the building up of neighbourhood integration, the development of neighbourhood capacities for problem-solving and self-representation, and the promotion of collective action to bring a community's preferences to the attention of political decision-makers.

— *Social Planning.* This orientation/approach was presented as being concerned with the assessment of community needs and problems and the systematic planning of strategies for meeting them. Social planning comprises the analysis of social conditions, social policies and agency services; the setting of goals and priorities; the design of service programmes and the mobilisation of appropriate resources; and the implementation and evaluation of services and programmes.

— *Service Extension.* This is a strategy that seeks to extend agency operations and services by making them more relevant and accessible. This includes extending services into the community, giving these services and the staff who are responsible for them a physical presence in a neighbourhood.

In Britain the notion of community development became associated for some with shifts within community work towards more radical approaches. In particular this involved a movement away from what could be described as an informal education perspective, into what would be better labelled social action (see above). However, the radicalism of many of the workers attracted into the work in the late 1960s and early 1970s in many northern countries was not to last. The waning of key social movements, the increased influence of managerialism, and more general economic and political shifts around marketization and globalization meant that there was in many countries, a gradual drift into a policy orientation and a focus on the implementation of social care and regeneration initiatives. In other words, there was a significant movement into approaches to what people described as 'community development' that looked to what Thomas described as social planning and service extension.

In some places there were countervailing forces to this movement away from education and from mutual aid and community. In Scotland, for example, the developing professional and political interest in community education kept a stronger focus on more locally-based and associational work. In a similar way the experience of non-formal education programmes in some countries retained an interest in the ways in which local people understood their situation and reflected more of a 'bottom-up' approach to policy formation.

4.1. Capacity Building

Some of the classic concerns of community development found expression in the early 1990s in the notion of 'capacity building'. There was an interest in developing the ability of local groups and networks to function and to contribute to social and economic development. On the whole, though, the idea of capacity building often remained associated with a technicist and economistic viewpoint - a concern with competencies, 'investing' and so on. There were those that looked to the 'bottom-up' and more convivial aspects of traditional community development. A few contributions also emerged that had a more thorough theoretical basis. Eade's approach, for example, and that of development agencies such as Oxfam, was linked into certain fundamental beliefs, for example: 'that all people have the right to an equitable share in the world's resources, and to be the authors of their own development; and that the denial of such rights is at the heart of poverty and suffering'. Strengthening people's capacity to determine their values and priorities, and to act on these, is the basis of development.

Capacity building is an approach to development rather than a set of discrete or pre-packaged interventions. So while there are certain basic capacities (social, economic, political and practical) on which development depends, Oxfam seeks to support organisations working for sustainable social justice.

From this flow a number of implications. That:

— capacity building must not be seen in isolation.

— all have capacities that may not be obvious to outsiders and it may take time to discover these.

— if it is to be inclusive, interventions must take into account different and sometimes negative, ways in which the impacts will be experienced.

— flexibility is important but this must not be at the expense of a loss of direction with regard to wider processes of social and economic transformation.

— capacity building is not 'doing development' on the cheap or against the clock. Nor is it risk-free.

The problem was that many of those interested in capacity building located it within a particular paradigm. It was capacity-building within a particular set of policy parameters. There was not often a disposition to build capacity that might oppose or fail to the 'importance' of state interests and priorities.

4.2. Community Participation

In the late 1960s there was some exploration of different models of participation and their relationship to community development. Since then concern around popular and community participation in key agencies such as the United Nations has been part of the discourse of community development. As Midgley et al have noted, the notion of popular participation and that of community participation were interlinked. The former was concerned with broad issues of social development and the creation of opportunities for the involvement of people in the political, economic and social life of a nation, 'the latter connotes the direct involvement of ordinary people in local affairs'. As such community participation can be seen as linking with older concerns with associational democracy and the like. In some countries the notion of community participation has reappeared in discussions around the need to bring some local services and facilities more directly into the control of local people. For example the 2005 election manifesto for the British Labour Party argued for 'new opportunities for communities to assume greater responsibility or even ownership of community assets like village halls, community centres, libraries or recreational facilities'.

This concern with local control and networks had some roots in the debates that emerged around social capital in the late 1990s and early 2000s. Significant press attention was given in the United States and the UK to Robert Putnam's arguments around the diminution of social capital in the USA (and the impact this had upon people's health, education and happiness). It also encouraged some important debates within academic and policy circles. While there has been some exploration of what a concern with deepening social capital might mean in terms of work in communities it has been, on the whole, rather disappointing. Part of the problem is that it entails policymakers and practitioners entertaining and making sense of issues within a markedly different frame of reference than that which dominates discussion and policy today. The work involved is long-term, dependent upon process and concerned more broadly with flourishing and happiness. State intervention is largely short-term, looking to outcomes and interested in economic growth and efficiency.

4.3. Community Work for Development in Africa

Africa in the closing years of the 20th Century will be remembered for two historic events. One was the rise of the popular movements that led to the end of the colonial empire and the downfall of apartheid; the other, a human catastrophe of immense proportions involving the massacre of nearly a million people in Rwanda. If the one was achieved through the mobilisation of the majority for the goal of emancipation, the other was fuelled by pressures to comply with an externally defined agenda for social development. These events represent the extremes of hope and despair that came to characterise much of the continent in the closing years of the millennium. Every country in the region contains, albeit to varying degrees, the mixture of factors that can lead to either outcome a future built on respect for human dignity, or one torn apart by conflicts such as those seen in Sierra Leone, Liberia, Angola and in the Democratic Republic of Congo.

Development, it seems, has failed. In many post-colonial countries real per capita GDP has fallen and welfare gains achieved since independence in areas like food consumption health and education have been reversed. The statistics are disturbing. In Sub-Saharan Africa as a whole per-capita incomes dropped by 21% in real terms between 1981 and 1989.1 Madagascar and Mali now have per capita incomes of $799 and $753 down from $1,258 and $898 25 years ago.

In 16 other Sub-Saharan countries per capita incomes were also lower in 1999 than in 1975.2 Nearly one quarter of the world's population, but nearly 42% of the population of sub-Saharan Africa, live on less than $1 a day. Levels of inequality have also increased dramatically but worldwide. In 1960 the average income of the top 20% of the world's population was 30 times that of the bottom 20%. By 1990 it was 60 times, and by 1997, 74 times that of the lowest fifth. Today "the assets of the top three billionaires are more than the combined GNP of all least developed countries and their 600 million people".

This has been the context in which there has been an explosive growth in the presence of Western as well as local nongovernmental organisations (NGOs) in Africa. NGOs today form a prominent part of the "development machine", a vast institutional and disciplinary nexus of official agencies, practitioners, consultants, scholars, and other miscellaneous experts producing and consuming knowledge about the "developing world". According to recent estimates, there are as many as three thousand development NGOs in OECD countries as a whole. In Britain alone, there are well over one hundred voluntary groups claiming some specialist in the field.

Aid (in which NGOs have come to play a significant role) is frequently portrayed as a form of altruism, a charitable act that enables wealth to flow from rich to poor, poverty to be reduced and the poor to be empowered. Such claims tend to be, as David Sogge puts it "shibboleths, catch phrases that distinguish believers from doubters. Indeed they are utterances of belief. At best they are half-truths".

4.3.1. Missionaries of Development

The market and volunteering have a long association; the first and most celebrated period of 'free trade', from the 1840s to the 1930s, was also a high point of charitable activity throughout the British empire. In Britain itself, the industrial revolution opened up a great gulf between the bourgeoisie and the swelling ranks of the urban proletariat. In the 1890s, when industrialists were amassing fortunes to rival those of the aristocracy, as much as one third of population of London were living below the level of bare subsistence and death from starvation was not unknown. At this time, private philanthropy was the preferred solution to social need and private expenditure far outweighed public provision.

Colonial powers had no desire to finance state welfare programmes for Africans. Government social services for the indigenous population were minimal. Social policy was geared towards ensuring the integrity of the structures of colonial rule. It was designed to secure a sufficient quality of labour to guarantee a reasonably efficient exploitation of the colony. The goals of social development (such as they were) were defined in the metropolis. Within that framework, policy formulation and implementation were usually decentralised, being delegated to the colonial governor and administration.

Social services were not, however, completely absent. In periods of serious outbreaks of epidemics in indigenous settlements, health services were provided principally to stave off the possibility of infections spreading into white society. Limited education also was provided when certain basic skills would be necessary for the administration of the colony or for the particular forms of exploitation.

But state expenditure to support white settler populations was usually generous. Although on the eve of independence there were significant changes in the extent to which investments were made in the social sectors, for the most part the state's function in these sectors was to provide only for a minority. For the majority of the rural population, it was left to a clutch of charities and missionary groups to exchange their spiritual wares for material support in education, health or other social services. In providing such services, they were also concerned with evangelising amongst the African population, discouraging what they perceived as ignorance, idleness and moral degeneracy, and promoting their own vision of civilisation.

If the welfare of Africans was not a primary concern of colonial administrators and missionaries, their control certainly was. Whites were universally agreed on the necessity for controlling the expectations and behaviour of blacks. African people did not always respond passively to colonial rule. The interwar years saw some of the first serious challenges to white authority in Africa, the emergence of significant, if nascent, nationalist and anti-colonial movements, of organised black labour and indeed of open revolt against the brute injustices of colonialism.

However, it was the period following the Second World War that witnessed the most significant popular mobilisation and the formation of numerous popular organisations (both formal and informal) throughout Africa. Initially, these grassroots movements were motivated not so much by desires for abstract concepts of self-determination, but by struggles for basic rights that were part of everyday experiences of the majority; the right to food, shelter, water, land, education and health care; rights to freedom of association, freedom of speech, freedom of movement, freedom from harassment and other forms of human rights abuses. It was these numerous civil agitation (urban and rural) that provided the impetus to the liberation movements.

The imperial response was frequently brutal. In Kenya, grassroots struggles came to a head in the 'Mau Mau' uprising of 1952 when the Kikuyu population of the so called 'white highlands' mobilised widespread popular support for a guerrilla war against the colonial settlers. Officially, 95 whites and 11,503 Africans were killed in the conflict, although most now agree that the number of African dead was actually far greater. Tens of thousands of Kikuyu men, women and children were also interned in concentration camps under emergency legislation. However, not all efforts to control Africans were wholly or even mainly based on brute force. Ideology played a far greater role.

As Ngugiwa Thiong'o explain. Colonialism imposed its control of the social production of wealth through military conquest and subsequent political dictatorship. But its most important area of domination was the mental universe of the colonised, the control, through culture, of how people perceived themselves and their relationship to the world. Economic and political control can never be complete or effective without mental control. To control a people's culture is to control their tools of self definition in relationship to others.

Missionary societies and voluntary organisations were key actors in the ideological war. They provided the administration not only with a cheap form of private welfare, but also with a subtle means of controlling the behaviour of blacks. While colonial philanthropy may have been motivated by religious conviction, status, compassion or guilt, it was also motivated by fear. In Britain and the colonies alike, politicians frequently alluded to the threat of revolution and actively encouraged greater interest in works of benevolence as a solution to social unrest. In short, charity was not only designed to help the poor, it also served to protect the rich.

Charitable organisations actively helped to suppress anti-colonial struggles. For example, in Kenya the Women's Association, Maendeleo Ya Wanawake (MYWO) and the Christian Council of Kenya (CCK) were both involved in government funded schemes designed to subvert black resistance during the 'Mau Mau' uprising. The CCK established a "rehabilitation programme" in response to the emergency. It offered "pastoral care" to internees in the concentration camps, a euphemism for a process of interrogation during which "loyal Africans" were screened from potential "terrorists". It also established community centres in Nairobi's more troublesome slums and shanty towns to extend these "rehabilitation" services to urban communities affected by the 'Mau Mau' uprising.

Voluntary welfare provision was easily adapted to the purpose of social control because it was conceived as a largely asocial activity. The programmes of care they delivered did not seek to redress the social circumstances that caused impoverishment, but instead concerned themselves with the apparent failings of Africans themselves. The problem was not injustice, but being 'uncivilised' and suffering from the 'native' condition. And charitable welfare was the sweetener that made the colonial condition more palatable.

But with the emergence of the anti-colonial revolution, missionary and voluntary organisations in the colonies faced a crisis. The nationalist movements that came into power did so on the basis of a 'social contract' with the popular movements that they led. Their credibility and legitimacy derived from their promise to end social injustices that characterised the colonial era. Given the extent of involvement of missionary societies and voluntary organisations in the suppression of nationalist struggles in Africa, the question arises as to how such organisations were able to survive and even prosper after independence, as many clearly did? The answer lies in the history of development discourse itself and the emergence of the 'development NGO' as an entity in the national and international arena.

While the idea and practice of 'community development' existed within the colonial period, voluntary bodies did not represent themselves or their work in terms of 'development' until much later when the US Government and international agencies began to distinguish half the world as 'underdeveloped' and to describe 'development' as a universal goal. The emerging discourse of development provided a convenient rationale for two distinct groups of voluntary organisations. The first group consisted primarily of overseas missionary societies and charitable bodies, like the CCK and the MYWO in Kenya, that were present in the colonies before independence.

Christian Aid evolved out of a network of such bodies. The second group is typified by organisations like Oxfam, Save the Children and Plan International, who had no direct involvement in the colonies. They were 'war charities', established to deal with the human consequences of conflict in Europe. The histories of these two groups of organisations are often conflicted in accounts of the origins of development NGOs. In fact, each group had very different motivation for adopting the development mantle and, at least originally, each had a very different relationship with the official bodies that dominated the field.

With the rise of the anti-colonial movement, colonial missionary societies and charitable organisations were clearly tainted in the eyes of the majority by their association with racist colonial oppression. Colonial rationales of 'trusteeship' were not longer acceptable. Faced with their potential demise, they transformed themselves completely.

Firstly, they 'indigenised' their administrations, gradually replacing white staff, clergy and secular managers with educated blacks. Secondly, they changed their ideological outlook, replacing the overt racism of the past with a new discourse about 'development' that was just beginning to take shape in the international arena.

The new discourse provided a solution of sorts. It offered an alternative language and set of practices that, at least on the surface, were free of racial signifiers. And it appeared to imply some connection with emancipation, the prospect of 'progress' that would benefit all. They 'discovered' the appeal of expressing concerns about poverty, and they began to condemn the racial prejudice that had created this poverty with as much conviction as they had justified racial exclusion in the past. The exigencies of black resistance and international politics had forced them to reconstruct themselves as indigenous 'development NGOs'.

Unlike their colonial counterparts, war charities had no undesirable associations with racist regimes. They had a popular base in Europe that was supportive of their goals of internationalist humanitarian relief. As the post-War reconstruction effort began in earnest in Europe with the implementation of the Marshall plan in 1948, mass suffering and starvation were no longer an imminent threat in Europe. The war charities were faced with basic choices. They could either wind down their operations entirely, or they could expand into new areas of activity and new continents. Oxfam, Plan International and Save the Children were amongst only a handful of organisations that decided to extend their existing humanitarian activities beyond Europe's boundaries.

So why did they make this choice? In part they were driven by organisational survival for its own sake, but they were also driven by ideological goals. Religion certainly played a large part in the founding beliefs of most, but it was the idealist tradition of liberal internationalism of their founders that now provided the motivation the same tradition that gave birth to the League of Nations in the interwar years. Idealists sought to promote world peace through international cooperation and actively encouraged people to gain a "truer understanding of civilisations other than their own". The 1960's marked the turning point in the history of war charities.

The Freedom from Hunger Campaign and the UN Decade of Development both had profound effects on these organisations. They embraced the new discourse of development with as much enthusiasm as colonial missionary societies and voluntary organisations were doing locally. They were seduced by arguments about development as a more noble pursuit than humanitarian relief alone, since it was said the former addressed the long-term causes of poverty, whereas the latter merely dealt with short-term symptoms. Oxfam, War on Want and Christian Aid in particular were sympathetic to these views and supported the Food and Agriculture Organisation's call for the relief of poverty through 'self-generating agricultural development'.

Their participation in development discourse helped to solve some serious marketing problems that organisations such as Oxfam experienced in its early overseas ventures. At first, the British public found it very difficult to comprehend the fact that there was widespread poverty and hunger throughout the glorious empire. The public's vision of Africa was informed alternately by images of exoticism and adventure. As Maggie Black acknowledges;

Whatever variations were provided in the picture of Her Majesty's brown and black-skinned subjects, one feature was axiomatic: they were not described in the same terms in political, economic, social as "us". Comparisons using the same set of criteria were not made because the people were not comparable; they were 'not like us'. Development resolved this marketing problem.

The discourse offered a confused audience a more palatable perspective on Africans and Asians. It was more palatable because it was similar in many respects to the racist discourses of the past, this time with a vocabulary consistent with the new age of modernity. It was no longer that Africans were 'uncivilised'. Instead, they were 'underdeveloped'. Either way, the 'civilised' or 'developed' European has a role to play in 'civilising' or 'developing' Africa.

Caught in the torrent of upheavals that characterised the victory over colonialism, it was easy for these Western NGOs to become romantic and blinkered by their own enthusiasm for 'bringing development to the people' in the newly independent countries. But the real problem was that the dominant discourse of development was framed not in the language of emancipation or justice, but with the vocabulary of charity, technical expertise, neutrality, and a deep paternalism (albeit accompanied by the rhetoric of participatory development) that was its syntax.

As with the racist ideologies of the past, the discourse of development continued to define non-Western people in terms of their perceived divergence from the cultural standards of the West, and it reproduced the social hierarchies that had prevailed between both groups under colonialism. On this basis, the so-called 'developing world' and its inhabitants were (and still are) described only in terms of what they are not. They are chaotic not ordered, traditional not modern, corrupt not honest, underdeveloped not developed, irrational not rational, lacking in all of those things the West presumes itself to be. White Westerners were still represented as the bearers of 'civilisation' and were to act as the exclusive agents of development, while black, post-colonial 'others' were still seen as uncivilised and unenlightened, destined to be development's exclusive objects.

Political independence was achieved in Africa through the ability of the leadership of the nationalist movements to capture the imagination of popular formations, uniting them in the promise that only through self-determination and independence could all their aspirations be achieved. Having grasped political self-determination from colonial authority, however, the new occupiers of the state machinery were reluctant to accord the same rights to others. The state was to be the 'sole developer' and 'sole unifier' of society.

The popular associations, political organisations and unions, that had brought the nationalist leadership into power gradually began to be seen as an obstacle to progress. They were gradually marginalised, replaced by the ascendancy of the expert supported by bureaucratic and centralised decision making under the guise of 'national planning'. Emancipation was no longer the flag around which the oppressed could rally Instead the concept of rights was codified and rarefied in laws and constitutions whose application was determined by the increasingly unaccountable, guardians of the state. 'Development' became the main preoccupation once political independence had been achieved.

The 'problem' was not, it appeared, emancipation or the denial of basic rights, but one of 'poverty' and 'basic needs'. While the one demanded popular mobilisation, the other inspired only pity and preoccupations about the technically 'correct' approaches to 'poverty alleviation'. While the vision of 'development' appeared to offer a more inclusive path to 'progress' than had previously been the case, in fact the discourse was little more than a superficial reformulation of old colonial prejudices. As Crush puts it, "development is fundamentally about mapping and making, about the spatial reach of power and the control and management of other peoples, territories, environments and places".

The discourse of development provided a means of subverting popular aspirations for radical change in the context of independence struggles while legitimating the continued marginalisation of non-Western peoples. After independence development worked to undermine popular mobilisation and to limit an expanding communist ideology, both of which threatened to obstruct the continued growth of Euro-American capitalism in the former colonies. And it achieved all this while providing very little in the way of tangible benefits to non-Western people.

There was no Marshall plan for Africa. The limited assistance post-colonial countries received in development aid was usually tied more directly to short-term Western interests. For all it limitations, however, the post-independence African economy did at least sustain a social infrastructure that, while not comparable to conditions in the West, nevertheless served a wide population. It remains one of the most remarkable, and yet least acknowledged, achievements of independence governments that within the space of a few years, access to health services and to education became effectively universal. The impact of these interventions was to be reflected in the subsequent dramatic changes in average life expectancy, in infant and child mortality rates, in the improvements in nutritional status of the young, in literacy levels and educational enrolment and achievements.

Substantial improvements in all these parameters were to be observed throughout the continent by the end of the 1970s as a result of these social programmes. These achievements challenge the current, largely ideologically motivated, caricature of the state as being 'inefficient' and unable to deliver effective services. Notwithstanding NGOs' early allegiance to the idea of development and, indeed, the scope and breadth of their activities during this period, official development agencies remained largely unenthusiastic about their work. In the imagination of organisations like USAID, the UN and the World Bank, development was the business of the state and NGOs stood some somewhere on the extreme margins of the field. While international NGOs had a license to run their projects in Africa, this freedom was conditional, based on an unspoken assumption that they accepted or did not comment on the manner in which the state exercised its power.

This arrangement suited official agencies on both sides of the West non-West divide, since key amongst the implicit goals of development in the cold war era was the co-optation of post-colonial governments to the economic and military agendas of Western powers. Consequently, the role of NGOs in the early post independence period remained marginal. While they carried out 'projects' providing services in peripheral areas that the state was disinclined to reach, the bulk of social services were provided by the state under its social contract with the people.

The work of NGOs was limited to project work where, armed with their manuals and technical tricks, they focused the attention of 'the poor' on finding participatory means for coping with the present rather than seeking justice for past crimes against them. Like their missionary predecessors, they offered the poor blessings in the future (albeit on earth rather than in heaven). And in their local offices they established the same racial divisions of labour and low salaries for local staff as had been customary amongst their missionary predecessors.

4.3.2. Neo-Liberalism and the Resurgence of NGOs

But by the late 1970s, events were on the horizon that were to qualitatively transform the 'development' arena and lay the basis for the proliferation of NGOs in the region that rekindled their missionary zeal. The so-called 'oil crisis' of the mid 1970s resulted in the creation of a finance capital glut in a world economy already suffering from recession. Europe and America were suddenly awash with capital with few opportunities for high rates of return. As a result, developing countries were courted to take loans to finance 'development'.

But this glut of international credit was short-lived. The 1980s saw significant increases in the cost of borrowing. The US government implemented an avowedly neo-liberal, monetary policy, which drove up interest around the world. Coincident with this, the emerging technological revolution in microcomputers and in gene technology attracted capital to new fields where the rates of profit were likely to be more substantial. Debtor countries were suddenly faced with servicing the interest on loans that absorbed the ever-greater proportions of export earnings. Debt had now become the central issue of 'concern' in development circles.

This was the period that saw the emergence of 'neo-liberalism' as the dominant political-economic ideology in the West, epitomised by the rise to power of Thatcher in UK and Reagan in USA. Central to this ideology was the concept of the nominalist state, a concept the realisation of which radically altered the landscape of development practice in Africa and throughout the post-colonial world. According to the neo-liberal consensus, the most important function of economic policy is to safeguard the 'right' of a minority to accumulate profits at the highest rate possible (euphemistically referred to as 'growth'). Only when this freedom is unrestricted, it is said, will others in society benefit from any associated spin-offs (the trickle-down effect).

The purpose of 'development' is, therefore, to guarantee 'growth' so that ultimately other freedom can be enjoyed at some indeterminate time in the future. State expenditure, according to this dogma, should be directed towards creating an enabling environment for 'growth', and not be 'wasted' on the provision of public services that, in any case, can ultimately be provided 'more efficiently' by private enterprise.

These are the mantras that came to be woven through almost every report on economic development since whether from the World Bank, IMF, WTO, or from bilateral development agencies in the North. This is the "madness" that Amartya Sen. points out, makes socially useful members of society such as schoolteachers and health workers feel more threatened by conservative economic policies than do army generals. It is the madness that contributed to social calamities such as the genocide in Rwanda.

The indebtedness of African nations gave the multilateral lending agencies the leverage they needed to impose their neo-liberal policy prescriptions, in the spirit of universality, across the board. The Bretton Woods institutions (with the support of the bilateral aid agencies) became the new commanders of post-colonial economies. Through the myriad structural adjustment programmes they initiated throughout the continent they could determine both the goals of development and the means for achieving them.

Adjustment legitimised their direct intervention in political decision-making processes. These institutions soon came to determine the extent of involvement that the state should have in the social sector, and insisted on the state imposing draconian economic and social measures that resulted in a rise in unemployment and the decline in real incomes of the majority. The result was to transform and restructure the social basis of power in African countries, strengthening those forces or alliances that would be sympathetic to the continued hegemony of the multilateral and of the multinationals in the emerging era of 'globalisation'.

Today, most commentators agree that the neo-liberal reforms the International Monetary Fund (IMF) and the World Bank imposed under adjustment programmes in the 1980s actually caused much of the growth in poverty and inequality we have seen in Africa and Latin America over the past two decades. Externally imposed constraints on health, education and welfare measures and social programmes, tax concessions on profits, liberalisation of price controls, and dismantling of state owned enterprises all have contributed to widening of internal disparities. Several studies have linked adjustment programmes to deteriorating health conditions in Africa and Latin America, pointing to increases in the incidence of child malnutrition, in the growth of infectious disease and in infant and maternal mortality rates.

It would be wrong to suggest that the mass of African people have accepted this situation passively. Popular dissatisfaction with adjustment and its related policies led to spontaneous demonstrations. Between 1976 and 1992 there were 146 protests against IMF supported austerity measures in 39 countries around the world. These took the form of political demonstrations, strikes and riots.

They took place almost exclusively in cities and they reached a peak in the mid 1980s. In many cases, the immediate response of governments was brute force. Demonstrations were violently suppressed, strikes declared illegal, universities were closed, and trade unions, student organisations, popular organisations, and political parties also became the target of repressive legislation or actions. However, such widespread opposition also forced the multilateral and bilateral aid agencies to rethink their approach to development promotion, particularly, how to present the same neo-liberal economic and social programmes with a more "human face".

The outcome of these deliberations was the 'good governance' agenda of the 1990s and the decision to co-opt NGOs and other civil society organisations to a repackag d programme of welfare provision, a social initiative that could be more accurately described as a programme of social control. So in the 1990s, the focus of attention of the international community was placed upon 'good governance', persuading African governments to permit political pluralism in the form of 'multipartyism'. But democratisation of the structures of the state had not occurred, and was certainly no longer in the interest of the ruling elites.

The state's role in the social sector had been effectively gelded in the process of structural adjustment. State actors' decisive role in determining economic policy had been appropriated by the multilateral institutions and, instead, they found themselves the focus of blame for the failed neo-liberal policies that had previously been imposed upon them by their critics. What was there left that could be offered that might stave off the possibilities of social upheavals. Pluralism in the political arena seemed the only possibility.

The bilaterals and multilaterals set aside significant volumes of funds aimed at 'mitigating' the 'social dimensions of adjustment'. The purpose of such programmes was to act as palliative that might minimise the more glaring inequalities that their policies had perpetuated. Funds were made available to ensure that a so-called 'safety net' of social services would be provided for the 'vulnerable' – but this time not by the state (which had after all been forced to 'retrench' away from the social sector) but by the ever-willing NGO sector.

The availability of such funds for the NGO sector was to have a profound impact on the very nature of that sector. This was a period in which the involvement of Northern NGOs in Africa grew dramatically. The number of international NGOs operating in Kenya, for example, increased almost threefold to 134 organisations during the period 1978 to 1988. According to the Overseas Development Institute, NGOs in 1992 distributed somewhere between 10% and 15% of all aid transfers to "developing countries".

While most of this money comes from private donations a significant proportion also comes from official sources. Britain's Department for International Development (DFID) allocates around 8% of its aid budget to NGOs. The US Government transfers nearly 40% of its aid programme through NGOs. The scale of official funding has increased considerably over the past two decades. In the early 1970s less than 2% of NGO income came from official donors. By the mid-1990s this figure had risen to 30%.

In the ten years between 1984 and 1994, the British Government increased its funding of NGOs by almost 400% to £68.7m. NGOs in Australia, Finland, Norway and Sweden all saw similar increases in official funding from the early 1980s onwards. As a consequence of increased levels of funding and increased attention, the number of development organisations in Western countries mushroomed and many established NGOs experienced spectacular growth. The number of NGOs active in African countries has grown equally. About 40 percent of the development NGOs working in Kenya today are foreign organisations, 204 out of a total number of 511 according to the most recent survey.

4.3.3. Agenda for Emancipation

In the era of globalisation, African states have increasingly lost authority to determine both the direction of social development and also the content of social policy. Externally imposed constraints on health, education and welfare measures and social programmes, tax concessions on profits, liberalisation of price controls, and dismantling of state owned enterprises all have contributed to widening of internal disparities.

And faced with the growing dominance of the multinational corporation in the domestic economy, there remain few legitimate ways for the indigenous capitalist class to accumulate. Their choices are limited either to becoming agents of the multinationals, or turning to crime, corruption, drug trafficking, sex exploitation, illegal migration and illicit arms. As UNDP points out, criminals are "reaping the benefits of globalisation."

The deregulation of capital markets and developments in information and communications technologies "make flows easier, faster and less restricted" for drug-trafficking, laundering money and weapons As the distinction between social organisation for criminal activities and for political purposes has become blurred in African society, civilians are increasingly being caught in the crossfire or becoming the targets either of armed opposition groups or of the increasingly desperate state machinery. Continued impoverishment, growing conflicts, the state reneging on its social responsibilities, it is into this arena that development NGOs have been plying their trade.

Africa's decline contributes to the continued justification for their work. NGOs will "do better the less stable the world becomes because finance will become increasingly available to agencies who can deliver 'stabilising' social services." As African governments increasingly become pushed into becoming caretakers of what might be described as the peripheral Bantustans of globalisation, are we seeing a return to the colonial paradigm in which social services are delivered on the basis of favour or charity and their power to placate? The mass mobilisation that led to the end of colonial rule in Africa were sparked by aspirations for social, economic and political emancipation. The gains of independence have all but been reversed.

NGOs are acknowledged today as "the preferred channel for service provision in deliberate substitution for the state". Official aid agencies have come to expect NGOs to act as a substitute for state welfare programmes, a solution to welfare deficiencies at a time when structural adjustment was hugely increasing the extent of welfare needs.

Development NGOs have become an integral, and necessary, part of a system that sacrifices respect for justice and rights. They have taken the 'missionary position' service delivery, running projects that are motivated by charity, pity and doing things for people (implicitly who can't do it for themselves), albeit with the verbiage of participatory approaches. It would be wrong to present the relationship between Western NGOs and official aid agencies in the 1980s as the product of some conscious conspiracy, as was clearly the case with colonial organisations like MYWO.

The precondition for NGOs' co-optation to the neo-liberal cause was merely a coincidence in ideologies rather than a purposeful plan. In charitable development, the proponents of neo-liberalism saw the possibility of enforcing the unjust social order they desired by consensual rather than coercive means. The role NGOs have played in expanding and consolidating neo-liberal hegemony in the global context may have been unwitting. It may not have been as direct or as underhand as some of the activities willingly taken up by colonial missionary societies and voluntary organisations. But that is not to say it is any less significant. Indeed, one could argue that it has actually been far more effective.

But the missionary position is not the only option. Local voluntary organisations have consistently expressed doubts about the lack of attention Western NGOs have paid to areas of activity other than overseas development, and have called upon them to intensify their awareness-raising activities at home. As far back as 1986, for example, African NGOs felt it necessary to remind their Western 'partners' of their wider responsibilities in a formal declaration made at the United Nations General Assembly:

We encourage Northern and international NGOs to recognise the linkages of many policies of their governments, corporations and multilateral institutions which their governments heavily influence and which adversely affect the quality of life and political and economic independence of African countries.

NGOs face a stark choice. If they stand in favour of the emancipation of humankind (whether at home or abroad), then the focus of their work has inevitably to be in the political domain, supporting those social movements that seek to challenge a social system that benefits a few and impoverishes the many. The closing years of apartheid in Africa were illustrative of the choice that NGOs face today: either they supported the emerging popular movements (in

South Africa and internationally) that supported the overthrow of a brutal system of exploitation, or they stayed silent and continued their philanthropic work, and became thereby complicity in the crimes of the system of apartheid.

Some consciousness of the need to engage in supporting emancipatory movements has been emerging, even amongst those Western organisations (such as Oxfam, Save the Children and Christian Aid) for whom development project work has been (and remains) their 'bread-and-butter', as well as amongst many local NGOs: their involvement in campaigns to end debt, their support for campaigns to protect and promote human rights these are but some of the examples of work motivated by an emancipatory agenda. Alternatively, they can continue their work in projects that serve, as was the case with their missionary precursors, to shore up those forces that have come to subjugate and imiserate the majority.

The challenge that both local and Western NGOs face in making this choice will be that funding at least from the bilateral and multilateral agencies will not necessarily be forthcoming to support the struggle for emancipation. But then, one would hardly have expected the apartheid regime in South Africa to have funded the movement that brought about the downfall of the regime.

References

Butcher, H., Glen, A., Henderson, P. and Smith, J. eds. 1993. *Community and Public Policy*, London: Pluto Press.

Calouste Gulbenkian Foundation. 1968. *Community Work and Social Change. A report on training*, London: Longman. 171 + xiii pages.

Henderson, P. and Thomas, D. N. eds. 1981. *Readings in Community Work.* George Allen and Unwin.

Twelvetrees, A. 1976. *Community Associations and Centres. A comparative study*, Oxford: Pergamon.

5

Community-Based Rehabilitation of Disabled People

Approximately two decades have passed since the concept of community-based rehabilitation (CBR) was presented as a strategy for improving the lives of people with disabilities. In this strategy community leaders work with disabled people, their families, and other concerned citizens to provide equal opportunities for all community members with disabilities.

In 1994 the competent services of ILO, UNESCO and WHO produced a "Joint Position Paper on CBR" in order to promote a common approach for the development of CBR programmes. During the seven years since the first paper was issued ILO, UNESCO and WHO have had more experiences working together in countries, as well as opportunities to work independently with countries in support of CBR. Because UNICEF has also had many country experiences in promoting and supporting CBR programmes focusing on children, this paper is now put forward by all four agencies.

5.1. CBR Strategy

CBR is a strategy within general community development for rehabilitation, equalisation of opportunities and social inclusion of all children and adults with disabilities.CBR is implemented through the combined efforts of people with disabilities themselves CBR is implemented through the combined efforts of people with disabilities themselves, their families and communities, and the appropriate health, education, vocational and social services.

The major objective of CBR is to ensure that people with disabilities are empowered to maximise their physical and mental abilities, have access to regular services and opportunities and become active, contributing members of their communities and their societies. Thus, CBR promotes the human rights of people with disabilities through changes within the community. CBR aims to include people who have disabilities from all types of impairments, including difficulty hearing, speaking, moving, learning or behaving. CBR also includes all age groups: children, youth, adults and older people.

5.2. Evolution of Concepts in CBR

Although the definition, major objective, and principles of CBR have not changed since 1994, there has been an evolution of concepts in CBR. Increasing emphasis on human rights and community participation helps to clarify the essential elements and approaches for implementing this strategy. Hence, it is clear that while CBR focuses on the rights of people with disabilities, it can also be a strategy that addresses the human rights of all citizens in the community. Having taken this important development into consideration, the word "rehabilitation" is perceived as a medical term and does not reflect the CBR concept.

5.2.1. Human Rights

The International Bill of Human Rights is comprised of the Universal Declaration of Human Rights; the International Covenant on Economic, Social and Cultural Rights; the International Covenant on Civil and Political Rights; the Convention on Rights of the Child; the Convention on the Elimination of All Forms of Discrimination Against Women; and the World Programme of Action Concerning Disabled Persons This International Bill of Human Rights forms the basis for the United Nations Standard Rules on the Equalisation of Opportunities for People with Disabilities, which states: "The principle of equal rights implies that the needs of each and every individual are of equal importance, that those needs must be made the basis for the planning of societies, and that all resources must be employed in such a way as to ensure that every individual has equal opportunity for participation."

CBR promotes the rights of disabled children, youth, women and men to live within their communities; to enjoy health and well being; and to fully participate in educational, social, cultural, religious, economic and political activities. CBR emphasises that girls and boys with disabilities have equal rights to schooling, and that women and men have equal rights to opportunities to participate in work and community activities.

5.2.2. Inclusive Communities

The term "inclusive" is now commonly used with reference to education provisions that welcome all children to participate fully in regular community schools or centres of learning, including children with disabilities. The principle of "inclusion" is also being applied to health and vocational services, cultures and communities. The concept of an inclusive community is particularly relevant to CBR. Although CBR contains the term community, the focus has been on disabled people and what the community can do to promote their inclusion. The name "inclusive community" puts the focus on the community itself. The community looks at itself and considers how policies, laws, and common practices affect all citizens. The community takes responsibility for tackling existing barriers to participation of disabled children, men and women. For example, many people in the community may have beliefs, attitudes, or prejudices that limit the kinds of opportunities that are open to disabled people. There may be physical barriers, such as the presence of stairs rather than ramps, or the lack of accessible public transport, limiting the participation of people with disabilities in routine activities of the community, including employment.

By placing the emphasis on the community, the term "inclusive community" has the advantage of focusing on all citizens and treating them equally, again reinforcing the fact that the rights of all people, including those with disabilities, must be guaranteed.

5.3. Developing CBR

We continue to support the broad approaches for developing CBR programmes: the participation of people with disabilities and their representatives at all stages of the development of CBR; the formulation and implementation of national policies to support the equal participation of people with disabilities; the establishment of a system for programme management; and the multisectoral collaboration of governmental and nongovernmental sectors to support communities as they assume responsibility for the inclusion of their members who have disabilities.

5.3.1. Participation of People with Disabilities

During the past two decades, in almost all countries, Disabled People's Organisations (DPOs) and organisations of parents with disabled children have been established and strengthened. Women with disabilities have started to form their own branches within the DPOs, as well as forming their own organisations. This has led to a significant increase in the participation and influence of all people with disabilities at local, national and international levels.

There have also been significant changes in the concepts of disability and rehabilitation. Rehabilitation is now viewed as a process in which people with disabilities or their advocates make decisions about what services they need to reduce limitations in their activities. The limited participation in education, work and social activities experienced by disabled people is no longer viewed as a result of their impairments, but primarily as a result of socialite barriers to their participation. The rights of people with disabilities to have the same opportunities as others in their communities and societies are well recognised. Many of these changes are the direct result of the increased activity and influence of people with disabilities, who now have central roles in monitoring the implementation of internationally accepted guidelines, such as the U.N. Standard Rules on Equalisation of Opportunities for Persons with Disabilities.

CBR programmes have always had the goal of promoting the participation of people with disabilities, but when CBR was initiated more than two decades ago, people with disabilities were not participating as planners and managers at national and district levels. Some community committees included people with disabilities, but others believed it was their responsibility to carry out activities for disabled people rather than with them. Now it is regarded as essential that programmes related to disability issues are planned and implemented with disabled people and their representatives. DPOs have the right and the responsibility to identify the needs of all people with disabilities, to make their needs known, and to promote appropriate measures to address the needs. CBR programmes can assist in forming and strengthening DPOs.

5.3.2. National Policies

National policies and local government involvement are essential elements of CBR programmes. The manner in which communities are linked to the national level varies, depending on the administrative structure of the country and the particular ministry that promotes CBR. However, national policies are needed to guide the overall priorities and planning for a CBR programme. The implementation of these policies requires adequate resource allocation.

The national government establishes policies and legislation relevant to disability, possibly including a specific policy for CBR. International instruments and declarations relevant to disability may form a basis for national policies: United Nations Standard Rules on the Equalisation of Opportunities for Persons with Disabilities; ILO Convention 159 and Recommendation 168 concerning the Vocational Rehabilitation and Employment of Disabled Persons; UNESCO Salamanca Statement and Framework for Action on Special Needs Education; WHO Alma-Ata Declaration establishing rehabilitative care as part of PHC; and UN Convention on Rights of the Child, especially Articles 2 and 23. National policies may also take account of regional proclamations concerning disability, such as the Proclamations of the Asian and Pacific Decade of Disabled Persons and the African Decade of Disabled Persons, or the Arab Proclamation on Disability.

5.3.3. Programme Management

CBR takes place at the community level. Nonetheless, it has an organisational framework at national and intermediate levels to ensure the most efficient and effective collaboration possible among the many sectors that contribute to a CBR programme.

5.3.4. National to District Level

If CBR is initiated by government, one ministry usually takes the lead and then provides the organisational framework. This is often the ministry responsible for social affairs, but sometimes it is the ministry for health. Sometimes the ministry for social affairs is linked with labour, health, or local government and community development. Of course, it is possible for any ministry to initiate CBR, including the ministry responsible for local government. Although one ministry initiates and co-ordinates CBR, the involvement of the ministries for labour, social affairs, education, and health, is considered essential to the success of CBR. These ministries collaborate not only with each other, but also with all ministries that deal with issues relevant to eliminating barriers to the participation of disabled people, e.g. ministries for housing, transport, and rural development. The ministry for finance is often not involved in CBR development, though it can be very helpful in implementation.

Each country decides how to manage its CBR program at different levels. Some countries may have co-ordinators, and perhaps committees, at all administrative levels. Experience has shown that the district level is a key point for co-ordination of support to the community. Therefore, it is particularly important to have district managers, and perhaps district committees, responsible for CBR.

The CBR Programme Managers usually work in the ministry that provides the organisational framework for the programme. For example, if the ministry for social affairs is in charge of CBR, the district social welfare officers will probably have CBR as one component of their work. If the ministry for health is in charge, the district officers for primary health care may be responsible for CBR. Ideally, some of the district level managers will be men and women with disabilities. The duties of a district level CBR programme manager, supported by intermediate staff, include supervising the training and the activities of community workers; monitoring the programme activities; co-ordinating the community committees within the district; and acting as liaison between the communities and the district level representative or committee for CBR.

5.3.5. Community Level

Because CBR belongs to the community, one approach for implementing CBR is through the leadership of the community committee headed by the chief of the village or the mayor of the town. This committee, perhaps called a community development committee, guides the development and affairs of the community. Such a committee is well suited to act as coordinator of the many sectors, governmental and nongovernmental, that must collaborate to sustain a CBR programme. For example, the community development committee can collaborate with the education sector to promote inclusive education, with the ministry of transport to develop a system of accessible transport for people with disabilities, and with voluntary organisations to form a group of volunteers who will take care of disabled children one half day each week so their mothers can do errands outside the home.

Community action for equal participation of disabled children and adults varies a great deal among countries and also within a single country. Even with the guidance of a national policy indicating that communities should take responsibility for the inclusion of their citizens with disabilities, some communities may not identify this as a priority for their - 6 - development. Or, the members of the community development committee may decide that CBR requires special attention and so they establish a separate committee linked to the community development committee. Such a CBR committee would be comprised of a representative from the community development committee, people with disabilities, family members of disabled people, and other interested members of the community. The committee for CBR will take the responsibility for responding to the needs identified by disabled people in the community; raising awareness in the community regarding the needs; obtaining and sharing information about support services for disabled people that are available outside the community; working with the sectors that provide support services to strengthen and coordinate those services; and working within the community to promote the inclusion of people with disabilities in schools, training centres, work places, leisure and social activities. In addition to these tasks, the committee may have to raise funds to support its activities.

Community CBR workers are a key component of CBR programmes because they provide precise information to disabled people about what they can do to improve their abilities to take care of themselves, to communicate, or to move around. The community CBR worker is also the person who provides information about services available outside the community, and acts as liaison between the families of disabled people and the programme manager.

It is the community CBR worker who provides information to disabled people and their families, e.g. advice about basic functional rehabilitation activities, construction of simple associative devices to improve independence in daily activities, use of sign language, or use of a walking cane by a person who is blind. The community CBR worker also acts as an advocate for people with disabilities by making contacts with schools, training centres, work places and organisations to promote accessibility and the inclusion of community members with disabilities. Without this information and advice provided by the community CBR worker, disabled people and their families may not be actively involved in a CBR programme.

Community CBR workers may be employed within the sector that provides the framework for CBR. They can also be volunteers working in cooperation with other community workers who are employed.

5.4. Multisectoral Support for the Community

A community committee for CBR should include community members who have disabilities and their representatives, as well as others who are knowledgeable about the general issues concerning disabled people. The committee members will know how to solve many of the problems in the community, but sometimes they will require additional information from the experts in the education, labour, health, social and other sectors. For example, family members may seek information about how to improve the function of a disabled person in the home; volunteers and community workers will need training in order to assist people with disabilities and their families; teachers may need to have training to effectively include children with disabilities in their classes; and business people will need advice on how to adapt workplaces so that people with disabilities can work.

Hence, information exchange is a key component of CBR. All sectors should support CBR by sharing information with the community, collaborating with each other, and strengthening the specific services they provide to people with disabilities.

5.4.1. Support from the Social Sector

Although the government's responsibility for social affairs varies among countries, issues commonly addressed include disability pensions, support for special equipment for disabled people, housing, vocational training, and co-ordination of referrals for individuals who require services from other sectors. If the social affairs ministry initiates CBR, social welfare officers may be managers of the programme.

A ministry for social affairs may not have personnel below the district level, but it is common that the staff posted in the district are very familiar with social and economic conditions throughout the district and also knowledgeable about resources within the district, including those in the nongovernmental sector. This information is very useful in a CBR programme, particularly for obtaining job skills training and work opportunities for men and women with disabilities. The staff from social affairs can advise individuals with disabilities as well as staff from other ministries regarding community resources.

5.4.2. Support from the Health Sector

The health sector promotes inclusive Primary Health Care (PHC) services, providing basic health care interventions for all persons of the community, including disabled children, youth, adults and elderly. This means that PHC provides routine services like health checks, vaccination, to all people with disability. In addition, PHC personnel provide support to CBR through advice on methods to limit the progression of disabilities, and refer to appropriate rehabilitation services when needed. To ensure that this occurs, it is necessary to train PHC personnel.

The health sector will also strengthen the rehabilitation referral services for supporting PHC personnel and for providing specialised interventions with the aim of maximising the independence of people with disability, for living in community. Health care and rehabilitation personnel will also be available to present health education programmes relevant to disability, to counsel disabled people and their families, and to confer with teachers and social workers, when a special issue is raised by a disabled person or family members.

5.4.3. Support from the Education Sector

The education sector makes an important contribution to CBR by helping regular schools to become more inclusive. This involves, for instance, adapting the content and methods of teaching to meet the needs of all children rather than expecting them to adapt to a rigid curriculum. In this way, the schools will be able to meet the needs of not only children with disabilities, but also the 10 to 15 percent of the children who are already in the schools and who experience difficulties and barriers to learning.

The regular education system will take responsibility for the education of all school-aged children, including children with disabilities who, in some countries, have been the responsibility of the social or health sector or NGOs. Depending on the context, children with multiple or severe disabilities who require extensive additional support may be taught within special units, but can also be taught in regular classrooms. Special schools may be effectively used as resources for regular schools in promoting inclusive education The education sector will, for example, adapt the initial and in-service training of both regular and specialised teachers in response to the new roles in the inclusive school, as well as ensure that buildings are physically accessible. The education sector will also take responsibility for the educational assessment of children with disabilities, which some countries have viewed as a medical responsibility.

5.4.4. Support from the Labour Sector

The local business community is more actively involved in providing skills training and work opportunities for persons with disabilities. Ministries for labour or other competent ministries may provide special services to assist men and women with disabilities to acquire vocational skills, find jobs, or initiate their own income generating activities.

In labour sector there is a growing emphasis on inclusive job training and employment. Women and men with disabilities are increasingly included in regular skills training programmes and seek work either in the local job market or through self-employment. Sheltered work in separate centres has now become a transitional option for some, but not all, disabled persons. Some disabled people attend sheltered workshops for a while, until they are ready to move on to other, more integrated forms of employment. Those unable to hold down a job on the open labour market, either with or without supports, continue to find employment in these workshops, which are undergoing change to be more in line with the current labour market situation.

5.4.5. Support from DPOs

National and local DPOs should be involved in planning and implementing CBR programmes. Members of DPOs can initiate discussions and promote actions to eliminate barriers to equal participation. They can also serve as resource people to advise other NGOs and the government services regarding the specific needs of disabled people and the most appropriate ways to address those needs.

Adults and youth with disabilities can also provide advice and support to each other, and to parents of disabled children, regarding opportunities and resources that will help them to achieve full participation in school, work and social life. Most importantly, DPOs can participate in implementing CBR and at the same time strengthen their role as advocates for the rights of all children, youth and adults with disabilities in their communities and countries.

5.4.6. Support from NGOs

Most communities have a variety of nongovermental organisations (NGOs) and groups that can contribute to a CBR programme. These may include for example, humanitarian organisations, women's and youth groups. Some of these may provide services to disabled people, while others can make special efforts to include people with disabilities in their activities.

National and International NGOs in the framework of Governmental policy, can also make significant contributions to the development of CBR e.g., by initiating CBR, by training CBR programme managers, and by helping to strengthen the services within the various sectors that contribute to CBR.

5.4.7. Support from Other Sectors

The business community can provide valuable support to CBR by providing on-the-job training and hiring people with disabilities. If there are opportunities for members of the community to obtain small grants or loans to start their own business, the business sector can ensure that these opportunities are extended to community members with disabilities. Newspapers, radio, television and the internet can provide the public with information about disability issues, and also present a positive image of individuals with disabilities at school, work or in social settings. All CBR stockholders can work closely with the media to identify priorities and to provide pertinent information.

5.4.8. Collaboration for Support to the Community

CBR will not work if each of the sectors mentioned above works in isolation. Collaboration is needed among the government support services, DPOs, and other nongovernmental groups. The following example suggests the types of collaboration that may occur. A social welfare officer may identify an older child who has never been to school, and who has difficulty learning and moving. The officer will work with the family to convince them to contact the health services and the school. The health services will assess the situation to determine if something could be done to improve movement. The school will assess the child's learning needs to enable the teachers to meet these needs. If the child needs braces, for example, and there are no resources to pay for them, the social welfare officer may request assistance from other sectors, including NGOs.

Support services that consider the "whole person", and not simply the delivery of a special service, will more likely collaborate with each other. Collaboration with other resource groups in the community is necessary because services alone cannot provide disabled women and men with employment or social acceptance.

5.4.9. Sustainable CBR Programmes

Countries' approaches for implementing CBR have varied a great deal, but their experiences have identified some common factors that affect the sustainability of CBR programmes. These include: 1) the recognition of the need for a CBR programme based on a human rights approach; 2) the willingness of the community to respond to the needs; 3) the availability of resources and support, from outside the community; 4) multisectoral collaboration, including collaboration with DPOs and NGOs; 5) the presence of community workers; and 6) the integration of CBR within government with allocation of adequate resources.

5.4.10. Recognition of the Need

When a new CBR programme is initiated not all communities believe that they should have such a programme. A community must recognise that the need exists before it starts CBR activities. The programme manager from the district level must work with each community to clarify this issue. The manager will ensure that it is disabled people themselves, and their families, who define their needs. During community meetings all needs can be discussed and the community can decide whether it wants to address the needs in a co-ordinated way through a community committee for CBR.

5.4.11. Community Response

If the community decides to address the needs of disabled people, the process of establishing a CBR programme can begin. The community development committee will decide if it will take charge of the programme, or if a special committee should be formed. Then decisions can be made about the selection of community workers and volunteers for CBR, and their training can take place. As the committee begins its work for CBR, priority needs will be determined and actions will begin to address those needs. Throughout this process, disabled people and their families will be actively involved. This process of agreeing and planning by the community is essential.

5.4.12. Availability of Resources and Support

If there is a government policy at national level that promotes community efforts in favour of people with disabilities, and if this is matched with adequate resource allocation, efforts for CBR can be strengthened. For example, the government can provide programme managers at district level; strengthen services for people with disabilities; and collaborate with the private sector to ensure that job opportunities are available to people with all types of disabilities.

5.4.13. Multisectoral Collaboration

The various sectors that support the community in a CBR programme each have an important role to play. It is very important for all ministries, as well as all nongovernmental sectors, to realise that in CBR all sectors work in partnership. Although one ministry provides the organisational structure, all sectors are equally important when activities are carried out to promote the full equalisation of opportunities for people with disabilities.

5.5. Community CBR Workers

Maintaining the commitment and motivation of the CBR worker is one of the major challenges of community leaders and CBR programme managers. Some incentive, such as regular in-service training, an annual award for the best worker, certificates of appreciation, or the provision of uniforms, may be offered to the volunteers. This will depend on the customs of the country and the community.Sometimes people with disabilities and their family members have become CBR workers because they are particularly concerned about the needs of all community members who have disabilities. These workers have proved to be very committed to CBR.

An integrated CBR programme with strong links to governmental structures has a greater impact compared to a CBR programme working in isolation. In the absence of governmental support, small CBR projects started by local community groups or NGOs can exist, but their impact may remain limited. If small projects can be linked with governmental services, they are more likely to have sustainability and continuity.

References

Calouste Gulbenkian Foundation. 1973. *Current Issues in Community Work. A Study by the Community Work Group*, London: Routledge and Kegan Paul.

Harrris, V. ed. 1994. *Community Work Skills Manual* 2e, Newcastle: Association of Community Workers.

Jacobs, S. and Popple, K. eds. 1994. *Community Work in the 1990s*, Nottingham: Spokesman. 177 pages.

Ross, M. 1955. *Community Organization. Theory, Principle and Practice*. 1967 edn.), New York: Harper & Row.

Smith, L. and Jones, D. eds. 1981. *Deprivation, Participation and Community Action. Community Work 6,* London: Routledge and Kegan Paul.

Stewart, S., Reynolds, J. and Elsdon, K. T. 1992. *Adult Learning in Voluntary Organizations. Volume 2: case studies 3 - 15*, Nottingham: University of Nottingham Department of Adult Education.

6

Technology for Social Work

An estimated 3.5 billion mobile phones are now in use around the world more people now have one than don't. This remarkable revolution widespread access to the most ubiquitous communication device in human history has changed the way societies and communities organise themselves and do business.

6.1. Innovative Uses of Technology Driving Change

Looking at the work of NGOs in three specific issue areas—health, the environment, and humanitarian relief—we found a number of creative and innovative uses of mobile technology for change. In exploring the various applications in these areas, we observed the following:

6.1.1. Innovation and Scaling

- Organisations are thinking in creative, innovative, and often very entrepreneurial ways about how mobile technology can advance their social impact.
- The potential to scale and replicate projects is significant. Although the vast majority of projects are ground breaking, often they are pilot projects that are small in scale. Many of the organisations we talked to recognise that scaling their projects beyond a relatively small pilot and replicating them elsewhere will be vital to realising the potential of mobile technology in the areas studied.

— Creative partnerships are key to bringing promising mobile initiatives to scale. For example, SexInfo, a text message-based health information service for youth, was made possible through collaboration between the San Francisco Department of Public Health and a local nonprofit. Now it is being scaled up in a similar way in two new locations. Similarly, both Satellife's project in Uganda and the EpiSurveyor project piloted in Kenya and Zambia are being replicated and scaled to use mobile devices for health data collection and analysis in several additional countries.

— Sharing information and technical exchanges could reduce the amount of time it takes to launch a solution and reduce the associated costs. Smaller organisations, in particular, continue to exercise a great deal of trial and error when it comes to utilising mobile technology in their work. ISIS-Inc., the parent organisation of the SexInfo project spent nearly six months researching cost effective ways of implementing its text messaging based health information service before a technology firm in Australia offered to provide a short code at no cost.

— More needs to be done to overcome the 'innovation silos' some organisations operate in, where advances and knowledge gained in the use of mobile technology do not necessarily transfer across organisational boundaries.

— We have seen in the health field that mobile technology is facilitating data collection; yet health providers and local and national governments are now facing the need to create back-end systems capable of aggregating and analysing a wealth of new data. Systems are complex and multifaceted and interventions in one area may require investments in others. In some cases, advances made possible through mobile technology demand more sophisticated back-end systems.

6.1.2. Social Impact

— Mobile initiatives provide greater opportunities for social impact that other information and communications technology (ICT) projects do not necessarily share. For example, physical access to mobile phones is obviously much greater compared to computers and other less readily available technologies. With rapid mobile phone penetration in many areas of the globe and growing mobile network coverage, access is increasingly assured. Likewise, mobile initiatives can be more affordable but the skills and training necessary to implement them less so.

— Mobile technology initiatives in this field are still emerging, with most of the projects we investigated at the 'proof of concept' stage. A report by the World Bank's InfoDev program states, "It is harder to find examples of analysis that moves beyond the project purpose to look at the conditions that might need to be in place to scale up interventions and what might be the impact of such activity."

— While we can point to solid outcomes for the programs, for example, the number of clients served or number of text messages sent, strong evidence-based information about the widespread impact of mobile initiatives on international development goals is elusive.

— Investment in knowledge-sharing and impact assessments are vital to realise what we believe is the enormous potential of mobile technologies to further development goals such as those outlined in the United Nations' Millennium Development Goals. Several donors, such as Canada's International Development Research Centre, are now investing considerable resources to assess over several years the impact of mobile technologies in improving health, for example, to build a more solid body of evidence about social impacts.

6.1.3. Challenges

— The costs of developing and deploying mobile technologies are often onerous for organisations, explaining, in part, why projects are small in scale. We found that many projects rely on heavily subsidised technology or transmissions or even direct donations by technology companies and mobile operators. While some players are willing to donate their services for smaller projects, there are questions as to whether scaled initiatives would receive the same level of support.

— The potential for scaling up 'mobile for good' initiatives may come with identifying commercial incentives.

6.1.4. Lessons Learned

- Many of the same lessons learned in information and communication technologies (ICT) development and deployment apply to mobile initiatives.
- Our research has uncovered a set of potential best practices for technology deployment: There need to be clear and realistic program goalsand solid knowledge about the needs on the ground and of the intended beneficiaries.
- Mobile solutions, as with any other ICT project, need to be appropriate to their environment to have impact, and be responsive to local needs and conditions.
- Users need to be involved in the planning and design of mobile systems and they need incentives (such as increased efficiency or time savings) to use the technology.
- Training for users needs to be a focus of mobile projects within an organisation.
- There needs to be a focus on the benefits of a given system rather then the technology per se. Governmental ICT policies and regulatory frameworks should be consistent and predictable and foster an environment for innovation.
- There are still significant barriers in this arena, despite efforts by trade associations such as the GSMA to increase awareness of these issues for development.
- We are hopeful that increased attention and investment into the real and concrete potential and actual use of mobile technologies will help improve lives around the world.

6.2. Mobile Technology in Health

The Millennium Development Goals (MDGs) acknowledge the centrality of health in reducing poverty and increasing human development. The role of mobile phones, as with other information and communication technologies (ICT), is under increasing scrutiny in the health arena, precisely because the stakes are so high and the potential gains from technology development so significant.

Take HIV/AIDS, for example. A 2007 report on the MDGs states: "The number of people dying from AIDS worldwide increased to 2.9 million in 2006, and prevention measures are failing to keep pace with the growth of the epidemic. In 2005, more than 15 million children had lost one or both parents to AIDS."

Furthermore, of the one billion people living in extreme poverty, 75 percent live in rural areas. A report by InfoDev notes: "Health conditions in rural areas are generally poorer, and access to information, services, and supplies is most limited." Informa Telecoms & Media estimates that in mid-2007, mobile networks covered 90 percent of the global population, and that in 2008 worldwide mobile phone penetration will hit 50 percent, with well over 3 billion subscriptions.

With rapidly increasing mobile coverage around the world and expansion to rural areas where Internet access is still years away, mobile technology holds great promise for making health prevention and medical care more effective for the world's poorest people. Mobile technology has been piloted in a range of health-related areas, including improving dissemination of public health information (e.g., disease outbreak and prevention messages); facilitating remote consultation, diagnosis, and treatment; disseminating health information to doctors and nurses; managing patients; monitoring public health; and increasing the efficiency of administrative systems. In all these areas, evidence exists that mobile phones can play a significant role. Further work is underway to look at the actual impact of mobile phones on improving health outcomes.

The Pan Asian Collaboration for Evidence-based e-health Adoption and Application (PANACeA), a project underway at the International Development Research Centre, is assessing the effect of mobile phones on improved While impact assessments and outcome measurements are hard to come by, there is evidence that text message reminders increase patient compliance in taking medication for such diseases as tuberculosis and HIV. Yet much of the published evidence about the use of mobiles in health remains in the proof of concept stage.

The case studies featured here explore areas where mobile phones show great potential: health workers making better treatment decisions because of information delivered via the mobile network (e.g., Academy for Educational Development (AED)-Satellife), people making informed choices about their health with better access to information delivered via mobile phones (e.g., SexInfo), and the collection of medical data on mobile devices for better patient and public health management (e.g., DataDyne and Cell-Life). In order to justify investing in the use of mobile technologies in the health sector in poor countries, much more attention needs to be paid to how such technologies effectively integrate and improve basic service delivery on the ground. Furthermore, the potential benefits in improved access, quality of care, and better clinical results need to be clearly demonstrated.

6.3. Confronting South Africa's HIV/AIDS Epidemic

Africa's HIV/AIDS Epidemic Medical workers and doctors in South Africa are confronted daily with nearly impossible odds: over onetenth of the South African population has HIV/AIDS, with younger age groups showing infection rates as high as 30 percent. With more than 5.6 million afflicted with HIV or AIDS, South Africa has the worst AIDS epidemic in the world. The South African government began supplying anti-retroviral drugs in 2004. By 2006, 33 percent of people living with HIV/AIDS were receiving anti-retroviral treatment.

A weak state health infrastructure and disparate system of rural clinics make consistent anti-retroviral treatment (ART) and patient monitoring extremely difficult. Eighty percent of the HIV/AIDS patients that do receive medical care rely on the government health care system. HIV/AIDS patients living in rural areas must travel long distances to reach a hospital. Frequently, they encounter a day-long wait as understaffed and under-resourced clinics attempt to cope with the high demand. Sometimes hospitals run out of the necessary drugs, and patients return home without medications. Secondary infections such as tuberculosis or pneumonia are common. For those patients fortunate enough to be receiving ART, effective patient care monitoring is essential to reducing the risk of high toxicity levels from treatment, and to ensure a regular treatment regime. If adherence to medication is not kept above 90 percent, HIV can develop mutations that lead to drug resistance, making first-line ART ineffective and worsening the epidemic.

6.3.1. Improving Treatment through Mobile Applications

Cell-Life, a non-governmental organisation based in Cape Town, South Africa, created its "Aftercare" program to work with the public health system and its health workers to provide home-based care for HIV/AIDS patients receiving ART treatments.

The mobile technology-based Aftercare program supports the effective treatment of HIV/AIDS patients, and covers other aspects such as voluntary counselling. Each Aftercare worker is assigned to monitor 15 to 20 patients.

The worker visits the patient in his or her home, and in a one-one session discusses the patient's current treatment. Using their mobile phones for data capture, Aftercare workers record information about patient medical status, drug adherence, and other factors that may affect a patient's ART therapy. Aftercare workers then relay this information via text message to a central Cell-Life database. The data sent via text message reaches the Cell-Life server, where a care manager uses a web-based system to access and monitor the incoming patient information.

The manager can also respond to Aftercare workers' questions and provide supplemental information to improve patient care. The information collected not only facilitates individual patient care, but is also used to build a database of information on the severity and prevalence of the South African AIDS epidemic in these regions. The goals of the program include reduction of treatment errors, increased volume of patient data, and increased comfort for the patients as they receive HIV/AIDS care. Outcome: Delivering Health Care for HIV/ AIDS Patients

The Cell-Life Aftercare project was conceived as a joint project with the University of Cape Town and the Cape Peninsula University of Technology. The partners built a monitoring and evaluation system into the Aftercare program, and initial results indicated that the quality of care for patients has improved. A Women's Net and United Nations Children's Fund (UNICEF) report billed Aftercare as "one of the most experienced initiatives combining mobile phone technologies and AIDS management." In part, the efficacy of Cell-Life's work in South Africa can be attributed to the high prevalence of mobile phones. South

Africa's mobile penetration rate is 41 percent, and mobile phone networks cover more than 90 percent of the country's territory.

The Aftercare program and technology were designed with end users in mind. It functions in a participatory fashion, is simple and works consistently, and provides feedback to the counsellors via text message when reports from the home health aides are received. The program has been able to keep costs relatively low by using data collection software that functions even on lowcost phones.

6.3.2. Sustainability and Scalability

Two major challenges for Aftercare's future identified in several evaluations are long-term financial sustainability and the difficulty of implementation on a larger scale. Scaling the project to more areas is expensive and difficult because the system can only be used on one network using prepaid accounts. And because the software is written only in English, it would have to be translated into South Africa's eleven national languages in order to be successfully scaled.

Ulrike Rivett, founder and director of Cell- Life, says: "The single greatest risk to effective patient monitoring is the lack of resources to roll out ART effectively. The areas with the highest prevalence of HIV have a shortage of skilled medical personnel, lack of good nursing and management staff and have limited financial resources," making mobile health solutions all the more valuable..

Cell-Life is also considering a migration to Java and GPRS (General Packet Radio Service) platforms to lower data transmission costs. They are also looking to enhance security measures and translate the program to other languages spoken in South Africa. In a country challenged by a high rate of HIV/AIDS, a weak state health infrastructure, and a disparate system of rural health clinics, the Cell-Life Aftercare program is demonstrating how an innovative mobile application can improve patient treatment.

6.3.3. Expanding the Cell-Life Model

Beyond securing the necessary funding, Cell-Life has identified a number of criteria that would influence the future of Aftercare. These include:

- Further development of its data management software.
- Expansion of its partnerships with other actors in the public health sector and commercial operators in South Africa.
- Better interoperability between its systems.
- Greater standardisation for medical record collection forms.
- The adaptation of the system to other chronic and acute diseases.

6.3.4. Relaying Medical Care Information in Rural Areas

In developing countries, health care is often delivered by a lone nurse practitioner in a one-room clinic. As they battle AIDS, tuberculosis, malnutrition, malaria, and other diseases, the practitioners frequently lack access to electricity or running water, let alone medical information, a telephone, or the Internet.

Often the quality of care a patient receives is limited to whatever knowledge the nurse retained from basic training. In Uganda, per capita spending on health is US $57 per year. In Rakai, a rural district about 200 miles southwest of the capital city of Kampala, there is one doctor for every 22,400 people; in the Mbale district, a rural agricultural district where coffee and bananas are grown, there is one doctor for every 15,000 people. With medical staff stretched so thin and working under challenging circumstances, access to wireless-enabled health care information becomes a critical lifeline just when it is needed at the point of care.

6.3.5. Using Wireless Personal Digital Assistants

To address this urgent need for point of care medical information, Academy for Educational Development (AED)-Satellife, a U.S. Based nonprofit organisation, has implemented projects in more than a dozen countries where health professionals working in resource poor areas use hand-held personal digital assistants (PDAs) to transmit and receive vital data via a wireless or mobile network.

6.3.6. AED-Satellife

AED-Satellife has used hand-held computers for the last six years to deliver medical information at the point of care. It delivers medical information including disease treatment guidelines, continuing education materials, newsletters, and essential drug lists and database. Nurses also receive national and international news articles on their devices. AED-Satellife also has customised software for data collection on hand-held so medical workers are able to track patients and keep records electronically. Clinics are required to regularly send data on public health programs and routine epidemiological data back to the regional health centers.

Holly Ladd, Director of AED-Satellife, describes how hand-held devices deliver vital information: "We have seen changes in practice, particularly around treatment for diarrhoea. We emphasise in the medical treatment alerts that we send to the hand-held devices in the clinics that rehydration therapy is strongly recommended as a first course of action, particularly with kids.

We have evidence that this is now used much more often as a first course of action in those clinics." Likewise, PDAs can streamline health data collection from remote areas. Ladd describes a recent typhoid outbreak that was detected early because clinics regularly reported cases with PDAs.

"The outbreak was contained because we could see that something was amiss. This would not have been possible with paper and pencil reporting, which is much more time-consuming," she says. AED-Satellife has pioneered the use of hand-held devices that can perform the same tasks as a desktop or laptop computer in healthcare settings in developing countries. The Uganda Health Information Network is an AED-Satellife Project operated in collaboration with Uganda Chartered health net and the Faculty of Medicine of Makerere University. It is the largest of AED-Satellife's current projects using PDAs in health clinics.

6.4. Humanitarian Assistance

Mobile technology plays an important role in communications efforts during the various phases of a humanitarian catastrophe from the early warning phase through the immediate disaster response and longer-term reconstruction efforts. Stories abound about how mobile technology has been used in recent disasters, from reestablishing communications networks vital to the work of first responders to providing a first line of communications for refugees trying to reconnect with a loved one.

Communication needs differ in each unique situation, ranging from mass broadcasting of text messages in the early warning phase, for example, to decentralised two-way communication among relief workers and affected populations in the aftermath of a disaster. Early warning systems involving mobile phones both cell broadcast and text messaging alerts are being considered or implemented in various countries. Because it can quickly and informally disseminate information from person to person, mobile communication is a good medium for information sharing both during and in the aftermath of a disaster.

The case study on the World Food Programme's use of text messaging to inform Iraqi refugees of food shipments illustrates both the challenges and opportunities of text alerts. There is evidence that neither the public nor emergency workers utilise mobile technology to its fullest potential. For emergency workers, key barriers include organisational and communication inefficiencies and breakdowns, as well as technical barriers such as overburdened systems unable to handle post-disaster traffic For the affected populations, emergency communication needs to take a priority and may necessitate prioritising that particular traffic over person-to-person communication. A 2005 Groupe Special Mobile (GSM) Association (GSMA) study found that in the immediate aftermath of a disaster the speed with which cellular networks can recover from damage often within hours plays a critical role in relief supply management and economic recovery.

As the case study on Telecoms Sans Frontiers illustrates, rapid restoration of networks is essential in the critical period right after a disaster. Our research underscores the importance of operators, governments, and relief organisations working closely together to ensure that mobile networks are available for critical communication, and that information is able to flow freely. The GSMA study states that: "in the case of developing countries in particular, mobiles are likely to be the dominant means of communication for affected members of the public. This flow of information not mediated by broadcasting agencies or public authorities ensures that people elsewhere quickly come to know what is happening and what help is needed. In the chaotic aftermath of a disaster, when people are displaced, buildings and infrastructure destroyed, no central authority can possibly hold all the necessary information and allocate resources in the place of greatest need." Hence, there is a need for government coordination with telecommunication carriers to ensure that there is rapid rebuilding after a disaster, and 'light touch' regulation to support this. Text messaging-based fund-raising appeals have grown increasingly popular in recent years, with private donations in many cases exceeding government expenditures in the wake of a disaster.

This was especially true after the 2004 Indian Ocean tsunami, when millions of dollars were raised via text messaging particularly in Europe. Even though donations are relatively small, their cumulative impact can be substantial. Looking ahead, there are a number of opportunities for improving the effectiveness of mobile technology in disaster relief. As mobile infrastructure grows worldwide, early warning and last minute information dissemination become more viable, especially if there are strategic investments and agreement on standards. Similarly, efforts are needed to coordinate relief organisations more effectively and increase their internal capacity to take strategic advantage of mobile technology.

6.5. Delivering Food Aid to Iraqi Refugees

6.5.1. Alerting Refugees to Food Aid Deliveries

Beneficiaries of the United Nations (UN) World Food Programme (WFP) are the poorest of the poor. As the front line agency mandated to combat global hunger and entirely reliant on voluntary funding WFP must make stark choices about whom it can provide with food assistance. This year, WFP aims to assist 73 million people in 78 countries knowing that there are a staggering 850 million hungry people worldwide. About two million Iraqis have fled their country since 2003, and an additional 60,000 are leaving each month. Syria has received the majority of these refugees and there are now an estimated 1.4 million Iraqis in Syria.

The WFP has estimated that about 50,000 of the Iraqis in Syria need food aid. Every month at distribution centers and warehouses of the Syrian Red Crescent, the WFP and Syrian Red Crescent provide eligible refugee families with basic food commodities, such as rice, lentils, and oil, and complementary items, such as sugar, tea, pasta, tomato paste, and bulgur.

Charged with coordinating these distributions, WFP alerts eligible families about food rations and directs them to the appropriate distribution centers. Previously, the WFP had used local nongovernmental organisations (NGOs) who work with refugees to help get the word out. Since not all eligible families had regular contact with local NGOs, however, a new strategy was needed. To facilitate this process, the UN agency recently instituted a text messaging program to notify refugees about the availability of food aid.

6.5.2. Using Text Messaging to Communicate News

With a responsibility for coordinating the logistics and emergency communications for other UN agencies and NGOs, WFP is constantly looking for innovative ways of stretching its donations to benefit as many people as possible. The Iraqi beneficiaries described in the case study are far from typical in that they have access to mobile telephones. Describing the genesis of the project, Haitham El Noush, program officer at WFP Damascus, says: "Last year we started distributing food to refugees in Damascus. But how were we going to announce distribution? We wanted to alert about 6,000 families in a pilot project when food was ready for pick-up.

Someone in the office came up with the idea to use a text messaging service to alert these families." In August 2007, WFP's program in Damascus contacted one of the mobile telephone operators in the country, to inquire about covering a portion of the costs of the text messaging. The operator agreed to provide an initial 800 text messages at no cost. El Noush notes: "The idea was new; this was the first time this was ever done. And it was simple: We sent a text message to people on our list to go to the distribution site and receive the food."

To bring the text message pilot program to scale, the WFP set up an account with a mobile marketing vendor to accommodate their bulk messaging needs. WFP buys text messages in bulk to secure a volume discount, and uses a list of phone numbers provided by the UN High Commissioner for Refugees (UNHCR) to target its food distribution alerts. WFP manages and distributes messages using a do-it-yourself dashboard on the mobile vendor's website. The message that is delivered to refugees provides a URL (uniform resource locator) where potential food aid recipients can verify whether they are eligible for food benefits.

6.5.3. Reaching the Right Recipients with the Right Information

One of the limits of a program like this is that the messaging is only as targeted as the phone numbers on the contact list. Because people switch phone numbers or share phones, delivery of a message to an intended recipient is not always assured, especially in a sometimes chaotic environment. As a result, during the first month of the program, some messages were delivered to people not eligible for food aid, who were subsequently turned away at the distribution center.

El Noush notes that, "people thought the text message was like an entitlement and then showed up and wanted the food but had to be turned down." Learning this lesson, recipients are now directed to a website to make sure that they are indeed eligible. However, says El Noush, even though "there are lots of internet cafes and people can have easy internet access, we still cannot be 100 percent sure that we don't exclude some people by this extra step.

At the same time, text messaging really is the most effective way to reach people everyone has a mobile phone and by sending some 35,000 messages we got a lot of visibility about the program." UNHCR is now asking individuals picking up food to update their phone number at the distribution center in the hope that this will reduce errors over time and ensure a more accurate list of numbers. Another challenge of texting is the limited space especially in Arabic. While a text message in English can accommodate 160 characters, a text message in Arabic can hold only 70. With such limited space, messages must be very clear to be understood by the recipient.

6.5.4. Improved Awareness and Targeting of Food Aid

The initial distribution of text messages to 800 families was successful in reaching targeted recipients of food aid, and the program expanded rapidly. In the first six months of operation in 2007, WFP sent out about 35,000 text messages to 140,000 eligible people approximately one message per registered family. While some text messages went to people not eligible for food, most were successfully delivered and the families expressed gratitude and appreciation. Says El Noush, "The text messages have the side effect of creating news in the city by word of mouth. We are finding the program to be very effective. You give good news to people on their mobiles. People reported that they felt happy when they received the text messages from us, and told us that they felt that someone cares about them."

6.5.5. Bringing the Food Aid Alert Model to Scale

WFP's food aid text message alert program has grown rapidly. The first effort reached about 6,600 people through some 800 messages; approximately one message per phone number available for each family. The second round of messaging targeted some 30,000 individuals. At the time of publication, the WFP's list had grown to include more than 142,000 Iraqi refugees in Syria that it is reaching via text messaging. The target for 2008 is to notify a total of 362,000 Iraqi refugees in Syria about the availability of food aid. Although this program has yet to be replicated elsewhere, the WFP is excited about the potential of the program. When conditions permit, as in the case of Iraqi refugees in Syria, communicating with large groups via text messaging can provide targeted delivery of essential information including where one might find one's next meal.

6.6. Facilitating Communication in Emergency Situations

6.6.1. Essential Emergency Communications for Disaster Relief

On the evening of 15 August 2007, a 7.9 magnitude earthquake struck the coast of Peru, bringing down buildings, cutting power supplies, and disrupting communications. More than 500 people died and 1,600 were injured, with tens of thousands more left homeless. As with other major international disasters, relief agencies across various government, nongovernmental, and intergovernmental bodies activated to deliver food, medicine, and supplies to those in need. Yet none of these groups could operate effectively without a communications system enabling them to share information among themselves, and with operational headquarters.

6.6.2. Deploying Rapid Response Emergency Communications

Telecoms Sans Frontiers (TSF), or Telecoms Without Borders, a nongovernmental organisation (NGO) headquarters in France, uses mobile telecommunications to help re-establish these vital communications networks in the response to and management of humanitarian crises.

Within hours of the earthquake in Peru, five staff and volunteers boarded a commercial aircraft from TSF's Latin America regional office in Managua, Nicaragua to Peru's capital city of Lima. With them, they carried everything they would need to set up emergency telecommunication operations satellite phones, mobile phones, routers, laptops, fax machines, printers, and scanners.

Within 24 hours of their arrival, the team had established temporary telecommunications centers in three of Peru's hardest-hit areas: Pisco, Inca, and Chicha. Over the next ten days, a broad range of disaster relief agencies used TSF's service to coordinate relief efforts and help save lives.

These included the Peruvian Ministries of Health and Education, the National Program for Food Assistance, the United Nations (UN), and local and international NGOs. Satellite phones were also made available so that local residents could contact family and friends. In all, more than 17 agencies and 1,400 families accession TSF's services over the course of its deployment.

6.6.3. Providing Vital Communications Services

When and Where Needed Most In 2006 and 2007 alone, TSF responded to 17 emergency situations around the globe facilitating relief efforts in southern Lebanon during the Lebanon-Israel conflict, helping survivors of a cyclone in Bangladesh, and assisting victims of the ongoing civil war in the Democratic Republic of Congo. The origins of TSF's work date back to the late 1990s when TSF co-founders Jean- Francois Cazenave and Monique Lanne-Petit were volunteering with humanitarian missions that took them to Kosovo, Afghanistan, and Iraq. Refugees would pass Cazenave slips of paper asking if he would contact their loved ones abroad.

TSF was founded in 1998 with the goal of providing disaster survivors with three minute phone calls that enable survivors to place a call to a loved one often to confirm family members' whereabouts or to request assistance. Today, its services have grown to include establishing communications centers for relief groups, including UN agencies. TSF has put in place a 24-hour emergency monitoring system and coordinates closely with the UN Office for Coordination of Humanitarian Affairs (OCHA) and the UN Children's Fund (UNICEF) before deploying to a particular location. Headquarters in Pau, in southwestern France, TSF has field offices in Managua, Nicaragua and Bangkok, Thailand.

The majority of the telecommunication experts TSF deploys are volunteers, who receive a modest stipend for their time in the field. Most are students or recent university graduates in their twenties or professionals over 50 with backgrounds in information and communications technology (ICT) and engineering. TSF's work in support of UN agencies is supported by a joint grant from the United Nations Foundation and The Vodafone Group Foundation. TSF is also supported by a diverse group of public and private sector donors, including the European Commission's Humanitarian Aid Office, and telecommunications and technology companies such as Inmarsat, Eutelsat, AT&T, Cable and Wireless, and Vizada.

6.6.4. Keeping Apace with Technology Developments While Staying the Course

A key challenge, according to TSF Information and Communications Coordinator Oisin Walton, is keeping up with changes in technology and determining how best to adapt new technologies to meet needs in the field. Currently, TSF maintains an inventory of 50 data transmitters, more than 100 phones, and assorted computers. A mainstay of TSF's work is the Inmarsat BGan, which offers voice, fax, and broad band Internet connections. For longer duration emergencies, TSF employs a Very Small Aperture Terminal (VSAT), a satellite dish that can facilitate data transmission from several satellite phones.

TSF's mobile "visio-emergency" video system allows for satellite transmission of live videos filmed at the site of an emergency.

Similarly, TSF can set up a video conferences system capable of linking field staff with headquarters. Looking ahead, Walton acknowledges that the sustainability of TSF's efforts is a key issue. The bulk of funds TSF receives are directed at immediate disaster service provision, and not at strengthening TSF's long-term capacity to respond to emergencies. TSF is making the case for the vital importance of disaster communications to corporations and other funding organizations that support more traditional relief measures such as the provision of food, water, shelter, and education.

6.6.5. Developing Services to Improve Emergency Response

Following each assignment, TSF staff conduct a thorough debriefing on what went well and where future improvement is needed. Among those areas being looked at is how to expand the use of TSF services by governments and large NGOs, many of which rely on their own telecommunications capacity, and the development of new services in cooperation with TSF's existing partners. TSF is exploring a number of ways to improve and expand its emergency services. For example, it is looking into what would be required to set up 'cyber cafes' in relief areas that would enable affected individuals to send mails to family and friends about their situation and needs.

It is also exploring how to play a greater role in prevention efforts through helping communities prepare in advance of an emergency, particularly in cases where annual weather patterns predictably lead to flooding or droughts. In Nicaragua, for example, following its emergency response to Hurricane Felix in September 2007, TSF installed an emergency communications network in the remote North Atlantic Autonomous Region of the country, where no traditional communications exist. The network will allow for improved response in the event of future emergencies. TSF is also looking at expanding its use of mobile technology, and setting up temporary Groupe Special Mobile (GSM) networks at base camps.

"With GSM networks being re-established faster and faster in emergencies, we are looking at ways of using more GSM technology." He adds: "When mobile networks are disrupted, we could deploy equipment capable of connecting to the network outside the affected area." TSF's work alongside UN agencies, national governments, and other disaster relief groups demonstrates the crucial role of mobile and other communications technology in all stages of disaster relief. TSF has consistently delivered rapid response emergency communications to support humanitarian activities, and has frequently provided a first line of communication for refugees and other populations affected by disasters. Continuing its work on building the capacity of mobile communications to play a role in disaster prevention and preparedness could be a promising area for TSF's growth. Another area for exploration is the use of mobile phones for money transfer services ('mtransactions') during disasters. M-transactions have the potential to meet a widespread need during challenging circumstances.

6.7. Text Messaging as a Violence-Prevention Tool

6.7.1. Providing Real-Time Information in Times of Crisis

Following the December 2007 presidential election in Kenya, waves of political and ethnic violence swept the country. The election, which returned President Mwai Kibanki to office, was marred by widespread allegations of vote rigging. To help stem the violence, human rights advocates in the country quickly mobilised by creating a text messaging 'nerve center.' That center served as a vital tool for conflict management and prevention by providing a hub for real-time information about actual and planned attacks between rival ethnic and political groups. The text messages, sent in by human rights advocates, religious leaders, and others, were then relayed to local Peace Committees for response. The initiative was funded by Oxfam Great Britain (Oxfam-GB) a development, advocacy, and relief agency as part of its emergency response. Oxfam-GB has employed several text messaging strategies as it develops its knowledge and evaluates the effectiveness of that platform as a fund-raising, awareness-building, and advocacy tool.

6.7.2. Connecting Communities in Crisis through Mobile Communications

As part of its emergency response during the crisis in Kenya, Oxfam-GB provided financial support to Peace Net, an umbrella body made up of Kenyan organisations and individuals dedicated to human rights, peace, and justice. "Before the elections, Peace Net was gathering information around Kenya to make sure nothing went awry," explains Philippic Crosland Tailor, Oxfam Country Programme Manager in Kenya.

"After the election, they decided it would be valuable to have people text into a nerve center, which could then pass information along to relevant authorities and the police. Sometimes if you put a few policemen or elders in place, you can prevent something unfortunate from happening." Oxfam-GB's contribution of roughly £36,000 was used to support Peace Net's field operations and headquarters costs during the crisis. Oxfam-GB also used its connections to negotiate a deal with Celtel, the second largest mobile phone network in Kenya, to halve its ordinary rates for those transmitting and receiving messages through the text message 'nerve center.'

6.7.3. Communicating by Mobile Phone to Avert Crisis

Through facilitating emergency communications, Peace Net's text message 'nerve center' was able to prevent violent incidents in the weeks and months following the election. For example, in the city of Eldoret, Peace Net mobilised local nongovernmental organisation (NGO) and religious leaders to form Peace Committees to offer early warning of violent activity and to serve as intermediaries. When one local citizen learned of a pending attack against a camp for internally displaced people, a text alert was sent to the text message 'nerve center.' It, in turn, alerted the Peace Committee in Eldoret, which took steps to avert the attack.

During another instance, following the murder of a member of the Kenyan Parliament, a group of young people made plans to attack residents of a particular ethnic community. Once the 'nerve center' was alerted, it notified Peace Committee members who persuaded the youth to go home. Text Messaging as a Violence-Prevention Tool (Kenya) "In the wake of a government ban on live broadcasting of incidence of violence, the SMS Center became a lifeline for information by linking Nairobi to incidence as they happened on the ground," says Barasa Meaning, Peace Net-Kenya program officer. "The initiative encouraged local level dialogue and mediation to stop violence and facilitated communication to security forces, the Kenya Red Cross, and UN Office for Coordination of Humanitarian Affairs. Civil society actors were linked to peace processes at the community level, enabling them to contribute to nonviolence advocacy."

6.7.4. Expertise to New Outreach Efforts

While encouraged by the successes of the text message 'nerve center' in preventing violence in Kenya, and its text message outreach efforts related to the Make Poverty History campaign, Oxfam-GB emphasises that its use of mobile applications remains in the preliminary stages, and has yet to develop into a cohesive strategy for employing mobile applications in the future. Part of the challenge lies in developing the necessary expertise. Oxfam-GB relied heavily on a mobile marketing firm for support and advice during the White Band campaign. Oxfam-GB's experience in using text messaging as an awareness-building tool mirrors that of many NGOs.

Because text message-based advocacy is relatively new, expertise is limited and few successful case studies exist. Setup costs are also a big factor. Particularly in the area of fund-raising via text messages, those NGOs that have claimed successes tend to be well known and represent causes that elicit an emotional response that drives people to take immediate action.

6.7.5. Increasing Organisational Reach through Mobile Phones

Looking ahead, Cioffi is encouraged by the potential for people to be able to make donations via the Internet on mobile phones that are wireless access protocol (WAP) enabled. "From our point of view," says Cioffi, "we see mobiles as a way that people can spontaneously donate. If they see a billboard or a poster, they can do so right away." Text messaging has emerged as an increasingly powerful tool in humanitarian crises helping to disseminate life-saving information, providing critical news updates, and mobilising people to make donations to help those in need. As the use of mobile phones keeps expanding, the power and reach of these strategies will only continue to grow.

6.8. Environmental Conservation

6.8.1. Using Mobile Phones to Protect the Environment

Around the world, mobile phones are being used in the environmental arena from efforts to promote wildlife conservation to environmental advocacy to educating and influencing consumers about the environmental impact of their purchasing decisions. In the area of conservation, mobile phones are used to track wildlife and provide an early warning system designed to mitigate human/animal conflict.

Central to these efforts is improving communication among local stockholders, nongovernmental organisations (NGOs), and government agencies. For conservation efforts to be successful, all stockholders, including local residents of sensitive areas, must be engaged and their interests taken into consideration. As the case study on wildlife conservation in Kenya shows, opening up communication channels using mobile phones can play a valuable role in community based conservation efforts.

Mobile technology is also being used to monitor wildlife. One pilot project initiated by Save the Elephants in Kenya employed Global Positioning System/Groupe Special Mobile collars to track elephant movements. Unlike the more expensive satellite/very high frequency tracking systems, mobile communication inexpensively pinpoints the elephant's location and text messages the coordinates back to the researchers. These efforts are in the beginning stages but show great potential for making animal tracking easier and more precise.

The case study on Greenpeace Argentina's efforts to protect forests and pass environmental legislation demonstrates the use of mobile phones in environmental advocacy. Text messages, because they are immediate and direct, offer an effective way to alert constituents about important news and move them to action. If the action is a phone call to a decision maker (e.g., a legislator), mobile communication is especially useful. There is growing evidence that mobile phones can move people to action more effectively than other media. A number of campaigns reported to us a response rate of 20 to 45 percent for text appeals, which is considerably higher than that recorded for mail alerts.

This data is supported by research from the commercial market that shows that text messaging works to influence decision-making and purchasing behaviour. Existing research studies reflect that mobile communication can influence how people feel about a product or brand, and affect their behaviour. One study concludes: "The reported increased likelihood to purchase is the most important finding of this research; on average this was 35%, but it was as high as 71% for one [text message campaign."

Given these findings, we sought to investigate some of the text message services that disseminate data on products and companies with the goal of getting consumers to buy or use environmentally sustainable products. While text messaging information lines are proliferating, we have not seen direct evidence that they influence consumer behaviour other than by inference based on data from the commercial sector. Lastly, we looked into using mobile phones as environmental sensing devices, an emerging area that is attracting both commercial and academic interest. Several pilot projects illustrate what may be possible in the future when it comes to applications such as monitoring air quality. Such applications are in the experimental stage and remain relatively expensive for widespread public use.

6.9. Text Messaging to Save Trees

6.9.1. Protecting Argentina's Forests

Every hour, trees covering an area the size of forty soccer fields are cleared from the old growth forests of Argentina, home to indigenous tribes and numerous endangered species. According to Greenpeace, 300,000 hectares of native forest are cleared in Argentina each year. To confront this rapid deforestation, Greenpeace Argentina used the web, mobile phones, and publicity on television and in newspapers to gather 1.5 million signatures for a petition supporting La Ley de Bosques, or the Forest Law.

6.9.2. Mobilising the Public for Environmental Protection

The Forest Law, Argentina's first federal forest protection act, was passed in 2007. It includes a one-year moratorium on clearing native forests, giving the forest service time to develop appropriate forest management regulations. The law, funded in part by an export tax on genetically engineered soy, also establishes public hearings and environmental impact studies. Greenpeace was able to effectively advocate for the Ley de Bosques by building a large database of supporters. Through a form on the organisation's website, individuals were asked to sign a petition supporting the Forest Law, and submit both mail addresses and mobile phone numbers.

About 300,000 phone numbers were collected from this web form, and an additional 50,000 were collected via other means, such as mail or through volunteers stationed on busy streets.

This 350,000 number mobile phone list is one of the larger active mobile phone lists used in advocacy today. By the end of the campaign, over 1.5 million people had signed the petition supporting the Forest Law. Greenpeace used their mobile phone network in several ways.

The organisation collected about 3,000 signatures for the petition via text messaging. Greenpeace also sent out text messages asking people to call specific legislators to lobby for the law. Text messages were sent out to specific target audiences, so that people would be directed to their legislator. Finally, Greenpeace used the mobile network to send urgent alerts about other actions or news.

Using text messaging for advocacy requires an active list of mobile subscribers who have agreed to receive communications from a campaign. Hernan Pablo Nadal, Greenpeace Argentina's online organiser, describes how Greenpeace expanded its mobile list: "Two years ago, we had 10,000 mobile numbers. By October 2007 with a lot of outreach, we had 45,000 numbers. With the campaign for the Forest Law, we gave signers of the petition the option of giving us their mobile number.

As a result, we now have 350,000 mobile activists and 1.5 million people on our list and a law on the books that protects Argentinian forests." The Forest Law campaign was not the first time that Greenpeace Argentina successfully used mobile phones for a campaign. In 2005, Greenpeace lobbied for a "Zero Waste" law in Text Messaging to Save Trees (Argentina) Environment Buenos Aires that mandated that the government reduce urban waste sent to landfalls by 50 percent by 2012, and by 100 percent by 2020. The city produces between 4,000 and 5,000 tons of waste each day. Using text messages, Greenpeace encouraged supporters to call their legislators and urge them to pass the bill during critical hearings, and prior to city council votes. Greenpeace also used text message alerts to coordinate lobbying meetings and demonstrations. As a result of this comprehensive approach, the Zero Waste Law was successfully passed. Outcome: A Rapidly Deployed Cadre of Activists

Greenpeace Argentina has established itself as one of the premier advocacy organisations in the country and region. Alongside the directaction flair for which Greenpeace is famous, its grassroots organising, online advocacy, use of social media, and innovative use of mobile technology has enabled it to win remarkable legislative victories in Argentina. Organisers are clear about what makes mobile messaging effective in an advocacy context: the ability to mobilise large numbers of people wherever they are at a given moment.

As demonstrated by its legislative victories, Greenpeace Argentina has been particularly effective at deploying this tactic during strategic times, such as in the lead-up to legislative deliberations. Greenpeace Argentina has also used text messaging to mobilise supporters to attend mass rallies. Says Nadal, "We mobilised our database of movie activist as even from inside the Congress building several times. City politicians from Buenos Aires are used to being pushed by Greenpeace, but this was a national campaign and representatives in Congress are not used to our pressure. Our constituents made some 300 calls an hour to legislators. That definitely made an impression."

6.9.3. Managing and Maintaining a Growing List

With relatively scant resources, Greenpeace Argentina has long shown that it can still achieve impact. The organisation used an in house technical team to write the software handling bulk text messaging, keeping costs low. Beyond those programming costs, Greenpeace Argentina spent about 1,000 euros per month on text messaging transmission charges, at about 5 euro cents per message.

As Nadal notes, "Negotiating the costs with the telecom carriers is imperative now that we have such a large mobile list of 350,000 numbers." With so large a list of mobile constituents, list segmentation or the process of targeting specific constituents based on some characteristic becomes important. Yet this would require merging mobile contact information with a sophisticated database of constituent information. Because the mobile constituent system that Greenpeace Argentina is using is home-grown, integrating it with their member and supporter database has presented challenges.

Response metrics for text messages are notoriously hard to determine, so it is not clear how many people read a message or forward it to a friend. Greenpeace Argentina reports anecdotal evidence that about 15 to 25 percent of mobile activists report back to the organisation that they participated in a particular action. This is a high response rate for a direct marketing effort, and can be explained in part by the strong commitment of the organisation's supporters. But as Nadal notes, "Mobile marketing for NGOs nongovernmental organisations is hard and is just starting.

There needs to be a greater depth of discussion with the carriers and vendors in many countries about what Greenpeace Argentina uses the euro as its benchmark currency because the organisation's headquarters are based in Europe. Nonprofit need." In Argentina, as in most other countries, text message marketing is almost entirely focused on commercial uses and often associated with selling content. Greenpeace is now exploring hiring a mobile vendor that is capable of handling the volume of supporters on its mobile list, and is also negotiating directly with Argentinian mobile carriers for more favourable text messaging rates.

6.9.4. Replicating the Greenpeace Argentina Model

The work of Greenpeace Argentina in using mobile phones in advocacy campaigns is closely watched not just by intermediaries such as mobile active. Org that are monitoring the industry but also by other advocacy organisations, and, of course, by Greenpeace affiliates in other countries. Several other Greenpeace offices will test the Argentinian method of mobile activism in 2008. Greenpeace Argentina, meanwhile, has set its own goals, including expanding its mobile infrastructure with a more robust platform; integrating its mobile activist list and constituent database for better list segmentation; increasing sending speeds and delivery rates; and generating better reports on actions taken. Greenpeace Argentina's text messaging campaign clearly struck a chord with the general population. The tremendous participation rates have not only empowered the organisation with a core group of mobile activists, but have also demonstrated the power of mobile phones to serve as an effective tool to influence political change.

6.10. Text Message Infolines for Community Information

Number of environmental groups are embracing text messaging as a means of engaging key stockholders, whether in their capacity as community members or consumers. This case study surveys several of these initiatives.

6.10.1. Alerting Consumers to Endangered Stocks

Imagine this scenario: A woman in Johannesburg, South Africa, stands at the fish counter in her local supermarket and texts the name of a fish to a phone number. Within seconds, she receives back information via a short text message informing her whether the fish is legally and sustainable harvested, and advising her whether "to tuck in, think twice or avoid completely." The shopper is using Fish MS, a text messaging-based service that provides point-of-sale information about the impact of fishing on fish stocks, enabling consumers to make informed choices about the seafood they purchase.

The Southern African Sustainable Seafood Initiative (SASSI), a project of the World Wildlife Fund South Africa, condensed available research on local fish stocks into wallet-sized cards that organised species into three colour-coded categories: green for species that are not over-fished; orange for fish that are legal to sell, but where stocks are jeopardised; and red, indicating fish that are illegal to buy and sell in South Africa. With the collaboration of local information technology company ivory Payment Technology and their programmers, SASSI moved this system to a mobile platform, enabling a wider group of consumers to access more regularly updated data. According to SASSI coordinator Jaco Barendse, mobile phones are "the ideal way to combine technology and information with the growing awareness that the ocean's resources aren't infinite."

And because the data are interactive (unlike the wallet cards), Fish MS also provides data about trends in consumer behaviour. "We can see that the market is responsive, especially to press stories," he says. "If something was in the news about a certain type of fish, you can also see the spikes in text-based queries about that fish the next day." Between December 2006 and February of 2008, the service received 30,000 queries from 7,254 individual users, indicating that some users send repeated queries.

6.10.2. Climate Change, Healthy Toys, Air TEXT

Fish MS was the first of a growing number of environmental text message information services that use mobile technology to provide just-in-time information about the environmental impact of products and companies. Text message 'infolines' work when consumers text the name of a product or company to a short code to receive back information, providing 'just-in time' information at the point of purchase. For the information lines described here there are no costs to the consumer other than standard text message charges.

6.10.2.1. Climate Counts

One of these text message-based information services is the U.S. Based Climate Counts, which enables consumers to check companies' environmental sustainability ratings, and compare them with their competitors. The information, in the form of a scorecard that is delivered via text message back to the user, reflects the self-reported efforts of companies to address climate change. Climate Counts has compiled an index based on whether companies have measured their climate 'footprint,' reduced their impact on global warming, supported (or suggested intent to block) progressive climate legislation, and publicly disclosed their climate actions. It is funded by U.S. Yogurt company Stoney field and powered by Mobile Commons, a mobile vendor that provides the messaging technology.

6.10.2.2. Healthy Toys

Healthy Toys is a project of two U.S. environmental organisations and Moms Rising, an advocacy organisation. It enables parents or guardians to verify whether children's toys or products are safe to use.

Users can send via text message the name of a toy or product and receive back information about the chemical content of toys. The database can be queried via mobile phone or the web, and contains more than 1,200 products

6.10.2.3. Air TEXT

Similarly, numerous air quality information services are available that push information about dangerous levels of pollution to citizens. In the United Kingdom (UK), Air TEXT is a free air quality information service for people in London. Users who sign up for Air TEXT receive voice or text message alerts when air pollution is forecast to be higher than normal. The service is aimed at people who suffer from heart and breathing problems, whose health or quality of life may be affected by air pollution. Similar services exist for specific locations in the United States. Unlike the text information services that function as a 'pull' service, where a consumer actively queries a database, most air quality information services function on a 'push' basis, that is, a consumer signs up and then automatically receives updates about dangerous air quality levels and pollution information via text message.

6.10.3. How 'Infoline' Services

Work All text infoline services rely on a platform to handle the query and delivery of messages, and a database that contains information pertaining to users' queries. When information is needed, a user actively queries a database via a text message keyword sent to a short code or a regular phone number. The user receives a text message response with the results from that database, customised to fit the 160-character limitation of most text messaging services. Alternatively, a user can sign up (such as on the Web) to receive text message alerts to his or her mobile phone. Most text messaging infoline services also follow a similar model in how they convey results.

Similar to the three-tiered system of Fish MS' response used to indicate whether a consumer should buy, consider, or abstain from buying a particular fish Climate Counts uses a three-point scorecard to indicate whether a company is 'stuck,' 'starting,' or 'striding' in its efforts to lower its carbon footprint. Research shows that it is helpful to associate an indexed result with a recommended action. An air quality numeric value, for example, is not as useful as a message that states "unhealthful air, stay inside."

6.10.4. Managing an Effective 'Infoline' Service

For groups with limited funds, text messaging infoline services can be expensive to set up and maintain. Gathering and compiling comprehensive data that are reliable, well indexed, and ready for queries are not simple tasks. In fact, all of the services profiled here already had data compiled and available through other channels, such as in print or on the Web. And all groups already had made considerable investments in collecting, verifying, and organising this information.

For these groups, all that was needed was to make the data they already had available via a mobile channel. Another cost to consider is the fee to the vendor that provides the delivery platform. Vendor costs range widely, depending on country and complexity of delivery, but average a few thousand U.S. Dollars per month. Lastly, groups need to consider the transmission costs for communicating via text messaging with their constituents.

Obviously, the more popular an infoline service, the more text messages need to be sent to consumers and the higher the message delivery charges will be. In-kind donations from telecommunications providers can drive these costs down, but this strategy can also raise questions about project sustainability. There are also significant social marketing challenges that limit user uptake.

Nongovernmental organisations offering these infoline services must deploy an intensive and effective marketing campaign to get consumers to remember to use the service, and which number to text to. Another limiting factor is that aggregating reliable and accurate data on hundreds or thousands of products, services, companies, or other data points is very expensive and time-consuming. Climate Count's database, for example, so far includes climate change information on only 56 companies.

6.10.5. Future of 'Infolines' Advocacy

At the present time there is still little evidence to demonstrate that these services are actually changing consumer behaviour. Overall usage, measured by total number of subscribers to infoline services described in this case study, is small, ranging only in the thousands. Yet the potential of this tool is clear. Just-in-time information sharing via text message infolines, as in the case of Fish MS, can transform consumers into activists whose purchasing power can exert pressure on retailers or fishing companies. Groups considering using an infoline service should ask themselves not only what information they want to relay to the consumer, but also what further steps they recommend the consumer take. In the final analysis, the real value of these services will be judged by their ability to use information to change behaviour, resulting in concrete and measurable actions by consumers and other constituents.

6.11. Environmental Monitoring with Mobile Phones

6.11.1. Need for Comprehensive Data on Urban Air Quality

The need to shatter our understanding of mobile phones as merely phones and celebrate them in their new role as measurement instruments," says Eric Paulos of Intel Research in California (United States), a pioneer in the so-called urbansensing movement. His desire is to add 'super-sensing' tools that transform ordinary mobile devices into tools that can collect and help track environmental trends.

More than 3.5 billion people carry mobile phones today, and researchers are beginning to notice mobile phones' ability to become the 'ultimate data collection machines.' Mobile sensing also known as 'participatory sensing,' 'urban sensing,' or 'participatory urbanise, enables data collection from large numbers of people in ways that previously were not possible.

By affixing a sensory device to a mobile phone, mobile sensing provides the opportunity to track multiple data points and collect dynamic information about environmental trends from ambient air quality to urban traffic patterns. Or as Debar Estrin, a prominent researcher in this field from the University of California at Los Angeles, put it: "We can now manifest the previously unobservable in science."

6.11.2. Empowering Citizens with Data Collection Devices

Mobile sensing represents an important shift in mobile device usage from communication tool to a 'networked mobile measurement instrument.' By aggregating thousands of data points transmitted by individual mobile phones, mobile sensing can paint a complex and dynamic portrait of the environment in which users are based.

There are efforts underway to use sensing-equipped mobile phones to monitor a range of environmental factors, from ambient air pollution to transportation and traffic patterns to noise pollution. The World Health Organisation estimates that more than 4.6 million people die annually from the direct impact of air pollution more than from car accidents every year. According to Paulos, in many cases our knowledge of ambient air quality is limited to "a small handful of government installed environmental monitoring stations that use extrapolation to derive a single air quality measurement for an entire metropolitan region." He argues that this "sparse sensing strategy does little to capture the very dynamic variability of air quality that depends on automobile traffic patterns, human activity, and output of industries."

To demonstrate the potential of citizen generated environmental data, Paulos and his team ran a small-scale project in Accrue, Ghana, where they equipped a small group of taxi drivers with devices that gauged the amount of pollution in the air. Accrue has generally poor air quality, generated by tail pipe emissions, dust, and the common practice of domestic cooking outside using wood, charcoal, and other fuel sources that can spread harmful pollutants across the city. To help monitor air quality, Accrue has a stationary monitoring system installed by the U.S. Environmental Protection Agency. This tool makes it possible to compare data from a stationary point with the mobile air monitoring of the Intel Berkeley research project.

6.11.3. Clearer Picture of Polluted Air

In the Accrue study, seven taxi drivers were provided with a dash-mounted global positioning system (GPS) device and a tube to hang from their passenger window. The tube contained a carbon monoxide sensor. Similarly, three students were each given a mobile clip sensor pack containing a GPS device, and a carbon monoxide sensor. The taxi drivers and students were asked to carry their sensors as much as possible during their normal everyday activities. Throughout the day, the sensing system automatically logged sensor data.

6.11.4. Harnessing the Potential of the Mobile Sensing

Intel's mobile sensing pilot in Accrue produced some interesting unanticipated outcomes, including a 'human aspect' that resulted from the participatory data collection process. Paulos tells the story of how Accrue taxi drivers, who met at the end of the day at the mobile sensing device charging station, began to share their data, look at roads and areas that were particularly polluted, and trade tips on how to avoid certain routes. He notes that this incident illustrates the potential of 'participatory sensing' to both yield rich and interactive environmental data critical for public health and pollution reduction, and motivate people to become active participants in their environment.

Another area for further exploration is the ability of mobile sensing to contribute to public health by linking health with environmental factors that have not been available before. For example, even though we know that there is a link between asthma symptoms and air pollution, previously it was not possible to directly correlate an individual's symptoms with their exposure to air pollutants.

Measuring people's lung performance while measuring ambient air pollution exposure could shed new light on the links between air pollution and asthma, perhaps resulting in better treatments. Research is also underway to assess whether it is possible to detect avian influenza viruses and other diseases through mobile sensing devices. Similar linkages may be possible in other issue areas, such as in emergency detection and warnings, which are important to public safety, and emergency and disaster response applications.

6.11.5. Securing a Future for Mobile Sensing

Users in mobile participatory data collection projects are divulging private information about their location and context. Security and privacy are therefore of concern. There is considerable discussion about how to ensure privacy while still transmitting useful information. This could include giving users the choice of only selectively sharing direct observations, and designing protocol that ensure a person's anonymity. Mobile sensing is an emerging area where costs and benefits to date are hard to determine because it is still so early in the research cycle.

However, it is also a rapidly developing area of inquiry that will likely see considerable activity and interest, not just on the part of university or commercial researchers but also on the part of citizen groups and environmental advocates. Using mobile phones as sensing devices and aggregating "crowd source" data into sophisticated and previously impossible environmental maps is an emerging field with only preliminary trials. Yet while still in early phases of concept development, the potential of mobile sensing to contribute to environmental conservation and related fields is clear. Ongoing research in this area will continue to provide fascinating data for researchers, citizen groups, and environmental advocates.

6.12. Protecting Wildlife and Human Wellbeing

6.12.1. Humans and Animals Competing for Land

The Laikipia District of north central Kenya is a popular tourist destination, teeming with wildlife. Covering 9,700 square kilometres, Laikipia comprises a patchwork of small farms, large ranches, privately owned conservancies, and government land. Some 5,000 elephants, the second largest elephant population in the country, inhabit the region. As farmers, ranchers, and these animals struggle to coexist, the region has gained a reputation for being one of the worst areas for human elephant conflict, with more than 3,000 incidents occurring annually.

Human-wildlife conflict is a growing phenomenon around the world as human populations place mounting pressure on ecosystems, wildlife habitat is reduced, and animal migration routes are made inaccessible. As a result, humans are susceptible to injury, and even death, and animals suffer attacks by humans. In Laikipia alone, an average of five people and ten elephants are killed each year as a result of human elephant conflict. "The tension in Laikipia stems from communities having their crops damaged by elephants," explains Dr. Max Graham, Associate at the Department of Geography, University of Cambridge (United Kingdom), who has been studying and working in Laikipia for almost a decade.

6.12.1. Push-to-Talk Technology Program Launched in Laikipia

Believing that mobile technology could offer a solution, the Groupe Special Mobile (GSM) Association (GSMA) Development Fund, together with Safari com Ltd., Wireless Zeta Telecommunications (Wireless ZT), Nokia, the Nokia Siemens Networks, and local conservation organisations, collaborated in launching a pilot project in Laikipia. Using GSM technology, the project sought to facilitate cost-effective communication among local communities, government wildlife service personnel, and private landowners through an early warning system that would allow farmers to preserve their crops while protecting wildlife. The pilot utilised 'Push to Talk on Cellular (Phones)' (PoC) technology, which combines the functionality of a walkie-talkie or two-way radio with a mobile phone. PoC enables communication between two individuals, or a group of people, and is particularly useful in connecting a user group intermittently over a period of time (e.g., a working day).

A benefit of PoC is that it can be used alongside voice and data services on a single handset. Users can make standard phone calls and send text messages, while also accessing two-way communication and group talk through the press of a button. Because network resources are used only for the duration of each talk 'spurt,' PoC technology requires less airtime, demands less energy, and is less costly than a conventional phone call. Equally important was finding a solution that would be sustainable and scalable over the long term.

To address this need, the pilot was designed to test the commercial viability of the proposed solution. If the product could be successfully sold at a discounted rate to non-profit it would stand a far better chance of making it in the marketplace. "The goal was to develop a sustainable project that an operator could use commercially as an incentive to keep it running in the field," explains Christina Greenwood, Project Manager, GSMA Development Fund, who worked on developing the pilot. "At the same time, we were looking to offer the service at subsidised rate, or with lower tariffs, to non-profit to make sure they could access it."

6.12.2. Managed Human Elephant Conflict

Based on data collected and exit surveys, the pilot was found to reduce the number and severity of human–elephant conflicts in the four areas covered. Said Dickson Kamau, Chairman of the Rumuruti Forest Association: "Push-to-talk has helped us a lot. Before they the game rangers would never come to scare the elephants back [to the forest] but with this they could not make excuses because there were many of us listening." One hundred percent of PoC users engaged in the trial found the service to be helpful in managing human–elephant conflict, with 72 percent of users reporting that PoC helped provide an early warning system to reduce crop raiding, and 41 percent claiming that PoC was most useful in improving communication among all stockholders.

A significant result of the pilot was reduced tension and improved trust among farmers and community members, the Kenyan Wildlife Service (KWS), private landowners, and local law enforcement officials. The PoC trial enhanced communication among these stockholders and, in particular, helped community members recognise that conservationists were there to help them. In Mwenji, for example, the trial focused on the monitoring of an electrified fence. When elephants tried to break the fence, security guards hired to patrol the perimeters of private ranches were able to report the incidents to community members and conservancy rangers who could take action.

"It forced the guys who were meant to act to act," says Graham. "Because there were ten people listening it created collective pressure and improved accountability." In Rumuriti, the trial had an unexpected effect. Local scouts assigned by a community association to patrol the area used the phones to alert KWS officials of the location of elephants to reduce incidents of human–elephant conflict. With the phones, they were also able to report illegal logging and animal theft in the area. The trial "helped with policing elephants and the forest," says Graham. "It was the first time we were able to empower the community to play such a role." In Ex-erok, the phones were used by security patrols to alert KWS officials to both elephant incursions and animal stock theft.

Graham cites three occasions when farm animals such as goats were recovered as a result of easy and fast communication.

The primary challenge this project faced was securing the right partners to address the diverse needs of the stockholder groups. Preparations for the program required coordination among a broad range of stockholders from telecommunications and technology groups to local nature conservancies. Only a multi-sector partnership could adequately cover all aspects of project work, from assessing the needs of Laikipia communities to the project's commercial feasibility. The project would only work if local communities adopted the technology solution.

Here, nongovernmental organisation partners such as the University of Cambridge Laikipia Elephant Project and Laikipia Wildlife Forum were essential. These groups developed trusted relationships with the community that engendered good will for the project. They also could identify community users, and assist with the training, monitoring, and assessment. While the results were positive overall, an important lesson emerging from the trial was the cost and time needed to keep the phones charged.

References

Pearse, M. and Smith, J. 1990. *Community Groups Handbook*, Nottingham: Journeyman.

Pierson, John. 2007). *Going Local: Working in Communities and Neighbourhoods*. London: Routledge

Principal Community Education Officers, Scotland. 1992. *Community Development in the Community Education Service*, Edinburgh: Scottish Community Education Council.

Putnam, R. D. 2000. *Bowling Alone. The collapse and revival of American community*, New York: Simon and Schuster.

Reynolds, J. *et al.* 1993. *A Town in Action: Voluntary networks in Retford. Volume 4 of Adult Learning in Voluntary Organizations*, Nottingham: University of Nottingham Department of Adult Education.

Robertson, C. and Shaw, J. 1997. *Participatory Video. A practical approach to using video creativity in group development*, London: Routledge.

7

Evidence Base for Social Work

The modernisation of health and social care services inevitably calls attention to the quality of the knowledge base that can underpin change and development. Research evidence forms a cornerstone of this knowledge base. However, it is pointless to portray evidence in this way unless we have research that gives reliable and valid messages for policy and practice.

7.1. Context of Modernisation

Concern about the research infrastructure has grown in recent years in parallel with the emphasis on evidence-based practice, and this has highlighted the need for 'practice-based evidence'. By practice-based evidence, we mean research directly derived from practice concerns and aimed at providing practice improvement.

The policies of modernisation adopted over the past years have also brought an increased emphasis on the evidence base, with some commissioning of research to provide this, but there is also a growing recognition that there is quite simply a lack of relevant and appropriate research that can help to move forward key policy developments: interprofessional practice and learning is one such example. From a central government perspective, policy makers may question whether they can rely on the R&D community to have sufficient engagement with policy to deliver useful and timely evidence, and the Cabinet Office Strategy Unit is increasingly encouraging a more applied approach to generating knowledge, including through the establishment of enhanced capacity for systematic review.

New proposals from the English Department of Health (DH) for the development of healthcare research give similar priority for research that is relevant to clinical practice. While there has been little increase in investment in social care research in recent years, there has been serious investment in the dissemination and utilisation of the limited research that is conducted. From early work by the Joseph Rowntree Foundation, with its innovative 'Findings' series, to the pioneering production of research reviews with clear application messages by the DH, there has been a growing knowledge base about the ways that knowledge itself can be disseminated.

This has been partnered in more recent years by work on the ways that research can be utilised, as shown in the Social Care Institute for Excellence's (SCIE's) programmes and products, and the activities of 'Research in Practice' and 'Making Research Count'. In Scotland, the Scottish Institute for Excellence in Social Work Education (SIESWE) has provided a focus for research utilisation relevant to education. This substantial dissemination and utilisation work has made the lack of attention to the development of the research products themselves all the more noticeable.

There is of course nothing new in noting the lack of strategic development, particularly in practice-based research. Modernisation and the growing integration of social care with health care has, however, created a pressing need and an important opportunity to change and develop the infrastructure for the production of research knowledge in social care.

7.2. Nature of Evidence

So far we have been using 'knowledge' and 'evidence' without detailed definitions, and it is time to clarify the meanings we will attach to these terms and the implications. Janet Lewis, the former Director of Research at the Joseph Rowntree Foundation, has succinctly captured the role of evidence in the knowledge base for social care in the formula:

> Knowledge = evidence + practice wisdom + service user and career experiences and wishes (italics added)

The importance of this definition is that there is no hierarchy: the three components will vary in importance depending on the question under consideration. Evidence, in this construction, is the product of research, defined as a form of structured enquiry capable of producing generalisable knowledge. The strength of this definition is that research-based knowledge should be of significant value in policy making because it is designed to deliver general messages of wide applicability. However, the capacity of research-based evidence to do this is limited unless we add that evidence deriving from research should be relevant and applied that is, that it derives from and addresses practice concerns, and is potentially capable of translation into applicable ideas. This gives the formula:

Evidence = research findings + interpretation of the findings.

7.3. Need of Evidence

We propose six main arguments for the need for evidence from research within the knowledge base for social care. First, there is the major impact of the decisions of social care professionals on the immediate life chances of service users and careers (for example, in child protection). In these areas evidence from research can be literally a matter of life or death, and 4 having the best informed practitioners is vital to the immediate outcomes for highly disadvantaged people.

Second, there is the impact over time of decisions on the longer-term life chances of service users and careers (for example, children in care, or long-term carers). Decisions taken over the weeks or months will affect, for example, the educational outcomes for children in care, which are themselves of fundamental importance to their future. To give another example, they will affect the mental and physical health of disabled users and long-term carers, again with substantial implications for their quality of life. Best informed practice should be the right of people whose long-term outcomes depend in part on social care decisions.

Third, good evidence may produce a challenge to fundamental assumptions about social care, and this may bring substantial advantages to service users and carers. When Copernicus developed evidence that the Earth rotates around the Sun, the outcome was not simply a new theory of planetary movement but also the possibility of an entirely different understanding of our place in the universe.

On a more relevant and personal scale, research has shown the value of the development of the Expert Patient Programme in healthcare, where people with long-term conditions manage their own care. This programme has the potential to revolutionise the concept of expertise and the relations between providers and patients. Evidence about the effectiveness of family group conferences has the similar potential to change fundamentally the role of the state in protecting children. Research on direct payments has helped to demonstrate the potential to place service users in control of service providers, rather than vice versa. The research has aided these major, and sometimes controversial, shifts in policies, which have the potential to enhance greatly the lives of service users and carers.

The importance of providing safeguards over compulsory or quasi-compulsory decision making is a fourth argument. There are substantial areas of social care where professionals have strong powers, or where the courts may make decisions regarding major aspects of people's lives. Providing the best available evidence is an important component of these processes of control.

Fifth, the evidence is needed for an informed public, who can then engage better with relevant debates about services. Although, at present, there may be relatively few members of the public who actively engage in these debates, it is right that citizens have access to the best evidence. Sixth, the evidence is needed for informed service user and career communities, and individuals. Direct involvement in services and engagement with the development of services requires access to the best evidence.

These are six strong arguments for the development of the evidence base, and for shifting social services towards an evidence-based approach, instead of its historic reliance on an 'authority-based' approach. The arguments are remarkably similar to those made for the need for evidence in healthcare. Investment in evidence is clearly of central importance for both social services and health services.

7.4. Strategic Frameworks for Developing Research

We turn next to some crucial questions in the strategy for knowledge production in social care, and comparable strategies in primary care. How has the production of this evidence been managed in social care? What sort of strategic frameworks have been developed to enhance the applicability of evidence to policy and practice? Are there lessons from the strategic developments in primary care? A framework for the development of research needs to address four key questions – it should:

— Clarify the scope of the field of knowledge to which it applies.
— Name the questions that need to be addressed if the framework is to progress the strategic development of the knowledge base.
— Define, in general terms at least, priorities for knowledge production.
— Outline the key resource issues over a medium to long-term period to provide this knowledge production.

Ideally, such a framework would be developed by drawing on a thorough analysis of the field, but there have been insuperable difficulties in doing that in social care, because of the scattered and incomplete data available.

7.5. Evidence for Practice

We have argued so far that there is a clear need for evidence in social work and social care, and that a strategic framework to produce this evidence is lacking. We have made the comparison between social work and primary care, and noted the benefits of a strategic approach and appropriate investment in the latter area.

But while there seems little doubt about the need for evidence, and the benefits of suitable planning to produce it, should this evidence for social care come from social work, or from a broad range of disciplines? Our argument here is that a wide range of disciplines can and should play a role in providing the evidence for policy analysis (particularly the discipline of social policy). However, just as primary care requires research from a discipline based in front-line practice, social care for similar reasons requires evidence from social work as the primary discipline rooted in social care practice.

First and foremost, social care is a practice discipline and, while it requires research from other areas to underpin it, also requires research based in its own practice for its own development. To discover causes is not necessarily to discover cures, or, to take an example from basic science, what works in the laboratory is not necessarily what works in the clinic. This is fully accepted in health, where, for example, medical research needs to accompany biological research. In a similar fashion, social care needs accompanying social policy research, but it also needs social work research that is practice-based and that will deliver practice change.

Second, all disciplines have their own priorities, based on history, on current fashions, perhaps also on student demand and on international pressures. These priorities may or may not be relevant for social care, but because social work is rooted in social care, it shares the concerns and the pressures of social care practice. Third, the focus of many disciplines is on discrete aspects of human experience, rather than on the need for an evidence base that addresses the many different issues facing social care. For example, building an evidence base for social care for children and families requires evidence from disciplines such as social policy, psychology and education, but none of these has a primary focus on social care. In contrast, the best social work research integrates knowledge from different disciplines to focus specifically on social care concerns.

Fourth, social work research is relevant to the entire range of social work and social care issues. Its focus is not just on the work of social workers, but on the practice of social care as a whole.

These are substantial reasons to develop social work research in order to improve the practice of social care. Research from social work is not the only relevant discipline, but, at its best, and because of its applied nature and of its relationship with users, carers and practitioners, it is in a position to develop the type of research that will underpin social care practice and service in the future.

Developing the evidence base for social work and social care practice In addition, the rigour of the best social work research is an important asset for wider knowledge production in social care. There is an established tradition of good quality research, albeit low in quantity, that provides a sound methodology, within its social science base, for the production of knowledge for social care. These arguments will lead us to promote strongly the need for a new strategic approach to social work research, and accompanying investment. However, the enhancement of social work research capacity is also relevant to studies undertaken in other disciplines. Evaluations of new programmes, for example, from a discipline base outside social work, will produce more relevant practice knowledge if they are influenced by a strong perspective from social work research. Such a perspective will help to ensure that research focusing primarily on causes also pays attention to cures, and that the practice and implementation activities that need to accompany new programmes are spelled out and well tested. Strong social work research is thus likely to help other research disciplines to improve the relevance of their work to the business of developing practice and policy in social care.

7.7. Social Work Research

It is critical to the case for social work research as a core discipline underpinning social care that the subject matter of social work research is not seen as limited to the activities of social workers. To reiterate the points made above, social work skills, knowledge and values are relevant to a wide range of social care activities and deserve study. Of course some activities require higher levels of skilled practice currently requiring (at least) a social work qualification, but we must not confuse 'social work research', with 'research on what social workers do'.

We are arguing for the importance of a strong social work research community to assist with knowledge production in social care. This offers, we suggest, a distinctive positive role in the production of relevant evidence. Some would argue it also offers a distinctive role regarding research methods.

Further distinctiveness is claimed in relation to its attention to participated practices and social justice in the conduct of research itself. The conclusion may be that the strategic framework should use this claim to distinctiveness to elevate the case for investment and recognition. However, modern forms of knowledge production are increasingly recognised as 'methodologically interdisciplinary', suggesting that the development of methods benefits from less, not more, insularity, and that method distinctiveness is more about emphasis than uniqueness. Moreover, central government customers and commissioners may find the concern with methodological distinctiveness immaterial, in the sense that they commission research that assists policy and practice rather than the development of particular approaches. An important question, therefore, is whether there is value in claiming distinctiveness for social work research methods, when the epistemological tide is running the other way and when this is not the key concern for at least some research users.

Two answers suggest themselves. First, it is important to analyse distinctiveness more closely, and to separate out the argument that social work and social care has its own knowledge base from that concerning the application of knowledge. No modern social science claims exclusive ownership of a knowledge base with fixed boundaries indeed, it is a mark of a modern discipline that it draws on a wide range of appropriate knowledge. In social work and social care, the core approach is to "place the issue, problem or person at the centre of investigation" and "to understand events through available knowledge"). The distinctiveness lies not in the knowledge base, but in the application of social science knowledge to social analysis and intervention.

This is most emphatically not to say that social work and social care does not create its own knowledge the theory and technology of task-centred practice or of family group conferences are sterling examples but it is to say that it is unhelpful to seek an identity for social work and social care in the creation of exclusive knowledge. Second, distinctiveness may be far less important in gaining recognition for knowledge production in social work and social care than relevance – that is, the contribution that the knowledge base makes to the understanding of social issues. In this sense, the role that social work has played in revealing child abuse, particularly sexual abuse, and in reducing violence towards children deserves recognition. So too does its work in documenting the effects of poverty, particularly on women, the effects of institutional care, particularly on children, and the effects of social policies that marginalise or exclude people.

Therefore, the argument is to concentrate on distinctiveness in terms of the way social work and social care generates and uses knowledge, rather than on a spurious and rather dated notion of an exclusive knowledge base. We need to concentrate on the focus of knowledge, and the usability of it. Relevance is the hallmark of social work research, not a particular approach to research methodology.

7.7.1. Research in Social Care

Much of the research evidence for social work and social care practice can only be obtained by research involving practitioners and service users and carers. Resolving the difficult issues that are entailed in this should involve these groups directly. This is an example where social work research can be research in social care, rather than research on social care. The values of social care need to be central to such involvement, and social work researchers are likely to be best placed to uphold those values.

In addition, social work researchers will be well placed to understand the situations that are unique to social work (for example, legal requirements, and models of decision making with families). Social work researchers would be likely to approach the business of research with a set of skills and values relevant to the practitioners, service users and carers they will meet. But while this is a very important element of the arguments for the contribution of social work research, it is not the main one, which, as noted above, hinges around relevance.

Social care knowledge production needs research that can be used in practice. It needs research that begins and ends in practice: that begins with practice-relevant questions, and that ends with relevant material that can be applied in practice. Relevance needs to be built in both during the design of the research and afterwards when useful ideas are being developed from it. Of course there are 'translation' issues from research studies, but they are significantly reduced if the research has at its heart knowledge and understanding of the practice that it is trying to improve.

7.7.2. Research Relationship with Service Users and Carers

The experiences, needs and wishes of service users and carers are central to the production of useful and relevant knowledge in social care. Social work research has engaged, quite substantially, with service users and carers, but how should this engagement develop within a new and invigorated focus on social care research knowledge production?

7.7.3. Reshaping the Relationship with Service Users and Carers

Knowledge production for social work and social care in the UK rightly has a reputation for rethinking the relationship with service users and carers. At the core of this reshaped relationship is the requirement that knowledge production incorporates attention to users' and carers' definitions of knowledge, process and outcomes. A key question in the development of a strategic framework for social work and social care knowledge is, therefore, the nature of the alliance with service users' and carers' movements.

This work needs to be undertaken at a number of levels. First, the framework needs to recognise that many of those producing knowledge are themselves users or carers, and many are producing evidence of national relevance. One way of recognising this knowledge is to review and summarise it, so that its further development may be planned: although several important reviews have been undertaken, they all have limitations in the range of substantive research addressed or in attention to methodological issues. Work by Carry has identified the common issues from a range of R&D on involving users in service improvement, and this work is now being extended to review the impact of career involvement.

The user group 'Shaping Our Lives' is developing a national user network that will give the user movement greater potential to identify common themes across its member groups. Second, the ethical issues surrounding knowledge production and user and career involvement must be addressed, and Butler's work produced as part of the Theorising Social Work Research Seminar Series is a good starting point that will now need to be set into the context of the Research Governance Framework Policy and Guidance/Research And Development/ The central principle is to recognise the right of users and carers to be involved in all aspects of the knowledge production process, including setting the priorities for commissioning and standards for the ethical conduct of research.

Third, this principle has important consequences for the way social work and social care uses its resources. Alliances are required with the user and career movements so that their resources to participate can be improved. Here it will not be enough to rest the case on ethical grounds: if inroads are to be made into areas of knowledge production such as commissioning, and the production of systematic reviews, where service users and carers currently play little part, the case will have to include attention to the methodological necessity of adopting the principles of involvement.

7.7.4. Practice and Research

Research is one of the key components of best practice, and we have also argued that research that begins and ends in practice that is genuinely 'practice-based evidence' is lacking in social care. However, this problem with the research can be turned, and has been turned by some commentators, into accusations that poor research use by practitioners is a result of their lack of research-mindedness, and of their failure to read, to implement or to produce research. Most of this criticism emanates from a narrow view of evidence-based practice, and it is often underpinned by a simplistic understanding of the way knowledge should apply to practice. Shaw has summed up this problem as follows:

> The assumption of most writers of this persuasion is that utilisation of evaluation findings is a relatively straightforward matter. Where it is a problem, it is typically put down to a breakdown in communication or the self-interested resistance of professionals. To regard theory and practice problems in this way is to relegate 'practice' to the subordinate, the acted-upon. This unwillingness among some knowledge producers, primarily in the academic sector, to engage with the way practitioners use knowledge in practice, or to build collaborative partnerships with the practice community, stands in sharp contrast to work elsewhere.

There is now a powerful body of research, derived from working alongside practitioners, on the nature of the practitioner/research relationship, on how practitioners reason, on the knowledge components of professional expertise, and on the requirements for constructing knowledge as guidance for practitioners. All but one of the researchers quoted in this paragraph work outside the UK, suggesting that the UK academic community has something to learn from its international colleagues about engaging with practitioners.

At one end of such a gradient, all researchers with a social work qualification will have an understanding of practice derived from their professional education and training. Senior managers, and senior social work academics, will fall into this group, and they probably are the farthest from practice of all those engaged with social work research. A more substantial group, comprising team leaders and lecturers, will be somewhat closer to practice. They will observe practice, talk to practitioners, and consider, sometimes in great detail, the elements of practice. They will meet service users and carers, but perhaps not all that often, for their engagement with practice is somewhat second-hand. It is the largest group, the practitioners, those directly responsible for services, who are, of course, closest to practice.

References

McDonald, D. and Tungatt, M. 1992. *Community Development and Sport*, London: Community Development Foundation. 42 + x pages.

Midgley, J. et al. 1986. *Community Participation, Social Development and the State*, London: Methuen.

Ministry of Education. 1944; 1946. *Community Centres*, London: HMSO.

Ministry of Housing and Local Government. 1969. *People and Planning. Report of the Committee on Public Participation in Planning*,. 'The Skeffington Report'), London: HMSO.

National Institute of Social Work. 1982. *Social Workers. Their Role and Tasks*. The Barclay Report). Bedford Square Press.

Office of the Deputy Prime Minister. 2002. *Tenants Managing: Evaluation of tenant management organizations in England*, London: Office of the Deputy Prime Minister.

Ohri, A., Manning, B. and Curno, P. eds. 1982. *Community Work and Racism. Community Work 7,* London: Routledge and Kegan Paul.

8

Social Movements and Campaigns

This chapter deals with the tensions conceptual, political and organisational between nongovernmental organisations (NGOs) and "social movements". Although the first is usually associated with the "North" and the second with the "South", the real distinction is primarily political. In broader terms, it should be remembered that there are both Right-wing and government created NGOs, in the same way that there are also Rightist and even xenophobic social movements.

The distinctions we make take place within a broader justice-oriented liberal to radical camp. The central question we pose is whether social movements (mass resistance) can absorb and reorient NGOs, or whether we will witness the NGO-isation of movements and politics. Neither a blanket indictment nor approval is in order here, because there are NGOs doing valuable work in collaboration with movements. All actors can be regarded as part of "civil society", but that term too is a site of struggle, particularly when the notions of civility as models of analysis and action are also shaped by existing power structures and the resistance they engender.

According to the 2002 United Nations Development Programme (UNDP) Human Development Report, nearly one-fifth of the world's 37,000 NGOs were formed in the 1990s. Much like social movements, NGOs contested spaces previously held by labour unions and political parties, in both the political and social arenas. Supposedly, the increase in numbers and presence were part and parcel of the advent of civil society and civil society organisations (CSOs) at the national and international level.

While the prevalent image of NGOs is that of entities independent and critical of governments, one cannot be naive. Powerful governments turn to, or even create, NGOs government-organised NGOs in order to further the interests of the state. While the NGO would argue endlessly that it is independent, the reality could be different, whether by direct control or by setting a political, financial or even ideological framework defined by the powers that be. The difference may be that even governments may claim that the NGOs they work with are independent, albeit the close working relationship on many issues raises eyebrows.

Other governments have no such qualms. For example, the United States (US) government makes no apology for the use of NGO-delivered "humanitarian aid" that happens to also serve Washington's political and military objectives. The alleged neutrality reveals its true face as military and relief activity becomes mixed, sometimes at the expense not only of the aid agencies' reputation, but also at the cost of aid workers' lives. According to a US relief agency official: The same official spent three weeks in a Chechnya cellar in part because his kidnappers questioned his group's neutrality. US Secretary of State Colin Powell, addressing NGOs in 2001, made it clear that In other words, NGOs should take up combat positions in the war on terror.

In the face of tragedies such as in Rwanda, many took comfort in the close working relationship between governments and the relief and development NGOs. Humanitarian assistance was the order of the day for victims of massacres. But the alleged altruism became confused when NGO relief agencies went to work in ex-Yugoslavia, accepting funds from governments that had created much of the destruction in the first place. North Atlantic Treaty Organisation (NATO) planes dropped cluster bombs, and its country donor agencies paid mine action groups to go clean them up. Were relief NGOs simply part of a larger division of labour, a cleanup brigade for NATO armies helping to "pacify" the populations in the critical postwar period? In much the same way, should money for small arms campaign work be accepted from governments dropping big bombs in Afghanistan or Iraq?

Andrew S. Natsios, administrator of the United States Agency for International Development (USAID), was even more explicit, stating that NGO relief entities that received US financing were "an arm of the US government". Organisations that did not link themselves strongly to Washington's foreign policy would leave USAID no alternative but to tear up their contracts and find new partners.

For their part, powerful multinational corporations, usually the subject of criticism by social movements and many NGOs, also count with funded "non-profit" friends. Some of the most prominent health-related NGOs receive support from key corporations in the same field. What credibility can these non-profit organisations claim when, according to a recent report of the Center for Science in the Public Interest (CSPI),

8.1. Development NGOs

In the course of the 1980s, more development NGOs came to include the notion of partnership with beneficiaries in their work. Nothing could sound more progressive save if it takes into account that many of the services provided by NGOs relieved government of its own social responsibility, thereby reinforcing the state-shrinking neoliberal model. For their part, national and international "donor" agencies look at NGOs as implementation agencies for a pre-defined "development" agenda and model. In a word, instruments of policy and politics defined in the North have little or no "partnership" at the level of decision making.

The combination of policy failures, on the one hand, and the pressure of social movements, on the other, forced modifications in official policy rhetoric and style. The World Bank's Poverty Reduction Strategy Papers (PRSPs) sought out what it termed CSOs to carry out consultations and assist in the development of "national ownership". Methodologies and policy framework discussions, however, were tightly controlled. Questioning of the broader development model and the extreme enrichment by a few and the ensuing income mal distribution were out of the question. After two years it was clear, according to various comparative studies, that the community-based organisations and their consultations had no or little impact on the development of poverty reduction strategies, let alone the sacrosanct macroeconomic frameworks upheld by the international financial institutions (IFIs) and the donor community in general. A Danish study concluded that:

The problem, however, is not one of guidelines or inclusion in the policy processes. Processes could vary, but the policy was largely predetermined in Washington and the local finance ministries. Small wonder that important social movements and unions refused to participate or be included among those "consulted". To the contrary, movements and their NGO support network maintained a hard stance toward the IFIs and the structural adjustment programmes (SAPs), insisting accurately as it turned out that the PRSPs were simply old wine in new bottles.

Critical voices were excluded from the consultation process, particularly where the intention of consultation was to help achieve consensus between government and civil society around "poverty reduction" programmes that did not address the sources of illicit enrichment and cutbacks in social services. The problem, they insisted, was more a question of "impoverishment" than poverty: a poverty reduction strategy was no substitute for a national development strategy, and poverty reduction needed to be accompanied by greed reduction. As the same study admitted, "in many cases, 'participation' has been confined to carefully selected CSOs; the process has often been more exclusive than inclusive".

Not surprisingly, social movements were excluded, or excluded themselves, from these and other exercises purporting to build "consensus" for softened versions of neoliberal development. It was not a question of obstinacy because there was, and is, a price to be paid for participation in PRSPs or other donor-driven "civil society" initiatives. Crucial social agendas, often necessitating broad-based unity, were sacrificed. A cleavage emerged between intellectual, urban-based NGOs, and poor urban and rural majorities. A comparative review of PRSP processes in Africa, Latin America and Asia undertaken by three independent NGOs found that: Eurodad, a European Commission-funded debt and development network based in Belgium, summed up the dilemma when posing the question:

Ironically, the field was left open for the organisational efforts of social movements determined not simply to "hear" the "voices of the poor", as the World Bank would have it, but also to allow the voices to self-organise not simply to be heard, but to force changes as well. Sustaining local organisation did not figure as a priority for government, let alone the IFIs, but it was the core of the mobilisation agenda of movements. Invariably, this meant engaging in debates forbidden by the IFIs yet central to development and self-determination, such as trade policies, privatisation, foreign investment regulation, food sovereignty, protection, labour policies, among others, and not least the search of economic self-determination as a means to help underpin real sovereignty.

8.2. Politics of Accountability

As membership organisations, most social movements and some NGOs refer to their own constituents as the ultimate authorities. But it is not the case with many NGOs, which increasingly are the target of criticism precisely for the confused line of accountability, and with it their claim to legitimacy. Critics could in reality care less about transparency other than when it serves as a convenient vehicle to put political adversaries on the defensive.

At the end of the day, accountability is not technical, but political. And accountability to donors makes for confused politics, reducing the rendering of accounts to bookkeeping matters as if the transparent use of funds were an indication of political impact and purpose. Indeed, rendering of accounts becomes a time-consuming end in itself. For example, international donor pressure forced the Aga Khan Rural Support Programme in India to track 89 different statistics, such as births and deaths, farm yields and school graduations in the rural villages where it was working. According to Christensen,

Yet, the more accountability to the donor, the greater the dependence on towing the donor's political line. The question remains: Accountable to whom and how? Who is to judge success: the donor or the recipients? And according to what standard, those within or outside the organisation? Clearly the system lent itself to abuse, possibly making the "accountability squeeze" inevitable. The trouble was that the new watchdogs were often found on the Right as with the NGO Watch Web site created in 1993 by the conservative American Enterprise Institute, itself an NGO. Political motivation were clear as the intent was to go after the more liberal and progressive NGOs making these, in turn, all the more "careful" in their programme orientation.

If measuring performance is more than an accounting matter, new standards are necessary to gauge non-financial political impacts. A worthy example is Action Aid International, an NGO with a $120 million annual budget committed to fighting hunger and poverty in 30 countries. It recently decided to do away with data-centred reports because, according to its impact assessment officer: In 1998, Action Aid International while acknowledging its accountability to 150,000 donors, governments and its own board decided that its primary accountability was to the poor people, especially women and children, that it served. Performance is now measured from the partner's point of view, who decide along with programme managers whether the initiatives are succeeding and how they should be changed.

According to Lisa Jordan of the Ford Foundation, "the tools for measuring are developed by someone, made for someone, using a select method". Methods cannot be divorced from politics, and hence it is not surprising that many monitoring systems were developed to "answer questions about NGOs that donors feel need to be answered". According to Jordan, there are problems with this approach and adds that. In fairness, progressive NGOs may find it difficult to address those moral issues while they are the subject of pressure and political attacks not only by their conservative counterparts, but also by governments, particularly in the South, that regard the "CSOs" as unwelcome intruders into what they regard as their exclusive political domains.

According to the Cardias report: From a political and South perspective, campaigns were meant to influence policy, not to substantival change it, let alone question the power structure that underpins governmental stances. And emphasising policy, to the point of becoming technocrats who relished debating their governmental counterparts, came at the expense of questioning the power relations, that is to say, real politics. In time, some NGO technocrats assumed governmental or intergovernmental positions, dealing with policy matters assuming liaison duties with civil society groups. Foundations and church charities each year selected "themes" for their campaigns, but in almost all cases the efforts were purposely, like presidential elections, short lived and simplistic in message, seeking out the broadest alliances on the skimpiest of propositions. That is, what many at this point in time regarded as conservative or feel-good liberal politics celebratory media savvy actions driven by marketing and publicity dynamics.

Globalisation, on the other hand, is nothing if not comprehensive and multifaceted. Corporations, governments, media and academic continue to advance intellectually and operationally across the board. The power structure is so confident that it can in fact afford, tolerate and even fund civil society campaigns on subsets of problems, for example, debt relief, trade access, child soldiers, land mines, small arms none of which seriously threatened the system of war and exploitation.

Governments and the World Bank now proudly point to their efforts to "engage" civil society (meaning NGOs) in "informed" discussions (meaning their information), insisting that their institutions were open to dialogue and even change (the small changes necessary to ensure that there are no big changes). Where many NGOs called for engagement, most social movements called for the dismantlement of the IMF and the World Bank. So, some debts could be cancelled, but structural adjustment packages were not indeed, write-offs of uncollectable debt were made contingent on following IMF prescriptions. Yet, the Clinton, Blair and World Bank administrations publicly proclaimed having responded positively to the Jubilee call. And some Jubileers believed them. Campaigners could now go home, because campaigns had clear end points. Those mobilised were now told to demobilise.

8.3. Market Access versus Market Models

In early 2002, Oxfam Great Britain launched a market-access campaign geared to lowering protectionist barriers in the North to key exports to the South. As with the debt campaign, Southern organisations questioned the strategy being proposed from the North to deal with the unequal trade problem and corporate-driven globalisation in general. Oxfam responded by calling its critics "globaphobes", referring broadly to the anti globalisation movement, of which Oxfam apparently did not feel a part. A senior Oxfam staff resigned over the terms of her organisation's new campaign priority that, she claims, calls, over the life of its three-year campaign.

8.4. Social Work and Institutional Racism

Social work as a profession aims to address the impact of social problems on the lives of individuals, families, groups, organizations, and communities. To achieve this, the members of the profession, the organizations through which they work, and the schools of social work must have the knowledge base, theories, and values to understand relevant social issues, especially for the purpose of creating positive change. This section aims to address one key and significant social issue, institutional (also known as structural) racism. It offers a vision for how the social work profession can address structural racism, in terms of both limiting its negative influence and creating conditions for effectuating realistic, achievable positive outcomes.

Although acknowledging the existence and pervasiveness of the forms racism may take, the emphasis here is not on whether individual social workers are engaging in biased or racist practices. The assumption is that people enter the profession with good intentions and the desire to help. Rather, the focus is on the societal, institutional, structural maintenance of racism and the social worker's role in reference to this macro-level issue. What is key is that the social work profession and the systems through which the profession has evolved historically, into the present, is part of a larger society in which policies, resources, and practices are designed to benefit some groups significantly more than others, while simultaneously denying the existence of racism as a variable, except in its most extreme forms. The responsibility of individual social workers is to recognize that structural racism plays out in their personal and professional lives and to use that awareness to ameliorate its influence in all aspects of social work practice, inclusive of direct practice, community organizing, supervision, consultation, administration, advocacy, social and political action, policy development and implementation, education, and research and evaluation. Furthermore, individual social workers have a responsibility to promote change within and among organizations, and at the societal level.

Although institutional racism as a social issue is not new to social work, its significance and centrality to the profession needs to be clarified and underscored. The need to address racism through social work education and social work practice was identified at the 2005

Social Work Congress convened by the National Association of Social Workers, the Council on Social Work Education, the National Association of Deans and Directors, and other cosponsoring organizations. The purpose of the congress was to choose 12 imperatives that a unified profession would dedicate itself to over the following 10 years. The 400 leaders of the profession who participated included addressing racism through education and practice in two of the imperatives:

— Address the effect of racism, other forms of oppression, social injustice, and other human rights violations through social work education and practice.

— Continuously acknowledge, recognize, confront, and address pervasive racism within social work practice at the individual, agency, and institutional levels.

Another significant basis for addressing racism is detailed in the NASW social policy statement Racism that was updated at NASW's 2005 Delegate Assembly. The fundamental point of the policy is that racism must not be tolerated. The policy specifically calls upon all social workers to continuously acknowledge, recognize and confront all forms of racism, within all of the institutions that are relevant to social work. The immediate impetus for this document, however, came from the NASW President's Initiative Task Force on *Weaving the Fabrics of Diversity*, which NASW President Elvira Craig de Silva first convened in August 2006. The Task Force identified the decisions of the 2005 Social Work Congress and the NASW Racism policy statement as giving the impetus for calling on the entire social work profession in the United States to take responsibility for addressing institutional racism, as it is manifested within the profession's own domain as well as in the broader society.

8.5.1. Institutional or Structural Racism

Institutional or structural racism, defined as the social, economic, educational, and political forces or policies that operate to foster discriminatory outcomes or give preferences to members of one group over others, derives its genesis from the origins of race as a concept. *Race* as a biological fact has been invalidated by biologists and geneticists, but race as a social construct is very real. Physical traits still have meaning as markers of social race identity. It is this social race identity that confers placement in the social hierarchy of society, and thereby access to or denial of privileges, power, and wealth. "The status assignment based on skin color identity has evolved into complex social structures that promote a power differential between Whites and various people-of-color". The emphasis on the use of physical features to classify and group people has its history from the extended encounter between European and non-European peoples that began in the late 15th and early 16th centuries. Discovering human beings in Asia, Africa, and the Americas who looked- and often acted- very different from themselves, Europeans concluded that these superficial differences were surely indicators of much more fundamental differences as well. This conclusion helped them to colonize, enslave, and even exterminate certain of those peoples. Europeans came to believe that races are in fact distinct and identifiable human groups; that there are systematic, inherited, biological differences among races; and that the non-White races are innately inferior to Whites-that is, to Europeans.

In the United States, the cognitive dissonance between the values and beliefs of the Protestant founders for human rights, liberty, justice, democracy, brotherhood, and equality alongside the practice of enslavement of Africans, the making of Mexican/Mexican Americans a foreign minority in the land of their birth, and genocide of Native Americans was resolved by classifying groups of people by virtue of their physical characteristics as being not only different, but innately inferior and thereby unworthy of rights and entitlements. From the very origins of this nation, the concept of race was used to institutionalize the benefits of one group of people while denying them to other groups of people.

The determination of who is or is not white in America has fluctuated over time. There have been times and places in which the Irish, Jews, Italians, and Latinos have been considered white or non-white. The changes in the U.S. Census Bureau nomenclature system over time demonstrate the fluidness in the U.S. society's perceptions of how people should be clustered. The categorization that had been "White/Non-White" is now a set of five major groups along with notation of national origin. Furthermore, the individual determines his or her own race and can choose more than one. The census also makes a clear demarcation between racial categories and the ethnic category of Latino/Hispanic who can be of any race.Contemporary United States continues to struggle with the cognitive dissonance between the espoused virtuous beliefs of this nation and its actual practices in relationship to those who are "different," meaning "not white." These struggles are captured in several of the terms often associated with a discussion of racism and related concepts.

Racism is the practice of discrimination and prejudice based on racial classification supported by the power to enforce that prejudice. Ethnocentrism is the view that one's own group is the center of everything and that all things are judged based on one's own group. Prejudice is the negative (or positive/idealized) attitudes, thoughts, and beliefs about an entire category of people formed without full knowledge or examination of the facts. And discrimination is acting on the basis of prejudice. Discrimination is often codified by laws, regulations, and rules. People experience oppression when they are deprived of human rights or dignity and are (or feel) powerless to do anything about it. Sometimes the negative act is in the form ofexclusion, in which people are denied the opportunity to participate in a certain right, benefit, or privilege. Sometimes the negative act is in the form of marginalization, in which people find that they are on the fringe of political, social, or economic consciousness. That sense of invisibility results in decisions being made by those in power that may be harmful simply because the needs were not considered. Assimilation means being absorbed into the cultural tradition of the dominant society and consequently losing one's historical identity.This is in contrast to acculturation in which there is an adaptation to a different culture but retention of original identity.

8.5.2. Social Work Response

These concepts are relatively familiar to most social workers, and many view their work as addressing various aspects of these problems. As a profession, social work "has traditionally been looked to for leadership and support in altering conditions that impede human potential and dignity". Social work organizations can easily point to work that is being done to address the needs of the dispossessed, many of whom are people of color. The social work profession can look back on its history as a force for social change in our society in which the beneficiaries were and are predominantly people of color.

Institutional racism is the manifestation of racism in social systems and institutions. It is the social, economic, educational, and political forces or policies that operate to foster discriminatory outcomes. It is the combination of polices, practices, or procedures embedded in bureaucratic structure that systematically lead to unequal outcomes for groups of people. In this environment disparities are often tolerated as normal rather than investigated and challenged. "These power-assigning social structures in the form of institutional racism affect the life opportunities, life-styles, and quality of life for both Whites and people-of-color. In so doing they compound, exaggerate, and distort biological and behavioral differences and reinforce misconceptions, myths, and distortions on the part of both groups about one another". In the United States, the ethnocentric focus is still primarily a white, Anglo-Saxon protestant orientation. The standards by which things are considered valued emanate from a Eurocentric perspective. Kivel noted the following examples of institutional racism over the history of this country:

— exclusions from unions, organizations, social clubs

— seniority systems (last hired, first fired)

— income differentials

— predatory lending practices

— inferior municipal services

— admissions based on test scores

— differential education based on preconceived potential or ability

— monocultural school curricula

In each of these situations, people of color experience disadvantages that flow from one generation to another in reference to income, decision making, health status, knowledge and skill development, and quality of life. The greater loss is to the country as a whole of the talents and perspectives of a significant proportion of the population.

Structural inequities have been solidified over time. The multigenerational effect of the privileges of free white people as compared with the effect of slavery, "Jim Crow" segregation, along with prejudicial immigration rules1 has resulted in a set of social structures that maintain and reinforce the barriers to the attainment of maximal human potential and dignity. A strong social movement will be the most powerful approach to change. On the surface, this is a natural challenge for the social work profession to address. However, these social structures are maintained by individuals, many of whom are just trying to make a living. Their participation in these systems is not fueled by intention to do harm, and many are oblivious to the fact that anyone has been harmed. Some, including many social workers, believe that they are "doing good."

The new challenge for the profession is to tackle forms of racism that are more subtle than slavery or segregation. To a large degree, the social traditions and values within the helping professions preclude active promotion of the types of racism that are overt or blatant. Many in this society, including the helping professions, denounce intentional discrimination or prejudice against a person because of that person's membership in a certain racial group. The press for political correctness suppresses some behaviors or comments, and most people, including social workers or others in the helping professions, would not describe themselves as "racist." Nor do they engage in forms of overt racism. However, even if every person in the world currently conducted themselves in a non-racist manner, institutional racism would still exist.

These structures are maintained, in part, by individuals who exhibit some of the more subtle forms of racism that even they would not necessarily believe in themselves. The challenge for social workers committed to change is to address both overt forms of racism and these subtle forms as they are expressed by others and themselves.

8.5.3. Subtle Types of Racism

Three subtle types of racism are captured in the concepts of *symbolic racism, aversive* racism, and micro-inequities.

Symbolic racism is expressed by those who may or may not perceive themselves as racist, but justify their negative judgment of others by asserting that the others do not abide by traditional values of the dominant group. People can perceive themselves as being fair and practicing equality by holding forth certain values, such as "individualism" or "work ethic" or "self-reliance," and take negative action because the focal group does not share those values. So they perceive themselves as operating based on certain "objective" standards or "universal truths" rather than in opposition to the group based on their race.

Aversive racism is another subtle form of prejudice. People who engage in the practice see themselves as non-racists, but they will do racist things, sometimes unintentionally, or they will avoid people without overt racist intent. What they believe about themselves and will attest to is the importance of fairness, equality, and justice, but because they have been exposed to the ever-present societal racism just by living in the United States, they will reflect it in their conduct. Finally, good people can do bad things to others in ways for which there is no formal grievance, but still have negative (sometimes unintentionally) effect. This refers to *micro- aggressions* or *micro-inequities. Micro-inequities* are "those tiny, damaging characteristics of an environment, as these characteristics affect a person not of that environment. They are the comments, the work assignments, the tone of voice, the failure of acknowledgement in meetings or social gatherings. These are not actionable violations of law or policies, but they are clear, subtle indicators of lack of respect by virtue of membership in a group". These are forms of racism that as members of this society we all commit. People of color may commit these acts or maintain these attitudes against other people of color. The charge is to become able to recognize them and move ourselves and others beyond them to facilitate systemic change.

8.5.4. Looking into the Mirror

Two other issues must be confronted as a precondition to releasing the energy required to successfully challenge institutional racism. One is *white privilege* and the second is *internalized racism. White privilege* is the collection of benefits based on belonging to a group perceived to be white, when the same or similar benefits are denied to members of other groups. It is the benefit of access to resources and social rewards and the power to shape the norms and values of society that white people receive, unconsciously or consciously, by virtue of their skin color. In contrast, *internalized racism* is the development of ideas, beliefs, actions, and behaviors that support or collude with racism against oneself. It is the support of the supremacy and dominance of the dominant group through participation in the set of attitudes, behaviors, social structures, and ideologies that undergirds the dominating group's power and privilege and limits the oppressed group's own advantages.The challenge for white social workers and social workers of color is to confront these inhibiting forces to the work required to successfully confront institutional racism. Individuals are called upon to acknowledge that by the accident of history, they are in positions that give them advantages over others. And then, they are being asked to advocate for changes that may disadvantage themselves or their family members. Others are called upon to dare to recognize their own potential power, mourn the loss of what might have been, and marshal their energies to seek correction in society's processes. Even those within the social work profession can be paralyzed against change because of benefits of white privilege or the blindness of internalized racism.

8.5.5. Racism and the Other Isms

Some people discount the effect of race on the outcomes for people of color. Many would argue that the issues for people of color are more a consequence of socioeconomic status than race. What they fail to recognize is that the overrepresentation of people of color in lower socioeconomic strata is due to institutional racism that has constrained them to life circumstances that kept them in that strata. Others equate the prejudice, discrimination, and bias based on age, gender, sexual orientation, or physical ability to the negative experiences due to race. Prejudice and discrimination based on these factors do in fact cause much strife in our society. Also, issues of privilege based on these factors must be confronted as seriously as privilege by racial identification. However, the experience of people of color in each of these categories is significantly worse compared with those who are white and in these categories. Furthermore, the intolerance that was first established on the basis of race provided the template to treat in a discriminatory manner those who do not "fit." If our society can successfully tackle its treatment of people who are "different" by virtue of the social category of race, it will have changed the manner in which it views, understands, and responds to "differentness" in other forms.

8.5.6. Manifestations of Institutional Racism in Social Work

Social work as a profession historically has had to confront two sometimes complementary and sometimes competing mandates. The preamble to the NASW *Code of Ethics* begins by stating:

> The primary mission of the social work profession is to enhance human well-being and help meet the basic human needs of all people, with particular attention to the needs and empowerment of people who are vulnerable, oppressed, and living in poverty.... Social workers are sensitive to cultural and ethnic diversity and strive to end discrimination, oppression, poverty, and other forms of social injustice.

The profession is expected to "enhance human well-being" and also "strive to end social injustice." The irony is that by being a "helping" profession, social work reduces the pressure on the larger society for social change. The continued marginalization of those who should or could be mobilized to act for social justice could be an unintended consequence of the profession's "helpfulness." The other dilemma is that success in changing the forces that promote discrimination, oppression, and poverty also changes the forces that support white privilege. NASW as a predominantly white association must acknowledge and commit to taking action against white privilege, if it is to be successful in achieving social justice for people of color.

8.5.7. Self-Assessment of the Profession

A thoughtful examination of the practice in the association, in social work organizations, in institutions, in agencies, and by individual social work practitioners would probably reveal examples of different subtle forms of racism. If the profession can understand the manifestation of the different forms of racism within the profession, it can gain a better understanding of the issues, discover strategies that work for change, and become authentic social change leaders against structural racism in a variety of societal institutions. Consider the following familiar scenarios:

— Support is given to policies and practices without analysis of the racial effect or worse.

Scenario A. A program designed to reduce disproportionate confinement of youths of color in juvenile detention settings reviewed its decision-making policies. It discovered that one assessment question was sending children of color into detention with greater frequency than white children. The question was "Is there a parent available for supervision immediately after school?" In this community, most of the families of color were single-family units, in which the parent was at work immediately after school. When the question was changed to "Is there a responsible adult available for supervision immediately after school?", the disposition patterns of that community changed.

Scenario B. A senior social worker of color, employed by a state agency to monitor mental health programs, finds that assessments of black families and children do not adequately consider the social context and family strengths. When she raises such concerns with white program leaders, she is frequently told that she is missing the clinical aspects of what is involved, even though she is an experienced clinician, herself.

— Board leadership and membership and executive leadership and management positions are occupied predominantly by white people, even in institutions that serve predominantly populations of color.

Scenario C. City X's population is 40% multicultural. The service community is 80% African American or Caribbean American. The three primary social service agencies providing services in this community have boards that are 100% white. The executive directors are white. The senior management positions are white. The front line service staff is 30% multicultural. The administrative clerks and housekeeping staff are 80% multicultural.

Scenario D. A Vietnamese social work administrator is recruited into a large family service agency to help the organization move toward becoming more diverse and multicultural. She soon finds that she is expected to address issues of diversity without the executive leadership and board members assuming greater responsibility, themselves. She finds it very difficult to express her concerns about this out of a realistic fear of being told that she is too sensitive.

— Organizations that are led by people of color are marginalized by organizations led by members of the dominant society.

Scenario E. In community Y, four social service agencies provide most of the services. A consortium of African American, Cuban, Haitian, and Puerto Rican–led community-based social service agencies wants to expand their services. The leaders of the four dominant social service agencies refuse to engage in dialogue with the consortium about partnerships. The state agency promulgates rules in the request for proposal that advantage the established agencies and disadvantages the consortium. Unless there is change these agencies will not have the opportunity to demonstrate whether they can effectively provide the appropriate services to the community. And in the current fiscal environment, they may not be able to survive as service providers.

— Investment in the development of knowledge about people and communities of color is limited.

Scenario F. State Z mandates that child welfare agencies engage in cultural and linguistic competence training. The agencies in this particular city conduct annual cultural competence training consisting of an eight-hour training session providing an overview of cultural competence and stories from four members of the community about their culture. Staff members who have been there for several years are bored after hearing the same presentation year after year. No other training is provided. Staff members are not expected to develop a personal professional development plan in relationship to cultural competence. There is no programmatic effort to link with the various cultural communities on an ongoing basis.

Scenario G. A coalition of agencies approaches a school of social work to urge that curriculum better reflect the needs of the Latino community. The school's dean says that she agrees with the request but the faculty has a great deal of discretion in determining the curriculum. She did not feel she was in a position to insist on implementation of the requested changes.

Scenario H. A social worker of color who runs a program foı children in foster care shared an experience in which a white clinician reported to him that an African American child's grandmother, who was the primary caregiver, was resistant to working with the agency after she had missed several appointments. The program director said that when he looked more closely at the situation, he found that the grandmother was caring for three of the child's siblings, including one who had recently required hospitalization. Instead of seeing her as resistant, he found her to be a significant asset to the child, but overextended and stressed. He concluded that the clinician did not understand the commitment of many African American families in assuming responsibility for children even when they are not the biological parents.

— There is limited investment in creating partnerships with communities of color for program or service design, implementation, and evaluation.

Scenario I. In response to the need to provide better aging services in rural communities, this social service agency has decided to expand services from its base in the major city in this southern community to satellite offices in the rural communities contiguous to the city. The executive director and management staff of the agency developed a service delivery structure after consultation with a wellrespected consultant in the field. Like other social service agencies, the service population in both the city and the rural communities are predominantly African American, along with an influx of immigrants from Mexico, El Salvador and Guatemala but the board and executive directors are white. Part of the process included meetings with physicians and religious leaders in the rural area. Prospective consumers of the services or their families were not involved in the planning, design, or implementation. They were asked to complete a satisfaction survey at the end of service, but they had no input into the questions or analysis of the results.

Scenario J. In an effort to make family and children's services neighborhood based, a public child welfare agency awarded contracts to several established white-run nonprofit organizations with little history in the communities they were coming into. Whereas one community-based agency had a long-standing reputation for its involvement with the public schools, hospitals, police precinct, and cultural institutions in its neighborhood, the other contracted providers made little effort to develop such relationships.

— There is preference to soften racist language so that one sees euphemisms such as, "culturally deprived" and "economically disadvantaged" rather than "culturally dispossessed" and "economically exploited".

Scenario K. In a study being developed as background for a state legislative committee, this policy analysis group notes significant racial disparities in mental health services for the African Americans in one particular region of the state. It is a community that has received numerous complaints regarding racial profiling by police, predatory lending practices, and cross burnings. Rather than explore and discuss racism as a potential factor, they focus on the cultural orientation of the residents to use faith communities as a source of healing. They shift the focus to the residents rather than the institutions and policies.

— Social workers of color experience micro-inequities promulgated by their white social work colleagues.

Scenario L. In recent interviews with social workers of color in a major city about their experiencing bias among colleagues toward them, several reported, independently of one another, having their perspectives and concerns treated as unimportant. Significantly, all of them said that they also experienced having the same perspectives and concerns valued when expressed by a white person. One black program director said that he repeatedly reported that an air conditioning unit in a room where groups were run was broken during a hot summer, but it was not repaired until another administrator, who was white, made the report.

— Employment criteria and credentialing requirements often create barriers for employment of social workers of color and generally do not require demonstration of the knowledge and skills required to effectively serve a culturally and linguistically diverse service population.

Scenario M. Native American social workers in County A have consistently found it difficult to meet the criteria of the social work regulatory body in their state. As they pursue tutoring in preparation for the test, they are amazed at how few test items seem to relate to the issues and needs of tribal communities or best practices with this population. They despair that they are having a hard time meeting the formal criteria of the state and of obtaining social work positions to serve their community, while at the same time, the state credentialing body is not setting forth an expectation that those who are credentialed are prepared to serve their tribal community.

Scenario N. A hospital social work director terminated the employment of four social workers because they did not comply with a policy requiring all staff to pass the state's licensing exam within one year of being hired. Each social worker had been highly evaluated. For three social workers, Spanish, Hmong, and Vietnamese were their primary languages and English was their second language. The fourth social worker, an African American, grew up in an inner-city neighborhood where the quality of education was inferior to that of more affluent areas. This resulted in lower test scores throughout her life. The director said that this was a significant loss to the department and hospital, which was in a low-income and immigrant community.

Each of these examples demonstrates the ripple effect of institutional or structural racism in our society into social work practice. The correction in each of these circumstances requires authentic efforts to name "racism" as a factor for exploration and action. The journey to effective transformation is not straightforward. The following section maps out strategies to address these issues within the profession.

8.5.8. Institutional Racism in the Social Work Profession

The approaches to address institutional racism in the social work profession discussed here are not necessarily comprehensive in scope but identify some significant dimensions, including short- and long-term approaches. Strategies geared toward different levels of social organization are also needed, starting at the level of the individual professional social worker, moving to the level of social work organizations and then to social institutions that impinge on the profession and on clients and their communities.

Addressing these levels are not mutually exclusive but are intertwined; they are separated out here to bring attention to the importance of each level. In the final section of this paper, the question "What can be done now?" will be addressed.

8.5.8.1. Personal Growth and Professional Development

All social workers need to dedicate time to their personal growth and professional development to become and remain effective in addressing institutional racism. Whereas social workers are likely to fall along a continuum from having little professional development to being knowledgeable and effective in this area, growth and development is an ongoing process of continuous learning throughout one's career.Multiple elements contribute to personal growth and professional development, beginning with the recognition of the importance of institutional racism as a variable in social work and the lives of clients and the communities in which they live. Coupled with this awareness is the need to make a commitment to acquire the knowledge and skills necessary to be both competent and effective.

8.5.8.2. Interpersonal Capacity and Collaboration

Social workers have limited capacity to address institutional racism on their own. Although individuals must assume responsibility for their own growth and development, it is essential for professional social workers to initiate discussions, both formal and informal, about the issues discussed here, with colleagues and members of the organizations within which they work. The conversations need to take place both as general discussions and in response to specific policies, practices, behaviors, and attitudes observed or planned in their professional context. This is often easier said than done, given the nature of institutional racism and that discussion is often experienced as threatening. Becoming skilled in initiating and maintaining discussions about institutional racism requires critical judgment, skill, and self-awareness that evolve over time.

8.5.8.3. Social Work Organizations Becoming Antiracist Entities

Social work and social work–related organizations include agencies, programs, and departments that provide social work services; schools of social work; and associations such as the National Association of Social Workers (NASW) and the Council on Social Work Education

(CSWE). Organizations need to move from remaining silent about, or ignoring, the manifestations of institutional racism to recognizing their existence and making a commitment to promote change.

This movement begins with the individual members of the organization engaging in their own professional development and growth while entering into interpersonal collaborations with colleagues and other members of the organization. It is essential, however, for organizational decision makers to assume leadership for addressing institutional racism and developing official goals, policies, and procedures that will enable the organization to evolve. In organizations engaged in service delivery this effort will include a commitment by boards of directors and ongoing analysis of how institutional racism can be ameliorated or reversed through programming, hiring, training, supervision, and other forms of institutional processes.

In educational institutions, effectiveness in addressing institutional racism will involve making a commitment to the incorporation of content related to institutional racism into curriculum and all forms of education. The goal is to graduate social workers who are on the road toward competency in addressing institutional racism throughout their careers. It also means examining ways in which the current curriculum promotes and supports values, beliefs, and practices that foster institutional racism and then engaging in change process as indicated. Leadership is needed from deans and directors, chairs of educational committees, as well as from admissions and field work departments and field work supervisors. Associations such as NASW and CSWE have a special leadership role to play in assuring that the social work profession embraces a commitment to address institutional racism. NASW, CSWE and other social work organizations that sponsored the 2005 Social Work Congress have already taken an important step by adopting decade-long racism imperatives. These organizations can play a decisive role in using this document and similar tools as vehicles for encouraging recognition and commitment among their constituents on a broad scale.

8.5.8.4. Focus on Client, Community, and Social Policy

Fundamental to addressing institutional racism is the need for professional social workers and social work–related organizations to understand the effect of racism on their clients and their communities. There is a need to better understand the relationship between the problems a client needs help with and the role of racism in the genesis of those problems, regardless of the race or socioeconomic status of the client. Social workers need to adapt their own practice approach in consideration of these factors. Social workers also need to be attuned to the differential effect of social policies that disadvantage communities of color while benefiting others, and advocate for fairness and equity in policy decision and resource distribution.

8.5.9. What Needs To Be Done

Society cannot be changed overnight. However,

— Social workers can assume responsibility for taking action to reverse the effect of racism on services to people and communities of color.

— Social workers can take action to engage their own organizations to become antiracist organizations.

— Social workers can partake in actions large and small to challenge the institutional or structural racism in their communities and the nation at large.

Both individual initiatives and collective organized efforts officially endorsed by social work organizations are required to make this happen. NASW and its local chapters have a unique opportunity to take leadership. Opportunities for leadership also reside with schools of social work and social work service delivery organizations. Social work leaders, from CEOs and program directors to members of boards of directors, have a special obligation to address institutional racism and can do so, given their sphere of influence and ability to influence organizational decisions and structures. The following opportunities can be taken immediately while building toward longer term and ongoing efforts:

8.5.9.1. Recognition/Create awareness

Efforts to address institutional racism begin with recognition of the dimensions of the problem and how it is manifested within the social work profession. It is especially critical to recognize how institutional racism is ignored through a process of denial. Only through recognition and building awareness can a commitment be made to create short- and long-term plans for institutionalizing positive change.

Action Steps

1. Study NASW policies relating to institutional racism, including the policy statement in *Social Work Speaks* on "Racism" and in this document, "Institutional Racism and the Social Work Profession: A Call to Action."
2. Become knowledgeable about the history and context of institutional racism, the relevant concepts that have been developed, and the manifestation of institutional racism in social work, both generally and locally, including within one's own organizational setting.
3. Encourage colleagues, staff, and the institutions with which you are affiliated to take action steps 1 and 2 above.

8.5.9.2. Education and Training/Build knowledge

Participate in organized learning experiences that deepen one's understanding of institutionalized racism. Studying the dimensions of institutional racism is a beginning, but is usually insufficient to fully appreciate the nature of racism and its manifestations. Educational opportunities led by seasoned trainers in addressing racism are especially useful in understanding the dynamics of racism. As individuals and organizations acquire greater understanding, effective and sustainable activities can be developed. Educational opportunities include participation in forums, workshops, classes, discussion groups, as well as relevant readings.

Action Steps

1. Identify opportunities for classes and workshops that address racism.
2. Organize forums on institutional racism, its manifestations within social work, the nature of white privilege, and other relevant aspects of racism.

3. Allocate time for reading about institutional racism.

*8.5.9.3. **Dialogue and Inclusion/Become partners and allies***

Practitioners and organizations must create opportunities for discussions between social workers of color who have experienced firsthand the effect of institutional racism and white social workers. White social workers need to listen to what their colleagues have to say about their experiences in the field and to their suggestions for practice based on their knowledge of working with clients of color. In addition, initiatives to address institutional racism need to include social workers of color in the decision-making process. Affirmative efforts must be taken to ensure that as many social workers of color as possible are participating in discussions about institutional racism and in planning activities to produce longer-term change.

White social workers can take leadership in helping other white colleagues understand the implications of white racial identity, white privilege, and the effect of racism on white people. It is important to realize that everyone is affected by racism. This is work that can more effectively be conducted by those who share the same racial identity.

Action Steps

1. Provide meaningful opportunities for social workers of color to share their perspectives on how institutional racism is manifested in social work andidentify opportunities to create positive change. Issues of safety, trust, and commitment may need to be addressed to enable participation.
2. Use the opportunities provided in action step 1 above to enhance understanding among all social workers.
3. White social workers need to create opportunities for dialogue with social workers of color, based on action steps 1 and 2 above.
4. White social workers need to create opportunities for dialogue with other white social workers to explore the effect of racism and white privilege on white social workers.

*8.5.9.4. **Planning/Plan for internal change***

Social work–related organizations can engage in longer-term strategic planning, identifying progressive steps that can be taken over a period of time, whether one, two, or three years, as well as envisioning what the organization would like to achieve in the longer term.

Action Steps

1. Engage in a visioning process, identifying how an organization can become a multicultural, antiracist organization.
2. Create expectations for the organization's CEO and board of directors to lead the organization in addressing institutional racism.
3. Identify methods of accountability to ensure that planning is implemented and evaluated on a regular basis. In addressing the question "accountability to whom?" accountability should include social workers of color as well as clients and communities of color.

8.5.9.5. Organizing for Social Change/Challenge the status quo

Social workers and social work organizations can embark on the planned strategies to promote change at the individual, agency, community, and societal levels. The specific tasks are governed by the focus for intervention and the unique circumstances of that entity.

Action Steps

1. Prepare a racial effect analysis of policies and practices of the agency or community, so that specific polices and practices can be identified for change.
2. Identify and support champions for change within the organization and the community, by establishing partnerships with consumers, families, and leaders selected by communities as their representatives, and social work colleagues of color.
3. Establish an atmosphere of intolerance for racist conduct within the organization, system, and community.
4. Use the available resources to challenge racist policies, practices, and behavior. Invoke legal strategies such as civil rights laws and engage official monitoring and enforcement agencies to fulfill their mandates.

References

Hoggett, P. ed. 1997. *Contested Communities: experiences, struggles, policies*, Bristol: Policy Press.

Jones, D. 1977. 'Community Work in the UK' in H. Specht and A. Vickery. eds. *Integrating Social Work Methods*, London: George Allen and Unwin.

Mayo, M. 1975. 'Community development: a radical alternative?' in R. Bailey and M. Brake. eds. *Radical Social Work*, London: Edward Arnold.

Mayo, M. ed. 1977. *Women in the Community. Community Work 3,* London: Routledge and Kegan Paul.

Scottish Executive. 2003. *Working and learning together to build stronger communities. Working draft Community Learning and Development Guidance, Edinburgh*: Scottish Executive.

Taylor, M. 1991. *Signposts to Community Development*, London: Community Development Foundation. 36 + x pages.

9

Community Work for Mental Health Promotion

Public health is the science and art of promoting health, preventing disease, and prolonging life through the organised efforts of society. This 20th century has seen greater gains in health for the population of the world than at any other time in history. These gains have been made partly as a result of improvements in income and education, with accompanying improvements in nutrition, hygiene, housing, water supply and sanitation. They are also the result of new knowledge about the causes, prevention and treatment of disease and the introduction of policies that have made intervention programmes more accessible. The greatest advances in health have been made through a combination of structural change and the actions of individuals .

Since its inception, World Health Organization (WHO) has included mental well-being in the definition of health. WHO famously defines health as: A state of complete physical, mental and social well-being and not merely the absence of disease or infirmity. Three ideas central to the improvement of health follow from this definition: mental health is an integral part of health, mental health is more than the absence of illness, and mental health is intimately connected with physical health and behaviour.

Defining mental health is important, although not always necessary to achieving its improvement. Differences in values across countries, cultures, classes, and genders can appear too great to allow a consensus on a definition. However, just as age or wealth each have many different expressions across the world and yet have a core common-sense universal meaning, so mental health can be conceptualised without restricting its interpretation across cultures. WHO has recently proposed that mental health is: A state of well-being in which the individual realises his or her own abilities, can cope with the normal stresses of life, can work productively and fruitfully, and is able to make a contribution to his or her community. In this positive sense, mental health is the foundation for well-being and effective functioning for an individual and for a community. It is more than the absence of mental illness, for the states and capacities noted in the definition have value in themselves. Neither mental nor physical health can exist alone. Mental, physical, and social functioning are interdependent. Furthermore, health and illness may co-exist. They are mutually exclusive only if health is defined in a restrictive way as the absence of disease. Recognising health as a state of balance including the self, others, and the environment helps communities and individuals understand how to seek its improvement.

9.1. Importance of Mental Health

Mental health and mental illness are determined by multiple and interacting social, psychological, and biological factors, just as health and illness in general. The clearest evidence relates to the risks of mental illnesses, which in the developed and developing world are associated with indicators of poverty, including low levels of education. The association between poverty and mental disorders appears to be universal, occurring in all societies irrespective of their levels of development. Factors such as insecurity and hopelessness, rapid social change, and the risks of violence and physical ill-health may explain the greater vulnerability of poor people in any country to mental illnesses.

The findings from a recent natural experiment in poverty reduction with the opening of a casino on an American Indian reservation go a long way in demonstrating the reality of social causation for disturbed childhood behaviour, for example. After introduction of the casino, the rates of such behaviour reduced. The mediating variable appeared to be improved parental supervision of the children. Economic levels have important implications for family functioning and child mental health. Mental, social, and behavioural health problems may interact to intensify each other's effects on behaviour and well-being. Substance abuse, violence, and abuses of women and children on the one hand, and health problems such as heart disease, depression, and anxiety on the other, are more prevalent and more difficult to cope with in conditions of high unemployment, low income, limited education, stressful work conditions, gender discrimination, unhealthy lifestyle, and human rights violations .

Mental health for each person is affected by individual factors and experiences, social interaction, socialite structures and resources, and cultural values. It is influenced by experiences in everyday life, in families and schools, on streets, and at work . The mental health of each person in turn affects life in each of these domains and hence the health of a community or population. Ethnographic studies in the developing world show how environments and social settings such as the slums of Mumbai shape local experience and the mental health of communities.

Some of the newest researches across the disciplines of genetics, neuroscience, the social sciences, and mental health involve elaboration of ideas about the impact that societies have on human life over and above the sum of the impact of the individual members of the society (Anthony in press). Yet mental health and mental illness by and large are viewed as residing outside the public health tradition with its fundamental concepts of health and illness as multifactorial in origin and of there being a continuum between health and illness. The consequences are twofold. First, the opportunities for improving mental health in a community are not fully exploited.

Second, organised efforts in countries to reduce the social and economic burden of mental illnesses tend to depend mostly on the treatment of ill individuals. Mental illnesses are common and universal. Worldwide, mental and behavioural disorders represented 11% of the total disease burden in 1990, expressed in terms of disability-adjusted life years (Days) . This is predicted to increase to 15% by 2020.

Mental health problems also result in a variety of other costs to the society . Depression was the fourth largest contributor to the disease burden in 1990 and is expected to be the second largest after ischaemic heart disease by 2020. Yet, mental illness and mental health have been neglected topics for most governments and societies. Recent data collected by WHO demonstrates the large gap that exists between resources that are available in countries for mental health and the burden caused by mental health problems. In contrast to the overall health gains of the world's population in recent decades, the burden of mental illness has grown.

This neglect is based at least in part on confusion and false assumptions about the separate concepts of mental health and mental illness. Until now, the prevailing stigma surrounding mental illness has encouraged the euphemistic use of the term "mental health" to describe treatment and support services for people with mental disorders and in other matters related to mental ill-health. This usage contributes to confusion about the concept of mental health as well as the concept of mental illness.

In most parts of the world the treatment of mental illness was alienated from the rest of medicine and health care at least until recently. In the isolated setting of asylums, practitioners saw many seemingly incurable patients. The supposed incurability of insanity and melancholy made practitioners believe the causes were entirely biological. The idea has since persisted that prevention of mental illness is "all or none" and, furthermore, that promotion of mental health is somehow far removed from the problems of the real world and could even shift resources from the treatment and rehabilitation of people affected by mental illness. The twin aims of improving mental health and lowering the personal and social costs of mental ill-health can only be achieved through a public health approach.

Within a public health framework, the activities that can improve health include the promotion of health, the prevention of illness and disability, and the treatment and rehabilitation of those affected. These are different from one another, even though the actions and outcomes overlap. They are all required, are complementary, and one is no substitute for the other.

9.1.1. Absence of Mental Illness

Mental health implies fitness rather than freedom from illness. In 2003, George Vaillant in the USA commented that mental health is too important to be ignored, it needs to be defined. As Vaillant points out, this is a complex task. "Average mental health" is not the same as "healthy", for averaging always includes mixing in with the healthy the prevailing amount of psychopathology.

What is healthy sometimes depends on geography, culture, and the historical moment. Whether one is discussing state or trait also needs to be clear is an athlete temporarily disabled with a fractured ankle healthy or the asymptomatic person with a history of bipolar affective disorder healthy or unhealthy? There is also "the two-fold danger of contamination by values" a given culture's definition of mental health can be parochial and, even if mental health is "good", what is it good for? The self or the society? For fitting in or for creativity? For happiness or for survival? Even so, Vaillant advocates that common sense should prevail and that certain elements have a universal importance to mental health; just as despite every culture differing in its diet, the importance of vitamins and the four basic food groups is universal.

9.1.2. Mental Health and Behaviour

Mental health status is associated with behaviour at all stages of life. A body of evidence indicates that the social factors associated with mental ill-health are also associated with alcohol and drug use, crime, and dropout from school. The absence of the determinants of health, and the presence of noxious factors, also appear to have a major role in other risk behaviours such as unsafe sexual behaviour, road trauma, and physical inactivity. Furthermore, there are complex interactions between these determinants, behaviours and mental health.

For example, a lack of meaningful employment may be associated with depression, and alcohol and drug use. This may in turn result in road trauma, the consequences of which are physical disability and loss of employment. Kleinman describes the clustering of mental and social health problems in "broken communities" in shanty towns and slums and among vulnerable and marginal migrant population: civil violence, domestic violence, suicide, substance abuse, depression, and post traumatic disorder cluster and coalesce. He calls for a research agenda and innovative policies and programmes "that can prevent the simply enormous burden that mental illness has on the health of societies resulting from the variety of forms of social violence in our era". The corollary is the need for the development and evaluation of programmes that on the one hand control and reduce such clusters, and on the other hand assist people and families to cope in these circumstances.

Physical health and mental health are closely associated through various mechanisms, as studies of links between depression and heart and vascular disease are demonstrating. The importance of mental health in the maintenance of good physical health and in recovery from physical illness is now well substantiated, as is the converse. Mental health status is a key consideration in changing the health status of a community.

Various types of evidence suggest that mental health and/or its determinants can be improved in association with planned or unplanned changes in the social and physical environment. This will be discussed in the following pages. Prudence suggests that sufficient justification exists for programme and policy interventions accompanied by evaluation of process and outcomes in countries of high or low income. It also suggests the need to monitor the effects on mental health of social, economic, and environmental changes in any country. These actions in turn will continue to expand the evidence base to encourage further prudent interventions designed to improve or maintain mental health, to suit each unique time, country, locality, and population.

9.2. Mental Health Promotion

Health promotion is an emerging field of action, often referred to as the "new" public health. It is often defined indirectly by first examining the idea of "health"; however, the term "health" is itself imprecise. "Health" can refer both to absent and present states. It is often used to mean the absence of disease or disability, but, just as often, health may refer to a state of fitness and ability, or to a reservoir of personal resources that can be called on when needed. People with different backgrounds and cultures may hold different conceptions of health.

When lay people describe what it means to be healthy, their responses reflect often the particular circumstances of their lives. Under some circumstances, they equate health with freedom from disease; in others, they equate health with autonomy or with vitality. Older people, for example, tend to define health as inner strength and the ability to cope with life's challenges; younger people tend to emphasise the importance of fitness, energy, and strength. People with comfortable living conditions tend to think of health in the context of enjoying life; people not so well-off tend to connect health with managing the essentials of daily living.

Nonetheless, some solid attempts have been made to construct a unified theory of health. Unified theories of health such as that propounded by WHO cover wide territory, including environmental and individual factors. The obvious implication is that the promotion of health must have foci on both the individual and the environment. This calls for the involvement of a much broader array of interventions and actors than does the traditional model of medicine, which centres on specialists trained to return function to individuals.

Health promotion has been defined as action and advocacy to address the full range of potentially modifiable determinants of health. Health promotion and prevention are necessarily related and overlapping activities. Because the former is concerned with the determinants of health and the latter focuses on the causes of disease, promotion is sometimes used as an umbrella concept covering also the more specific activities of prevention.

9.2.1. Determinants of Health

Determinants of health are those factors that can enhance or threaten an individual's or a community's health status. These can be matters of individual choice, such as whether to smoke tobacco or not, or can relate to social, economic, and environmental characteristics beyond the control of individuals. Examples include the person's social class, gender, ethnicity, access to education, quality of housing, and presence of supportive relationships, and in the community the level of social and civic participation, availability of work, air quality, and building design.

9.2.3. Levels of Intervention

There is mounting evidence that it is possible to intervene at several levels, from local to national, to improve health . The factors over which individuals have little or no control require the collective attention of a society as encapsulated by the Ottawa Charter of Health Promotion. The five action strategies identified by the Charter remain today the basic blueprint for health promotion in many parts of the world.

9.2.4. Health Inequalities

Inequalities in health are related to a wide range of social factors, including those already noted. Inequalities also result to a degree from individual differences in genetics, health related behaviour, and choices regarding education, work, and play. To the degree that inequalities are a consequence of social injustice, there exists not merely inequality, but inequity as well. At all levels, from local to national, examples can be found of policies and interventions that assist people living in social and economic disadvantage to have better health. According to WHO, health promoting policies are needed not only in the health care sector, but also in the economic, environmental, and social sectors for positive impact on the determinants of health and improved health equity.

9.2.5. Political Dimension of Health Promotion

Discussions about what should be done are shaped by the nuances of a particular situation in a particular place at a particular time. Under what conditions, for example, does a health risk warrant an information campaign, a stern advisory, or a policy of forced commitment? Scientific evidence can never provide a fully satisfactory answer, and political considerations enter naturally into the decision-making process. Health promotion politics involves advocating both individual and collectivist interventions for social change.

9.3. Health Promotion Practice

Despite diverse settings, health promotion work exhibits common features based on collaboration and recurrent cycles of programme planning, implementation, and evaluation. Influential models emphasise the intention to build people's capacity to manage their own health and to work collaboratively. Virtually all health promotion practice models include:

— A careful study of a community's needs, resources, priorities, history, and structure in collaboration with the community: "doing with" rather than "doing to".

— Agreement on a plan of action, gathering of resources, implementation, and monitoring of action and change processes. Fluidity is needed in planning and acting to meet the demands of new or changing conditions, as well as constant surveillance of and reflection over practice.

— An emphasis on evaluation and dissemination of best practices, with attention to maintaining and improving quality as dissemination unfolds.

9.3.1. Principle of Prudence

A resolution to employ an evidence-based approach to health promotion was adopted by the 1998 World Health Assembly. Generating evidence of the effectiveness of health promotion can be challenging, however. Health promotion is social action. Controlled laboratory experiments, therefore, are often inappropriate ways to generate evidence of its effectiveness. Instead, consensus about effectiveness is based on methodological triangulation that leads to a converging interpretation of evidence of different kinds, from different places, generated by different researchers.

The "principle of prudence" recognises that all evidence has weaknesses, that we can never know enough to act with certainty, but that we can in many cases be sure enough of the quality of the existing evidence to make recommendations for action. Much of the evidence of health promotion's effectiveness must be derived from community based research. There cannot be total reliance on traditional, quantitative measures. Including qualitative methods gives a better understanding of what works and what does not. Although such "real world" research is a complex undertaking, it is nevertheless possible to develop a body of dependable knowledge.

Major successes in health promotion over recent decades have occurred in several arenas of action, including tobacco control and heart health. The implementation and evaluation of a heart health promotion programme in Finland is a good example of this. In a number of cases, these efforts have been supported by international conventions and collaborations.

9.3.2. Strength of the Evidence

There are two focal issues with regard to health promotion evidence: the strength of the evidence and its implications for research, practice, and policy development. The strength of evidence is influenced by the design of interventions and related methodological issues such as the validity and effectiveness of efforts to minimise bias. A useful strength of evidence typology that has reference to three elements of scientific enquiry falsifiability, predictability, and reputability results in four types of evidence:

— *Type A:* What works is known, how it works is known, and reputability is universal.

— *Type B:* What works is known, how it works is known, but reputability is limited.

— *Type C:* What works is known, reputability is universal, but how it works is not known.

— *Type D:* What works is known, how it works is not known, and reputability is also limited.

Health promotion research operates in an environment where numerous cultural, social, economic, and political factors interact. Complexities are involved that rarely resolve sufficiently to produce Type A evidence. Health promotion strives, therefore, for Type B evidence, and this has important implications for practice. It is unlikely that the effectiveness of a health promotion intervention can be guaranteed beforehand; hence, evaluation research needs to be combined with health promotion practice.

9.3.3. Positive Mental Health

The evidence for promoting mental health depends on defining, measuring, and recording mental health. Over the last 30 years, research has contributed to an understanding of what is meant by the term "mental health", although this understanding has been constrained by the fact that much of the evidence that is accessible widely is recorded in the English language and obtained in developed countries.

Mental health has been variously conceptualised as a positive emotion (affect) such as feelings of happiness, a personality trait inclusive of the psychological resources of self-esteem and mastery, and as resilience, which is the capacity to cope with adversity. Various aspects and models of mental health contribute to our understanding of what is meant by positive mental health. A number of aspects are described in the accompanying box.

9.3.4. Intrinsic Value of Mental Health

Mental health contributes to all aspects of human life. It has both material and immaterial, or intrinsic, values: for the individual, society, and culture. Mental health has a reciprocal relationship with the well-being and productivity of a society and its members. Its value can be considered in several related ways:

— Mental health is essential for the well-being and functioning of individuals.

— Good mental health is an important resource for individuals, families, communities, and nations.

— Mental health, as an indivisible part of general health, contributes to the functions of society, and has an effect on overall productivity.

— Mental health concerns everyone as it is generated in our everyday lives in homes, schools, workplaces, and in leisure activities.

— Positive mental health contributes to the social, human, and economic capital of every society.

— Spirituality can make a significant contribution to mental health promotion and mental health influences spiritual life.

Mental health can be regarded as an individual resource, contributing to the individual's quality of life, and can be increased or diminished by the actions of society. An aspect of good mental health is the capacity for mutually satisfying and enduring relationships. There is growing evidence that social cohesion is critical for the economic prospering of communities and this relationship appears to be reciprocal.

9.3.5. Culture and Mental Health

As already noted, although the qualities included in the concept of mental health may be universal, their expression differs individually, culturally, and in relation to different contexts. It is necessary to understand a particular community's concepts of mental health before engaging in mental health promotion. The broad nature of mental health also means that it is not just the preserve of the mental health professional.

Each culture influences the way people understand mental health and their regard for it. An understanding of and sensitivity to factors valued by different cultures will increase the relevance and success of potential interventions. A Xhosa mother in apartheid era South Africa whose explanation for not comforting her crying son was to ensure he grew up strong enough to leave the country and join the armed struggle exemplifies this. Young soldiers in Angola experienced disruption to their developmental experiences and education.

Their reports of feeling different and having difficulty relating to others enabled tailored approaches to helping them adjust to peacetime society. Stigma is a major concern to people affected by HIV/AIDS. Efforts to understand this group's concepts of mental health make a major contribution to developing relevant intervention programmes. A culture-specific approach to understanding and improving mental health may be unhelpful, however, if it assumes homogeneity within cultures and ignores individual differences. Today, most cultures overlap and are heterogeneous. The beliefs and actions of groups need to be understood in their political, economic, and social contexts; culture is one of several factors to be considered.

9.3.6. Social Capital and Mental Health

On the one hand, millions of dollars are committed to alleviating ill-health through individual intervention. Meanwhile we ignore what our everyday experience tells us, i.e. the way we organise our society, the extent to which we encourage interaction among the citizen and the degree to which we trust and associate with each other in caring communities is probably the most important determinant of our health. In the renaissance of thinking in recent decades about social collectivity and health promotion, the concept of "social capital" has been prominent. It is invoked to reform previously individualised lines of research on the social determinants of health generally and mental health in particular (Anthony in press). Extending beyond the tools and training that enhance individual productivity ("physical capital" and "human capital"), social capital "refers to features of social organisation such as networks, norms, and social trust that facilitate coordination and cooperation for mutual benefit".

Economic and social environments also affect social capital. Social capital is not an individual perception or resource. Challenges remain in defining and measuring it without reduction to the individual level. Potential detrainments include exclusion of nonmembers and minority groups, and excessive demand on members of social organisations. A consensus is growing, however, that social capital facilitates collective action and can promote social and economic growth and development by complementing other forms of capital.

Research over the last two decades has demonstrated links between social capital and economic development, the effectiveness of human service systems, and community development. Social scientists have investigated how higher social capital may protect individuals from social isolation, create social safety, lower crime levels, improve schooling and education, enhance community life, and improve work outcomes. Researchers have begun to analyse the relationships between social capital and mental health.

The relationship between social capital, health, and mental health, and the potential of mental health promotion to enhance social capital are current topics of research and debate. Population health measures or risk factors are usually considered as the aggregate of the individual characteristics in the population. Consideration is usually one of binary associations between one (or more) environmental factors and individual health. The power of social capital lies in its potential to understand the environment in another way the interaction between environmental and social factors and connected groups of individuals.

This perspective of networks of individuals interacting with environments has the power to explain an array of collective outcomes beyond that explained by aggregated individual health outcomes

(Anthony in press). Much work remains to be done in accounting for the mechanisms underlying the health community link and the interrelations between social capital and mental health. It is also unclear if the relations between these two variables are multidirectional, and of causality or correlation. However, social networks are believed to promote social cohesion, informal caring, protection during crises, better health education, and better access to health services, and to enforce or change society norms that have an impact on public health (e.g. smoking, sanitation, and sexual practices).

9.3.7. Mental Health and Human Rights

A climate that respects and protects basic civil, political, economic, social, and cultural rights is fundamental to the promotion of mental health. Without the security and freedom provided by these rights it is very difficult to maintain a high level of mental health. A human rights framework offers a useful tool for identifying and addressing the underlying determinants of mental health. The instruments which make up the United Nations (UN) human rights mechanism represent a set of universally accepted values and principles which can guide countries in the design, implementation, monitoring, and evaluation of mental health policies, laws, and programmes. As legal norms and standards ratified by governments, they generate accountability for mental health and thus offer a useful standard against which government performance in the promotion of mental health can be assessed.

Human rights empower individuals and communities by granting them entitlements that give rise to legal obligations on governments. They can help to equalise the distribution and exercise of power within society, thus mitigating the powerlessness of the poor. The principles of equality and freedom from discrimination, which are integral elements of the international human rights framework, demand that particular attention be given to vulnerable groups. Furthermore, the right of all people to participate in decision-making processes, which is reflected in the Bill of Rights and other UN instruments, can help ensure that marginalised groups are able to influence health-related matters and strategies that affect them, and that their interests are considered and addressed. Mental health promotion is not solely the domain of ministries of health. It requires the involvement of a wide range of sectors, actors, and stockholders. Human rights encompass civil, cultural, economic, political, and social dimensions and thus provide an inter sectorial framework to consider mental health across the wide range of mental health determinants.

9.4. Conceptual Framework for Mental Health Promotion

The Victorian Health Promotion Foundation in Australia developed a conceptual framework for action to guide its mental health promotion efforts. Central to this framework is a focus on three of the determinants of mental health, identification of priority population groups and areas and settings for action, and a description of the anticipated benefits. While mental ill-health is present in all population, it is more common among people with relative social and economic disadvantage. Integral to Vic Health's health promotion framework is the desire to reduce health inequities. In Vic Health's view, to be successful in this, efforts need to:

— Focus on social and economic determinants of mental health.
— Involve the full range of health promotion methodologies that work at the population and sub population levels.
— Engage those working across sectors and settings.

Due to the relationship between social and economic factors and mental health, success in promoting mental health and well-being can only be achieved and sustained by the involvement and support of the whole community, and the development of partnerships between a range of agencies in the public, private, and nongovernment sectors.

In order to recruit the cross-sector engagement required, synergies across sectors need to be located and a common language developed, which has a focus on health as opposed to illness. Given the scarcity of resources and the global effort required for managing and reducing the mental health burden, it is also critical that any perception of competing for resources with the health treatment sector is avoided.

Government policy, research, and practice take place in systems or organisations that have little involvement with each other. In order to develop effective mental health promotion activity at a population level, integration mechanisms across these "silos" must be developed. Long-term and integrated planning, implementation, and investment are required. Evaluation needs to occur and progress will be slow. Long-term gains are not always the drivers attractive to governments in the short-term, so effective ways of managing political discourse must be developed. Health promotion is an emerging field of activity, with mental health promotion being one of the most recent areas of focus.

While the rhetoric of health promotion includes the use of multiple methods to change the structural determinants of health, challenges lie in the development of workforces within health and other sectors with the conceptual and practice skills required. It is also critical that interdisciplinary collaborations are forged between those working in health and sociopolitical domains at the academic level. This will require an ideological as well as a cultural shift in the competitive academic environment. Finally, competition across sectors and disciplines will obstruct progress. The development of international collaborative arrangements is fundamental to ensuring that mental health promotion activity takes place in developed and developing countries and is informed by shared wisdom and expertise.

9.5. Effective Health Promotion

The personal, social, and environmental factors that determine mental health and mental illness may be clustered conceptually around three themes:

— The development and maintenance of healthy communities. This then provides a safe and secure environment, good housing, positive educational experiences, employment, good working conditions, and a supportive political infrastructure; minimises conflict and violence; allows self-determination and control of one's life; and provides community validation, social support, positive role models, and the basic needs of food, warmth, and shelter.

— Each person's ability to deal with the social world through skills like participating, tolerating diversity, and mutual responsibility.

— This is associated with positive experiences of early bonding, attachment, relationships, communication, and feelings of acceptance.

— Each person's ability to deal with thoughts and feelings, the management of life, and emotional resilience.

— This is associated with physical health, self esteem, ability to manage conflict, and the ability to learn.

The fostering of these individual, social, and environmental qualities, and the avoidance of the converse, are the objectives of mental health promotion. In each nation or community, local opinion about the main problems and potential gains, and the evidence about the social and personal determinants of mental health will shape the activities of mental health promotion. As noted earlier, health promotion and prevention are necessarily related and overlapping activities: the former is concerned with the determinants of health and the latter focuses on the causes of disease.

The evidence for prevention of mental disorders contributes to the evidence base for the promotion of mental health. Beyond that, however, the evidence for effectiveness of mental health promotion is being extended through evaluation of experience in various ways and in different countries and settings. This provides growing confidence in developing interventions, even while the principle of prudence recognises that we can never know enough to act with certainty.

The activities of mental health promotion are mainly sociopolitical: reducing unemployment, improving schooling and housing, working to reduce stigma and discrimination of various types, and specific policy initiatives such as wearing seat belts to avoid head injury. The key agents are politicians, educators, and members of nongovernment organisations. The job of mental health professionals is to remind them of the evidence for the importance of these key variables. Health practitioners may be more directly involved in prevention of illness, devising and applying programmes in primary health care and other settings, and in health policy.

A combined approach to health promotion and prevention of illness categorises interventions according to the levels of risk of illness (or scope for improving health) in various population groups, and makes it clearer what type of collective action is required:

universal (directed to the whole population, e.g. good prenatal care), selected (targeted to subgroups of the population with risks significantly above average, e.g. family support for young, poor, first pregnancy mothers) or indicated (targeted at high-risk individuals with minimal but detectable symptoms, e.g. screening and early treatment for symptoms of depression and dementia). The approach to gathering evidence is influenced by recognising that:

— The evidence for direct causal pathways is generally strongest for the most immediate influences on health or disease.

— Most health states have multiple causes interacting over time.

— Important factors such as family environment or child abuse and neglect will influence the level of physical and mental health as well as the risk for several types of illness in later life.

— Other life events and circumstances will interact favourably or unfavourably to contribute to health and resilience or the development of illness.

Mental health promotion has been seen to ask for peace, social justice, decent housing, education, and employment. The call for inter sectoral action has sometimes been diffuse. Specific evidence-based proposals with measurable outcomes are required. However, asking individual health promotion projects to demonstrate long-term changes in ill-health, productivity, or quality of life is often unrealistic and unnecessary.

What is required instead is a marshalling of the evidence linking mental health with its critical determinants (aetiological research), and programme design and evaluation to demonstrate changes in the same determining or mediating variables. Programmes and policies can aspire, in other words, to produce changes in indicators of economic participation, levels of discrimination, or social connectedness. Identifying and documenting the mental health benefits of these changes, and developing indicators of these determinants, are complementary areas of work needing further support. An evidence base for mental health promotion does exist but it needs boosting with aetiological research and programme and policy evaluation.

9.5.1. Linking Research with Practice and Policy

Important advances in establishing a sound evidence base for mental health promotion have occurred in recent years. Consensus exists on clusters of known risk and protective factors for mental health and there is evidence that interventions can reduce identified risk factors and enhance known protective factors. The International Union for Health Promotion and Education (IUHPE) report for the European Commission endorses that mental health promotion programmes work and that there are a number of evidence-based programmes to inform mental health promotion practice. The accumulating evidence demonstrates the feasibility of implementing effective mental health promotion programmes across a range of diverse population groups and settings.

An important challenge is to strengthen the evidence base in order to inform practice and policy globally. While researchers are more likely to be concerned with the quality of the evidence, its methodological rigour, and its contribution to knowledge, different stockholders in the area may bring other perspectives to bear on the types of evidence needed. As described by Nut beam, policy-makers are likely to be concerned with the need to justify the allocation of resources and demonstrate added-value, practitioners need to have confidence in the likely success of implementing interventions, and the people who are to benefit need to see that both the programme and the process of implementation are participatory and relevant to their needs. Another major task is to promote the application of existing evidence into good practice on the ground, particularly in disadvantaged and low-income countries and settings. This entails identifying programmes that are effective, feasible, and sustainable across diverse cultural contexts and settings. The challenge is therefore twofold: translating research evidence into effective practice and translating effective practice into research so that currently undocumented evidence may make its way into the published literature.

9.5.2. Shifting to Positive Mental Health

Mental health promotion reconceptualises mental health in positive rather than in negative terms. This shift in focus to positive indicators of well-being calls for methodological refinement in establishing positive indicators of mental health outcomes. This shift also calls for a focus on research methods that will document the process, as well as the outcomes, of enabling positive mental health and identify the necessary conditions for successful implementation.

9.5.3. Effective Programme Implementation

The systematic study of programme implementation has been relatively neglected. The challenge has been identified as using evaluation methods and approaches that are congruent with the principles of mental health promotion practice Robertson , which cross methodological boundaries, and which evaluate initiatives in terms of their process as well as their outcomes). The notion that there is a hierarchy of evidence, particularly one that focuses almost exclusively on evaluation outcomes from expensive randomised controlled trials (RCTs), restricts the current body of evidence to that research conducted mainly in high-income countries. A continuum of approaches is needed ranging from RCTs to more qualitative process oriented methods such as the use of case studies, narrative analyses correlational studies, interviews, surveys, and ethnographic studies . Implementation research is critical to the understanding of how and under what conditions programmes may be effective. Collections of this kind of data will contribute to advancing knowledge on best practice in real settings.

9.5.4. Applying the Evidence to Low-Income Countries

The evidence debate needs to extend beyond a concern with the quality of research design to focus more directly on the quality of the interventions and their wider practice and policy implications. Currently the evidence debate has taken place in the English language literature within a Euro–American context: "evidence is least available from areas that have the maximum need, that is developing countries and areas affected by conflicts". The development of user-friendly information systems and database is required in order to make the evidence accessible to practitioners and policy-makers. In particular, there is an urgent need to identify effective programmes that are transferable and sustainable in settings such as schools and communities. In this respect, it may be useful to explore the application of programmes based on community development and empowerment methods, such as the community mothers property gramme and the widow-to-widow peer support programme. These programmes, among others, have been shown to be highly effective, lowcost, replicable programmes successfully implemented and sustained by nonprofessional community members in disadvantaged community settings.

The implementation of school-based programmes for young people also appears to be a key area for development in low-income countries. In the absence of large resources, the challenge in many countries is to document innovative forms of practice and to bring them to the attention of others. Documentation, even newsletters and brochures, may be lacking. A lack of documentary evidence does not mean that there is not good practice, however. Dissemination research to examine how existing evidence can be applied across diverse cultural settings is necessary.

International cooperation is necessary to assist low-income countries by means of technical support in publishing guidelines for effective implementation of lowcost, sustainable programmes. The ultimate test of the evidence base is how it can be used effectively to inform practice and policy globally that will reduce inequalities and bring about improved mental health for individuals, families, and communities in most need.

9.6. Social Determinants of Mental Health

The socioeconomic determinants of health have been well studied. In brief, people who are more socially isolated and people who are disadvantaged have poorer health than others. More socially cohesive societies are healthier, with lower mortality . Many studies have shown the powerful health associations of social connectedness. The evidence on the personal, social, and environmental factors associated with mental health and mental illness has been reviewed by a number of authors Concurrent with 20th century advances in learning from the brain sciences and neuroscience, there has been an evolution of ideas about the social determinants of mental health and mental disorders.

At the beginning of the 21st century, we have returned to a position of widespread enthusiasm about our genetic endowment and the social shaping of its expression. At present, the predominant motif is not from eugenics as practised at the population level via the now rejected modes of ethnic cleansing and selective sterilisation. Instead, a prevailing motif is that gene expression can be shaped by exogenous agents and may be shaped by social experience. It will be important for the lay public and for socialite leaders to grasp these ideas as they emerge and are developed during the 21st century. Choices about the socialite response depend in part upon our capacities to predict the occurrence of harm or benefit and in part upon our benefit risk analysis with respect to deployment of resources. In this context, the accuracy of our predictions is disclosed in the evidence and is more or less objective, but the benefit risk evaluation and the choice of interventions depend upon an expression of shared consensus about values.

An immediate challenge for society's leaders is to create or refine the social structures and processes we use to evaluate the available evidence and to mobilise resources to promote mental health. New discoveries and increasingly definitive evidence about the determinants of mental health are of limited value unless there are social structures and processes to put the new discoveries and evidence into action.

As the 20th century ended, there was an increasingly acidic critique of "risk factor epidemiology", by which is meant a selectively narrow research focus on individual-level characteristics and behaviours that signal increased risk of mental disorders or general medical conditions. At the same time, considerable pessimism developed about how little was gained when prevention programmes were focused upon individual-level behavioural change. Indeed, this type of critique was not new. Earlier critics such as Claus Bahne Bahnson pleaded for more research using designs that avoid old controversies about the greater or lesser significance of biological or sociological or other factors but rather integrate these several levels in a larger matrix expressing the whole process. To the extent that disturbances in mental health such as suicide-related behaviour may be regarded on one level at least as a social phenomenon, the critique is more than a century old.

There is still much to be learned from public health research across disciplines, as well as the experimental paradigms of laboratory research on non human primates.

9.6.1. Links between Physical Health and Mental Health

Positive mental health is a set of key domains encompassing well-being and positive states of mind. It can influence onset, course, and outcomes of both physical and mental illnesses. For example, research has shown links between depression and anxiety and cardiovascular and cerebrovascular diseases. The role of mental disorders in increasing vulnerability to physical morbidity and poorer outcomes is well documented.

Psychological beliefs such as optimism, personal control, and a sense of meaning are known to be protective of mental health as well as physical health. Even unrealistically optimistic beliefs about the future may be health-protective for men infected with HIV . Similarly, physical health is a positive attribute influencing both mental and physical illnesses and their outcomes. These interrelationships are encompassed in holistic concepts of health. The results of a recently released New York City Community Health Survey reveals that poor general health is three times more common among people who report significant emotional distress. The latter experience high rates of many chronic conditions that put them at risk for early death, including high cholesterol, high blood pressure, obesity, asthma, and diabetes.

They often engage in behaviours that lead to increased risk for health problems, including sedentary habits, binge drinking, smoking, and eating a poor diet. In studies on the health of elderly people, the interrelationship between physical and mental health also becomes evident. For example, findings on daily living practice among Thai elderly suggest the importance to their physical and mental health of good food habits, regular exercise, seeking knowledge about health, religious activity involvement, good relationships with others, and well-planned management of income and expenses resulting in life satisfaction.

Holistic concepts of health are basic to many indigenous beliefs on the nature of health and wellbeing. This is illustrated by the definition of health accepted by Australia's ancient indigenous culture. The National Aboriginal Health Strategy Working Party) defines health as: Not just the physical health well-being of the individual but the social, emotional, and cultural wellbeing of the whole community. This is a whole-of-life view and it also includes the cyclical concept of life-death-life.

This definition encompasses mental health, which has been defined as social and emotional wellbeing, and spiritual, environmental (such as land and place), physical, social (including community and culture), and emotional factors. These are seen as interacting with each other in complex ways. Such interactions are hypothesised to occur through psychological and psychophysiological mechanisms. More recently, the influence of specific psychiatric disorders in contributing to adverse cardiac disease trajectories and death has been established. Thus, there is a body of evidence highlighting the value of an holistic approach to health in terms of mental health and physical health and illness. The natural consequence of such correlations is that promoting positive mental health may be seen as significant in terms of health globally and both physical and mental disorders.

9.6.2. Mental Health Concepts of Recovery

Realising that mental health is more than the absence of illness can be helpful to people with mental illnesses and their careers. Protective health resources and positive health can coexist with sometimes severe psychopathological symptoms, for instance in a person living with schizophrenia. This suggests the value of developing more comprehensive clinical approaches with an additional focus on the person's positive health, strengths, capabilities, and personal efforts towards recovery in prevention, diagnosis, treatment, and rehabilitation. The recovery model empowers consumers and those involved with them with its emphasis on strengths and a positive future orientation. Assessing and building on strengths helps people to "live well" with mental or other illness and avoid being further diminished by it.

9.6.3. Developing Indicators of Mental Health

A considerable body of practice informs the development and use of population indicators in mental health and mental health promotion: epidemiological studies of mental health, cross national studies of quality of life, findings regarding the relationship between social determinants and inequalities and health and mental health outcomes, psychometric studies, and observations from health surveillance and monitoring.

In proposing mental health indicators, the different perspectives of health promotion practitioners and mental health practitioners need to be appreciated, although these are not antithetical. Thus, either through a focus on population or a focus on individuals, both acknowledge that positive mental health is set within a larger sociopolitical, economic, and cultural environment which in turn influences the distribution of material and social resources through a variety of institutional and individual mechanisms. Ultimately, individual biology and genes are conditioned by and interact with these environments. As a consequence, indicators of positive mental health will of necessity reflect differing levels of influence.

Emerging frameworks or conceptual models of positive mental health, while at an early stage, already acknowledge the need to specify a range of indicators at differing levels of developmental influence on mental health. These influences entail multisectoral interests (e.g. health, welfare, education, justice). They also include macro-level measures of cultural, social, and political-economic structural processes; distil measures of the social organisation and behaviour of communities, schools, local neighbourhoods, and workplaces; proximal measures of the demographic, material, and social circumstances and behaviours of families and peers; and direct measures of the psychological, biological, social, material, and demographic characteristics of individuals. Clearly, developing a framework to capture all or even some of this is an extensive undertaking. Some efforts in this regard have been made, however.

Broad-based macro-level determinants of mental health are measured by, for example, the Human Development Index (HDI) which was reviewed in 2000 by the UN. The HDI was developed as a measure of achievement and focuses attention on human outcomes as well as the economic performance of a country. The Gender-related Development Index (GDI) and Gender Empowerment Index (GEI) are other examples of macro-level national indicators. They are relevant in characterising some aspects of basic human development, giving measures of mental health an appropriate context.

There are also several measures that attempt to rate the overall level of mental health distress in individuals or document specific behaviour, such as suicide. For example, the Kessler-10 is a self-report questionnaire that yields a measure of psychological distress; the SF-36 is an interviewer-rated indicator of mental health distress.

Information collected on individuals includes demographic determinants, exposure to stressful life events, level of social support, and quality of life. Demographic determinants, such as age, sex, level of education, income, and current employment, are essential to characterise population and to provide a descriptive context for implementation of mental health promotion. Stressful life events are associated with poor mental health and extensively studied in the social sciences. Social support is often conceptualised as an environmental variable; however, research shows that it is influenced by genetic factors. Correlated with personality, and relatively stable over time. Importantly, social support is not latent within the environment but rather is reciprocally maintained through the actions of individuals. Its association with health and, more particularly, positive mental health has been documented in longitudinal work.

Social support covers three domains: the extent to which individuals are attached to others, the individual's cognitive appraisal of the support, and the response of others in the provision of support. A number of measurement devices have emerged from its long history of interest in the social sciences. Examples are the 27-item Social Support Questionnaire and the Medical Outcomes Study Social Support Survey (MOSSSS). Quality of life measures not only measure mental health but also usually contain items and domains that directly probe aspects of mental health.

9.7. Effective Interventions

Evidence exists for the effectiveness of a wide range of exemplary mental health promotion programmes and policies. Their outcomes show that mental health promotion is a realistic option within a public health approach across the life-span and across settings such as perinatal care, schools, work, and local communities. In many fields of life, well-designed interventions can contribute to better mental health and well-being of the population. Over the last two decades, numerous studies in mental health promotion and mental disorder prevention have proven that such programmes can be effective and lead to improved mental health, social, and economic development.

Topic-specific literature overviews have confirmed that programmes can be effective to improve behaviours such as child abuse , conduct problems , violence and aggression , and substance use, and in different settings, including schools and workplaces. Similarly, meta-analyses have been undertaken to assess programme efficacy in the fields of harmful drug use for children and adolescents, mental health for children, interventions for infants and children up to six years of age, prevention of child sexual abuse and prevention of depression.

The following review of the best examples of effective mental health promotion is based primarily on evidence from controlled trials, including quasi-experimental studies, and studies using a time series design. Where relevant, evidence is taken also from observational and qualitative studies. This counts especially for the evidence from interventions in low-income countries where resources are lacking for expensive controlled studies. The programmes and policies illustrate the wide variety of strategies to promote mental health in the population across different system levels and stages of the life-span.

9.7.1. Macro Interventions with Mental Health Impact

9.7.1.1. Improving Nutrition

There is strong evidence that improving nutrition and development in socioeconomics disadvantaged children can lead to healthy cognitive development and improved educational outcomes, especially for those living in impoverished communities. The most effective intervention models are potentially those which combine nutritional interventions (such as food supplementation) with counselling on psychosocial care (e.g. warmth, attentive listening). These have also been suggested to be cost-effective. In addition, iodine plays a key role in preventing mental and physical retardation and impairment in learning ability. Iodine supplementation programmes ensure that children obtain adequate levels of iodine. Global efforts such as those supported by UNICEF have led to 70% of the world's households using iodised salt, which protects 91 million newborn from iodine deficiency and indirectly to preventing related mental and physical health problems.

9.7.1.2. Improving Housing

Poor housing has been used as an indicator of poverty and as a target to improve public health and reduce inequalities in health. A recent systematic review on the health effects of housing improvement suggests a promising impact on health and mental health outcomes, such as improvements in self-reported physical and mental health, perceptions of safety and crime reduction, and social and community participation.

9.7.1.3. Improving Access to Education

Low literacy is a major social problem in many countries, particularly in south Asia and sub-Saharan Africa. Illiteracy and low education tend to be more common in women. Lack of education severely limits the ability of individuals to access economic entitlements. While there are impressive gains in improving literacy levels in most countries through better education for children, there is much less effort directed to today's adults without literacy skills. Ethnographic research in India suggests programmes aimed at improving literacy, in particular for adults, have tangible benefits in promoting mental health. The positive mental health impact was mediated through a number of pathways, including acquisition of numeracy skills which reduced the risk of being cheated, greater confidence in expressing one's rights, and a reduction of barriers to access opportunities.

Evidence also indicates the success of initiatives using subsidies to close gender gaps in education. For example, in the first evaluation of a school stipend established in Bangladesh in 1982, enrolment of girls in secondary school rose from 27% to 44% over five years, more than twice the national average. Evaluation studies in Pakistan have illustrated that improved physical access to school, subsidised costs, and culturally appropriate design can sharply increase girls' enrolment in education. Better education increases female cognitive-emotional and intellectual competencies and job prospects, and might reduce social inequity and risks of certain mental disorders such as depression.

9.7.1.4. Strengthening Community Networks

Community interventions have focused on developing empowering processes and building a sense of ownership and social responsibility within community members. An example of a community intervention is the Communities that Care (CTC) Programme which has been implemented successfully across several hundred communities in the USA and is currently being adopted and replicated in the Netherlands, England, Scotland, Wales, and Australia. The CTC is a field-tested strategy for activating communities to implement community violence and aggression prevention systems. The strategy helps communities use local data to develop actions that occur simultaneously at multiple levels: community (e.g. mobilisation, media, policy change), school (changing school management structures or teaching practices), family (e.g. parent training strategies) and individual (e.g. social competence promotion strategies).

The CTC strategy supports communities in selecting and implementing existing evidence-based programmes that fit the risk profile of their community. To date this operating system has only been evaluated in the USA with pre–post designs and comparisons with baseline data involving about 40 communities in each field test. Outcomes have indicated improvements in youth behavioural outcomes, parental skills, and family and community relations, and decreases in school problems, weapons charges, burglary, drug offences, and assault charges.

9.7.1.5. Reducing Misuse of Addictive Substances

A strong evidence base indicates the negative impact of alcohol, tobacco, and drug use during pregnancy. These effects include an increased likelihood of premature deliveries, low birth weight, restricted long-term neurological and cognitive-emotional development of children (e.g. lower intelligence, temperament, ADHD, conduct problems, poorer school achievements), and perinatal mortality. Being born prematurely and low birth weight are in themselves known risk factors for adverse mental health outcomes and psychiatric disorders. In general, substance abuse by the mother is associated with the offspring becoming dependent on substances during adolescence and young adulthood. Educational programmes to stimulate pregnant women to abstain from or reduce substance use can therefore have long-term mental health benefits.

9.7.1.6. Intervening after Disasters

Psychological and social interventions during the reconsolidation phase after disasters have been recommended to improve the mental health of the affected population and to prevent psychopathology. These interventions include availability of community volunteers, provision of non-intrusion emotional support, psycho education, and encouraging preexisting positive ways of coping.

9.7.1.7. Preventing Violence

Community-based efforts to prevent violence include public education campaigns, improved urban infrastructure, and community policing. These efforts not only prevent violence, but also have effects on mental health and well-being of the affected population.

9.7.2. Meso and Micro Interventions

During the early stages of life there is more development in mental, social, and physical functioning than in any other period across the life-span. What happens from birth to age three influences how the rest of childhood and adolescence unfolds. A healthy start in life greatly enhances the child's later functioning in school, with peers, in intimate relations, and with broader connections with society. The major dimensions of a healthy start to life are physical and psychological well-being, including freedom from poverty, violence, armed conflict, HIV-AIDS in the family , physical disease, infirmities, injuries, abuse, neglect, exposure to drugs prior to birth, malnutrition, and reduced chances for healthy attachment to the mother. The start of life in turn influences the likelihood of later behavioural problems, including opposition-defiance, aggression and conduct problems; shy withdrawn behaviour; attention deficit and hyperactivity; and readiness for school, including verbal, language, and social skills. Policies attempting to target the well-being of families, such as policies to alleviate economic hardship, family-friendly policies at the workplace, or access to child care, can lead to overall mental and physical health improvements in children and future adults

9.7.3. Pre-School Educational and Psychosocial Interventions

There are many community programmes for families with young children, such as family reading programmes in libraries, health screening clinics, organised recreation, and television programmes that teach elementary reading skills and socioemotional values. In the USA, the Perry Preschool Project demonstrated very long-term effects from a half-day preschool intervention combined with weekly home visits. Children in the intervention, who were African-American and came from impoverished backgrounds, had improved cognitive development, better achievement and school completion, and fewer conduct problems and arrests. Significant benefit was found at age 19 and age 27 on lifetime arrests (40% reduction) and repeated arrests (a 7-fold reduction) .

Speech and language skills of children born in impoverished families or families from minorities can often develop more slowly than those of other children. There is strong evidence that early interventions starting at age two that promote basic reading skills and engage children in conversations with their parents about picture books improve reading skills and facilitate the transition to school.

Questions have been raised regarding whether home-based interventions and parenting approaches are an effective use of resources. The few cost-effective evaluations undertaken in this area seem promising. Moreover, interventions having a simultaneous impact on the physical and mental health of parents and their babies might prolong their impact throughout children's lives and between generations.

Reducing violence and improving emotional well-being in the school setting Many countries are committed to universal systems of primary education. Although this is not the case in all developing countries, the number of youth attending school is increasing. In addition to their central role of fostering academic development, schools serve an important role in the health and social-emotional development of students. Despite variation in the amount of time that children spend in school, they are the primary institution for socialisation in many societies.

For this reason, and because of the convenience of conducting interventions in a setting where young people spend much of their time, schools have become one of the most important settings for interventions for children and youth. To function effectively, children need social and emotional competencies. They also need the confidence to use those skills constructively and opportunities to practise their skills in order to help develop a sense of identity. This process is often called "social and emotional learning". The website of the Collaborative for Academic, Social and Emotional Learning (CASEL) offers a rich source of evidence-based programmes to enhance social emotional learning, as well as materials that can be down loaded to support the implementation of such programmes across communities, countries and regions.

9.7.4. Effective School-Based Interventions

There is ample empirical evidence that providing universal programmes to groups of students can influence positive mental health outcomes. Several types of interventions in schools can be identified as achieving improved competence and self-worth, as well as decreasing emotional and behavioural problems. While some interventions target the school in an integrated approach, others target only one part of the school system (e.g. children in a given grade) or a specific group of students that are identified to be at risk for emotional or behavioural problems. Generally, universal school based programmes have focused on a range of generic risk factors and mental health problems, such as academic failure, aggression, and bullying, and have demonstrated increased individual competence and resilience as well as reductions in depressive symptoms.

As students get older and are faced with new challenges, such as peer pressure to engage in delinquent behaviour or substance use, social-emotional skills become particularly important to maintaining health and positive development. School based skill-building programmes that are geared for middle and high school students often serve as both mental health promotion and substance abuse prevention programmes, particularly when problem-solving is geared towards addressing these issues. The Positive Youth Development Programme (PYD) is an example of a school-based programme focusing on this type of student skill building. The curriculum promotes general social competence and refusal skills related to alcohol and drug use, and is found to produce significant improvements in students' skills and in teacher reports of social adjustment.

9.7.4.1. Changing School Ecology

A positive psychosocial environment at school ("child-friendly schools") can positively affect the mental health and well-being of young people. The components of positive psychosocial environment at school include providing a friendly, rewarding, and supportive atmosphere; supporting cooperation and active learning; and forbidding physical punishment and violence.

9.7.4.2. Multicomponent Programmes

Programmes that focus simultaneously on different levels, such as changing the school ecology as well as improving individual skills, are more effective than those that intervene on solely one level. Examples of effective multicomponent programmes include the Linking the Interests of Families and Teachers (LIFT) programme, which demonstrated reductions in student aggression, particularly for those most at risk; and the developmentally sequences Seattle Social Development Project , which addresses multiple risk and protective factors across the individual, the school, and the family over a six-year intervention, leading to significantly stronger attachment to school, improvement in self-reported achievement, and less school misbehaviour.

9.7.4.3. Reducing the Strain of Unemployment

Retrenchment and job loss can cause serious mental health problems. In a sample of USA mothers living in poverty, not working and receiving welfare was associated with negative cognitive and behavioural outcomes for children, lower maternal mental health, less social support, and more avoidant coping strategies. It has been recommended that work reforms should be developed and implemented with the goal of moving poor women out of low-wage work and into work that allows them to become economically self-sufficient over the long-term. Priorities include the provision of a living wage, post-secondary education, and job training.

Similarly, counselling or job search training for low-income unemployed groups can be an effective strategy to enhance coping with unemployment and to reduce the negative outcomes of unemployment for mental health. The JOBS Programme, for example, has been shown to have positive effects on rates of re-employment, the quality and pay of jobs obtained, and job search self-efficacy and mastery, as well as reduce depression and distress. The JOBS Programme has been successfully disseminated internationally in the People's Republic of China, Finland, and the USA, and is currently being implemented in Ireland.

9.8. Stress Prevention Programmes at the Workplace

There is evidence that work characteristics may cause or contribute to mental health problems (e.g. burnout, anxiety disorders, depression, sleeplessness), gastro-intestinal disorders, cardiovascular illness, and musculoskeletal disease, and produces social and economic burden to health and human services. Interventions to reduce work stress may be directed either at the coping capacity of employees or at the working environment. Stress management training, stress inoculation techniques, relaxation methods, and social skills and fitness training can increase coping capacity. Several meta-studies show that such methods are effective in preventing adverse mental health outcomes in work environments.

Interventions to reduce stressor in the work environment include task and technical interventions (e.g. job enrichment, ergonomic improvements, reduction of noise); interventions targeted at improving role clarity, conflict management, and social relationships; and interventions that combine work-directed and person-directed interventions. These social interventions may cause but do not guarantee positive effects.

9.8.1. Improving the Mental Health of the Elderly

In the year 2000 more than 600 million people were aged over 60 in the world. This figure is expected to increase by 70% in the next 20 years. This rapid increase in the ageing population brings an increase of age-related physical and mental health problems, including an increased risk of dementia and age-related chronic diseases, and decreases in general mental well-being and quality of life. Different types of universal interventions have been successful in improving the mental health of elder population. Successful interventions include social support and community empowerment interventions and interventions promoting healthy lifestyle. Such programmes include exercise interventions, providing hearing aids, and a befriending programme

9.8.2. Moving forward in All Countries and Settings

Policy-makers, service providers, local authorities, and practitioners need to take full advantage of the interventions that have been developed, implemented, and tested elsewhere. However, retrieving relevant scientific knowledge from the fast-growing number of publications on evidence-based interventions is time-consuming. Especially in low-income countries, access to scientific journals and books is a serious problem.

Several organisations have developed or are currently developing internationally accessible database on evidence-based prevention and health promotion programmes, including those targeting mental health issues. Examples of such database are those provided by the USA Centres for Disease Control and Prevention (CDC), the Cochrane library, CASEL, the Substance Abuse and Mental Health Services Administration (SAMHSA), and the Implementing Mental Health Promotion Action (IMHPA) database developed by the Nijmegen Prevention Research Centre in relation with the European Union (EU) and WHO. The emerging evidence is limited, however, in that it is often based on only one or two welldesigned outcome studies mostly performed in affluent countries. Recently a new generation of studies has emerged aiming to compare outcomes of a programme or policy across countries or cultures.

Our knowledge on the robustness of findings across sites and their sensitivity to cultural and economic circumstances is still meagre. This is a serious problem in the context of the many recent efforts to disseminate "best practices" or "model programmes" across communities, countries, and regions. We need to be cautious in assuming that a programme that may work in one place will work again when implemented in different communities under different circumstances. Initiatives to disseminate effective or promising practices and to stimulate their adoption and implementation elsewhere should be combined with efforts to perform new outcome studies and to develop a supportive research policy.

The development of the evidence base for mental health promotion as a whole as well as for individual programmes is an incremental affair. It is not realistic to expect that every country, province, or district has the political will and the means to perform a range of controlled-outcome studies for each intervention they implement. Especially in low-income countries, the lack of resources pushes authorities and practitioners to take decisions on opportunities to promote mental health with a minimum of scientific evidence.

This stresses the need to study not only the outcomes of programmes but also their working mechanisms, principles, and effect moderators. Such knowledge and its translation into guidelines can support policy-makers, programme designers and practitioners in adapting programmes and policies to local needs, resources, and culture (reinvention), and increase the likelihood that these interventions will be effective. It also underlines the need to use the full spectrum of research methodologies, including less expensive qualitative studies, to build incrementally an evidence base that has validity for the country or community in question.

9.9. Mental Health Promotion in Low-Income Countries

Mental health is inextricably linked with human development, both because the social and economic determinants of human development are strongly associated with mental health and because poor mental health will compromise longevity, general health, and creativity. The factors that influence human development are those that influence mental health and it is likely that a dynamic relationship exists between human development and mental health.

A central challenge for mental health promotion in settings where infrastructure is poorly developed, human and material resources are scarce, and human rights practices cannot be taken for granted is that many of the social changes necessary for improved mental health are far more wide-reaching than some may immediately consider within the ambit of mental health promotion practice. The programmes discussed here focus on three areas of action: advocacy, empowerment and social support.

9.9.1. Advocacy

Advocacy aims to generate public demand for mental health and to persuade all stockholders to place a high value on mental health. Advocacy related to the mental health effects of alcohol abuse is an example.

The Global Burden of Disease study showed that alcohol abuse is a leading cause of social and family disruption, and morbidity and mortality, especially in men in developing countries. There is a growing awareness about the epidemic of alcohol abuse disorders, particularly in Latin America, Eastern Europe and South Asia. In India, the scale of social problems related to alcohol abuse has propelled the problem into a political issue: in recent years, entire elections have been fought, and won, on this issue.

One community-based approach to combating alcoholism and promoting the mental health of families in rural India began with participatory research to estimate the burden and impact of alcohol abuse in the community. The research demonstrated the enormous burden of the problem and identified a number of key prevention and promotion strategies. These included education and awareness building, action against drunken men, advocacy to politicians to limit the sale and distribution of alcohol in bars and shops, and mass oaths for abstinence.

The programme was implemented through a community movement led by young people and women and Daramukti Sangathana (Liberation from Liquor) village groups. The programme has led to a marked reduction in the number of alcohol outlets in the area and a 60% reduction in alcohol consumption. As a result, there is now more money for food, clothing, and welfare, and a reduction in domestic violence .

An unblinded matched community-based trial was conducted in Yunnan, China to investigate the effectiveness of a multifaceted community intervention to prevent drug abuse among youths. The programme, like the one in India, involved multiple sectors and leaders in the community and emphasised community participation and action, education in schools, literacy improvement, and employment opportunities. It led to a significant reduction in the incidence of drug abuse and a marked improvement in knowledge and attitudes towards HIV/AIDS and drug use .

9.9.2. Empowerment

Empowerment is the process by which groups in a community who have been traditionally disadvantaged in ways that compromise their health can overcome these barriers and can exercise all the rights that are due to them, with a view to leading a full, equal life in the best of health. An example of empowerment programmes that have had a mental health impact is the micro-credit schemes for alleviation of debt.

In many developing countries, indebtedness to loan-sharks and consequent economic uncertainty is a source of great stress and worry. These vulnerabilities arise because of the failure of the formal banking sector to extend short-term loans to the poorest in the community, who often lack the literacy or "creditworthiness" that are essential for accessing loans. Such uncertainties are compounded for small farmers who rely on seasonal rains for agriculture and face increasing competition from large, transnational companies. The combination of failures of the seasonal monsoon and competition has been identified as a major reason for debt in India, and the associated stress has led to hundreds of suicides in recent years.

The economic vulnerability of farmers in developing countries suggests the potential for mental health promotion in revising the process by which local banks assess the creditworthiness of people who belong to the poorest sectors of society. Radical community banks and loan facilities such as those run by SEWA in India and the Grameen Bank in Bangladesh have been involved in setting up loan facilities in areas where they did not exist and making loans to poor people who formerly did not have access to such facilities and services. Some evidence of the ability of such banks to promote mental health are available.

The activities of the Bangladesh Rural Advancement Committee (BRAC) span health care provision, education, and rural development programmes. The latter programmes are implemented at the level of individual villages, through Village Organisations (VO) that include the poorest members of each community. The primary activities are raising consciousness and awareness and compulsory savings. Once established, VO members can access credit for income-generating schemes. BRAC has carried out evaluations of a number of its programmes in different settings. Data used for evaluation come from baseline, seasonal, and ethnographic surveys, as well as from demographic surveillance. These data show that BRAC members have better nutritional status, better child survival, higher educational achievement, lower rates of domestic violence, and improved "wellbeing" and psychological health.

The empowerment of women and violence prevention in the community are the focus of other programmes and policies that have an influence on health.

9.9.3. Social Support

Social support strategies aim to strengthen community organisations to encourage healthy lifestyles and promote mental health. Inter sectoral alliances prove effective. An example of this is the promotion of maternal mental health. Poor maternal mental health has been shown to compromise the mother and development of babies. Interventions to improve the mother's health will improve the mother child relationship and outcomes for the child. For example, a trial from Zambia showed that mothers who received supportive and counselling interventions took more action to solve infant health problems, which is an indicator of maternal empowerment.

Women-to-women programmes in Peru have also been shown to increase maternal self-esteem (Broadhead et al. in press). Promoting childhood development in the midst of adversity has received attention in a recent WHO review. Nutritional and educational interventions were shown to improve psychosocial development in disadvantaged population. Interventions that combined nutritional and psychosocial components (such as parent stimulation) had the greatest impact. Full-scale programmes that include both components have been implemented in some of the world's poorest countries. Despite the favourable findings, however, it is important to recognise that children who are nutritionally or socioeconomically disadvantaged never fully catch up with children who are well nourished or privileged. There is a need to develop and test models of combined interventions that can reach a larger proportion of children and to evaluate the impact of such child focused interventions on adult mental and physical health.

Life skills education is a model of health promotion that seeks to teach adolescents to deal effectively with the demands and challenges of everyday life. Life skills include decision-making, problem-solving, creative and critical thinking, effective communication and interpersonal skills, self-awareness, and coping with emotions and stress. Life skills are distinct from other important skills that young people acquire as they grow up, such as numeracy, reading, and practical livelihood skills. There is evidence, entirely from developed countries so far, that life skills education is effective in the prevention of substance abuse, adolescent pregnancy, and bullying; improved academic performance and school attendance; and the promotion of mental well-being and health behaviours. This model is now being advocated, field-tested and implemented in a number of developing countries.

Those interested in promoting mental health in lower-income countries need to consider the extent to which the very concept of "mental health promotion" may imply a set of attitudes and assumptions that are not universally held. Mental health promotion programmes, intertwined as they are with fundamental assumptions about how people can and should live their lives, can be accused of amounting to strategies of cultural or biomedical imperialism. It is important to respond to this possible criticism by being reflexive about activities, but also important to avoid a form of radical relativism to disempower and dissuade exploration of what we know from other contexts to be good for mental health.

9.9.4. Effectiveness and Cost-Effectiveness

The evidence currently available on the health outcomes of government policies is patchy, at best. In short, there is good evidence for some interventions, particularly for individual-level interventions, but not for others. This is best illustrated by a recent extensive overview which aimed to synthesise evidence on policy interventions which either directly addressed mental health needs or which aimed to address factors strongly associated with poor mental health; the latter category included joblessness, homelessness, and low income.

Interventions for which there was evidence of effectiveness included home-based social support for pregnant women at high risk of depression, and social support and problem-solving or cognitive-behavioural training for unemployed people. Some interventions appeared to be harmful, including psychological debriefing after trauma. Other interventions appeared to be effective in addressing the determinants of poor mental health, rather than poor mental health itself, by offering educational, employment, welfare, or other supportive interventions.

Preschool day care seems to be beneficial, as it increases the chance of being in well-paid employment in adult life and thus reduces the risk of poor mental health. Many effective interventions aimed at tackling alcohol and drug misuse were also identified. There are many plausible policy interventions which may be expected directly or indirectly to affect mental health but for which strong evidence appears to be absent. Perhaps the most important of these plausible interventions is income supplementation. Poor mental health is consistently associated with poverty and deprivation, and it might be expected that increasing the incomes of the worst-off in society would improve mental and physical health. Yet good evidence of the positive health effects of income supplementation still seems to escape us.

Referring to the studies of income supplementation that had not assessed impacts on health, review authors bemoan a "lost opportunity". The same phrase can be applied to the evaluation of many other social interventions. This "absence of evidence" should not be mistaken for "evidence of absence". Plausible interventions can be applied in the absence of outcome evaluations, based, for example, on observational aetiological research; however, this example does illustrate again the need to foster evaluative research on the mental health and other outcomes of policies. Evaluative research like this, on the mental health outcomes of behavioural, organisational, psychological, or policy interventions, is still relatively uncommon in most countries. In addition, primary economic data on the relative costs and benefits of these interventions is lacking.

9.9.5. Difficulties with Evaluative Research

Five reasons have been suggested for the absence of evaluations of the impacts of policies on mental health. First, the window of opportunity in policy-making is short, leaving little time to develop complex outcome evaluations requiring long lead times; second, the policy environments change rapidly and data become obsolete quickly; third, experimental evaluations are often ill-suited to answer policy questions; fourth, the effects are often small and widely distributed, meaning that large samples and large units of randomisation are required; and, finally, funding for this type of evaluative research is limited .

While many of these obstacles can be (and sometimes have been) overcome, it is reasonable to suggest as Storm does that there is still a valuable role for longitudinal observational studies which can inform mental health policy by providing mental health monitoring data. The call for more robust outcome evaluations does not therefore preclude the contribution that can be made from observational data on determinants and indicators of mental health.

Policy-makers demand better evidence of the effects of upstream interventions such as policies. However, there are particular problems with collecting such evidence, as many of the major social determinants of mental and physical health are not amenable to randomisation for practical or political reasons. Examples include new roads, new housing, and area-based regeneration, all of which have been theorised to affect mental health. Recently, researchers in the field of health inequalities have recommended that more use should be made of "natural" experiments (e.g. changes in employment opportunities, housing provision, or other policy initiatives) as opportunities for estimating the health impacts of non-health sector policies. There is clear potential for positive mental health to be promoted through non-health policies, and assessments of the "spill over" effects of such policies will make an important contribution to the mental health evidence base.

9.9.6. Housing and Mental Health

There is some evidence from evaluative research which suggests that housing improvement improves mental health. As with employment, there is already good association evidence, in this case implicating a poor housing environment with poor health, but there are relatively few evaluations of the actual health impacts of housing policies. For example, a recent systematic review of the literature identified only 18 studies that had monitored health gains following major housing improvement. The studies themselves were diverse in terms of sample population, location, and type of housing improvement (e.g. they ranged from installation of central heating through to complete refurbishment and associated neighbourhood improvements), and the outcome measures varied widely.

However, evidence of a consistently positive mental health impact emerged. In one large prospective controlled study the degree of improvement in mental health was directly related to the extent of housing improvement, demonstrating a dose-response relationship. This consistent pattern of improvements in mental health suggests that, at least in affluent countries, improving housing does generate mental health gains. A number of other housing-related factors have been linked to variations in mental health, most notably housing tenure, housing design, moving house, and neighbourhood characteristics . Housing relocation has also been associated with loss of community, uprooting of social networks, and unsatisfied social aspiration, all of which may undermine mental and physical health.

9.9.7. Mental Health Impact Assessments

Clearly while policies aimed at improving public housing may have positive mental health effects, there is also significant potential for negative impacts, suggesting again the need to monitor and evaluate the actual health gains (and losses) caused by major changes to housing or other social policies. Expanding this monitoring and evaluation activity will be crucial for the success of mental health impact assessment, which (as with generic health impact assessment) aims to recommend changes to public policies, programmes, or projects in order to maximise any health benefits arising; mitigate any negative effects; and/or prioritise areas of investment to enhance mental health.

Successful and meaningful mental health impact assessment depends on, among other things, the availability of good evaluative evidence on the nature, size, and likelihood of predicted mental health impacts. Various sorts of evidence are clearly important too, particularly as evaluations of public health interventions are often scarce. Data from qualitative studies, for example, can be used to identify the existence, nature, and possible mechanisms for unprotected negative or positive impacts of interventions. Longitudinal life-course data can examine the long-term health effects of exposures to poor social and economic conditions and can identify aspects of the social environment or indeed population where interventions may be most appropriately targeted. Cross-sectional epidemiological data can be used to inform and prioritise proposed interventions based on the strength of observed associations, as for existing data on unemployment and poor mental health.

9.9.8. Cost-Effectiveness

Primary economic data on the relative costs and benefits of interventions is sparse. Economic evaluations are likely to be of key importance to decision-makers when determining whether or not to implement interventions. Economic evaluations aim to answer questions about the best use of resources. The application of economic theory and practice provides a useful set of methods for assessing the worth of promotional activities. Yet, as a methodology economic evaluation has not been extensively applied to health promotion. Studies in the area highlight the challenges associated with conventional methods for economic evaluation in the setting of health promotion, the long-term nature of anticipated benefits, and a shortage of sensitive suitable outcome measures.

As with clinical evaluation, the preferred design for economic evaluations is an RCT. The use of an RCT may be constrained by the fact that promotional activities are often pitched at the whole of a community rather than a specially recruited group. It may also be unethical or impractical to randomise subjects. For these reasons other methods of evaluation can be employed, such as cluster randomisation (comparison of whole population, such as groups of children in different areas), modelling, and observational studies. Although such studies lack the explanatory power of a control group they are more feasible to carry out and provide a closer representation of the real world. They are also able to study long-term costs and effects of upstream interventions over many years. Potential consequences of a mental health promotion strategy require appropriate and comprehensive measurement. Table 1 provides a set of potential domains of outcome that could qualify for inclusion in an economic study. The target beneficiaries may be individuals, communities, or population. At each level it is necessary to consider a number of consequences of the intervention, including intermediate outcomes (e.g. a change in behaviour), and final outcomes in terms of health (improved quality of life) and non-health (social productivity increased).

Changes in health may account for only one outcome and therefore consideration of non-health benefits of health promotion is required. The development of measures of community-level outcome is a needy area of research. As shown in Table 1, it is likely that resources or expenditures will be incurred at a number of levels, including by national or regional governments, local providers or communities, and individuals.

These will include costs associated with developing, implementing, and maintaining the health promotion programme; training costs; and, in particular, media costs. Measurement of these costs has posed a considerable challenge to date, owing to the many agencies involved as well as the joint nature of these cost components with other programmes, but some clear progress is now being seen in a number of related areas. For example, the costs of developing and maintaining programmes for the reduction of smoking, heavy alcohol use, unsafe sex, and cardiovascular disease risk factors have been recently compiled for different regions of WHO.

9.10. Mental Health Promotion Policies

The scope and outcome of mental health promotion activities is potentially wide. At the conceptual level, mental health can be and should be defined broadly. At a more practical level, it is useful to distinguish between interventions that have the primary goal of improving the mental health of individuals and communities, and others that are mainly intended to achieve something else but which enhance mental health as a side-benefit.

An example of the former is policies and programmes that encourage schools to prevent bullying and that improve parenting skills; policies and resources that ensure girls in a developing country attend school and programmes to improve public housing could be considered examples of the latter. This distinction helps narrow the scope of what can be called mental health promotion interventions and the allocation of relative responsibilities. Monitoring the effect on mental health of public policies relating to housing and education is, for instance, becoming feasible. The mental health programme or interests in a country or locality would need to advocate for this, watch that it occurs, and help use the findings. Other groups will need to do the work, however, and ensure that policies and practices are shaped by the findings.

The activities of mental health promotion may usefully be mainstreamed with health promotion, although the advocacy needs to remain distinct. Bearing in mind the intimate connection between physical and mental health, many of the interventions designed to improve mental health will also promote physical health and vice versa. Health and mental health are affected by non-health sector policies and a range of community interventions. The actions that promote mental health will often have as an important outcome the prevention of mental disorders.

The evidence is that mental health promotion is also effective in the prevention of a whole range of behaviour-related diseases and risks. It can help, for instance, in the prevention of smoking and of unprotected sex, and hence of acquired immunodeficiency syndrome (AIDS) or teenage pregnancy. These are not mental disorders. In fact, the potential of mental health promotion in preventing mental disorders is rather low compared with the potential contribution to the prevention of health-damaging and antisocial behaviours.

Mental health promotion: an important component of mental health policy Mental health promotion needs to be integrated as a part of policy in order to give it the status and strategic direction required for its successful implementation. Mental health policy is an organised set of values, principles, and objectives for improving mental heath and reducing the burden of mental disorders in a population. When well-formulated, mental health policy identifies and facilitates agreements for action among different stockholders, designating clear roles and responsibilities. If mental health policy is developed as part of broader social policy (rather than as a stand-alone policy or subsumed within a general health policy) the emphasis on mental health promotion is likely to be more substantial. There are more opportunities to engage a variety of stockholders representing different sectors in the development and implementation of the policy.

9.10.1. Components of Policy

A policy is composed of a vision statement, a statement of the values and principles underlying the policy, a set of objectives that help operationalise the policy, and a description of the major areas of action to achieve the policy objectives.

9.10.2. Vision Statement

The vision statement incorporates the main elements of the policy and sets out what is to be expected or achieved some years after its implementation. It should set high expectations as to what is desirable in the realm of mental health while being realistic within the resources available.

9.10.3. Values and Principles

Values refer to the judgments about what is considered desirable. Principles refer to the standards to guide actions and should emanate from values.

9.10.4. Objectives

Objectives are measurable goals that break the policy's vision into achievable tasks. They should aim to improve the health of a population and respond to people's expectations as well as provide financial protection against costs of ill-health.

9.10.5. Areas for Action and Srategics

Areas for action and strategies take the objectives of the mental health policy forward. Effective mental health policy considers the simultaneous development of several areas. Mental health promotion works at three levels: strengthening individuals, strengthening communities, and reducing structural barriers to mental heath . This framework is useful for conceptualising the entry points for promotion within a mental health policy. Structural barriers to mental health can be reduced through initiatives to reduce discrimination and inequalities and to promote access to education, meaningful employment, housing, health services, and support to those who are vulnerable.

9.10.6. General Framework

A general framework for considering mental health promotion strategies for whole communities and population is ideally supported by a government's social development as well as health and mental health policies. The framework has three aspects: a concept of mental health, strategies to guide mental health promotion, and a model for planning and evaluation.

9.10.7. Mental Health Promotion Strategies

The Ottawa Charter of Health Promotion provides a foundation for health promotion strategies and can be considered a guide for the promotion of mental health. It draws attention to individual, social, and environmental factors that influence health. The Ottawa Charter provides a sound framework for this positive approach, with its new public health philosophy and its emphasis on healthy policy, supportive environments, and control of health issues by people in their everyday settings. Its main strategies are building healthy public policies, creating supportive environments, strengthening community action, developing personal skills, and reorienting health services.

9.10.8. Building Healthy Public Policies

All public policies, not only those concerned with health, are considered relevant to health promotion.The Ottawa Charter recognises that most socialite structures and actions have an effect on health. Mental health promotion has an advocacy role to enhance the visibility and value of mental health to individuals and societies.

9.10.9. Creating Supportive Environments

Environmental health strategies have long been recognised as important to health. However, the focus has been largely on tangible areas. More attention needs to be given to the social and macro environments and the mechanisms through which they exert their influence on health. The complex interactions between an individual and their environment are contextual and mediated by individual experiences and skills, and social and cultural factors. A challenge for the promotion of mental health is to recognise the effect of these factors on environments and to develop interventions to modify them and indicators to evaluate impact and outcome.

9.10.10. Strengthening Community Action

Community action of people striving to achieve a mutual goal enhances social capital, creates a sense of empowerment, and increases the capacity and resilience of the community.

9.10.11. Developing Personal Skills

Information and its dissemination are critical to improving people's understanding of mental health. The concepts of health literacy are being used as guides to mental health literacy and contribute to mental health promotion.

9.10.12. Reorienting Health Services

The Ottawa Charter seeks to reorient health services from the medical model to a more inclusive holistic approach. A healthy health policy aims to achieve a balance between the two models. A complementary approach where "soft strategies" with their foundations in sociological domains are applied with the "interventions strategy" based on evidence from RCTs is suggested.

9.10.13. A model for Planning and Evaluation

A simple planning model helps implement the principles and strategies discussed. The determinants of mental health need to be described and operationalised in each setting with the aim of developing interventions.

9.10.14. Community Development as a Strategy

Community development is a people-centred approach. It aims to develop social, economic, environmental, and cultural well-being of communities with a particular focus on marginalised members. It has a participatory emphasis on identifying solutions to community problems based on local knowledge and priorities. Work done in rural areas of India exemplifies some aspects of the relationship between community development and promotion of mental health, even where the objectives of the programme may not include a specific focus on mental health.

Poverty, inequality, gender discrimination, and domestic violence are major contributors to mental illness within village settings in rural India. Related factors that have been linked with mental ill-health in the literature are also found, including low self-esteem, learned helplessness, less security, higher levels of adverse life events, social isolation, distress, unemployment, financial and economic deprivation, low social status, low levels of education, and female gender.

A large primary health care programme in rural Indian villages directly targeting poverty, inequality, and gender discrimination has led indirectly to significant gains in mental well-being. A key to the success of community development in these villages, and therefore to the improvement in mental health, has been an approach that is mindful of the needs, interests, and responsibilities of men and women, and that has focused on reducing the vulnerability and increasing the participation of women. As the interventions succeeded, the people realised the empowerment of working together and they became open to approaching other issues affecting the village such as health needs and caste discrimination.

9.12. Developing Sustainable Interventions

Sustainability in health promotion refers to the capacity of an intervention to continue to deliver benefits or health gains beyond the initial funding or "demonstration project" stage. Programmes are said to be sustainable if, given limited resources, efforts towards achieving the benefits continue. The research and theory on sustainability in the general field of health promotion has generated a number of useful examples, although the accumulated experience in mental health promotion alone is small.

A number of studies have shaped our thinking about sustainability. Goodman and Steckler led the way with a study that identified a cohort of programmes funded 10 years earlier and traced their progress. Their interest was in what factors predicted which programmes "lived" and which "died". The results surprised people. A key factor was the presence of a champion higher up in the host organisation, that is, someone who could advocate for the programme in the key decision-making forum. This research spawned a range of enquiry focusing attention on the factors in organisations that promote sustainability. The work drew attention to the fact that the way a programme is set up in the first place affects the likelihood of its continuation. The main features that are known to be associated with programme sustainability are:

— There is evidence that the programme is effective.
— Consumers/funders/decision-makers were involved in its development.
— The host organisation provides real or in-kind support from the outset.
— The potential to generate additional funds is high.
— The host organisation is "mature" (stable, resourceful).
— The programme and host organisation have compatible missions.
— The programme is not a separate unit but rather its policies, procedures and responsibilities are integrated into the organisation.
— Someone in authority (other than the programme director) is a champion of the programme at high levels in the organisation.
— The programme has few "rival providers" that would benefit from the programme discontinuing.
— The host organisation has a history of innovation.

— The value and mission of the programme fit well with the broader community.
— The programme has community champions who would decry its discontinuation.
— Other organisations are copying the innovations of the programme.

Research in sustainability is increasing but what to measure has become more complicated. Most work is focused on the presence or absence of programmes. But as Green points out, the proper goal of programme investment in health promotion is not the continuation of programmes per se, but the sustained capacity to address the problem at hand. This sustained capacity can take many forms and may remain very strong long after the name, the logo, and even the staff of the original programme have disappeared.

This directly ties research on sustainability to research on capacity building in health promotion . The new dynamic we need to address is less about adding programmes than it is about sharpening the functioning and capacity of systems e.g. primary health care systems, school systems to be more health-enhancing. The new frontier in sustainability research therefore is less about the technological aspects of programmes and more about programmes as change processes within organisations or communities. Programmes are opportunities to "recalibrate" systems to higher or better levels of functioning.

The new frontier also includes a more systematic analysis of the context within which programmes are provided and factors within that context (such as preexisting morale and interagency relationships) that might predict why some programmes wither over time while others flourish. An inter sectoral approach to mental health promotion The drivers of health lie outside the health sector. The Ottawa Charter "puts health on the agenda of policy makers in all sectors and at all levels" The Jakarta Declaration on Health Promotion goes even further in emphasising the need for inter sectoral collaboration:

There is a need to break through traditional boundaries within government sectors, between government and nongovernment organisations, and between public and private sectors. Cooperation is essential this requires the creation of new partnerships. This is even more important for mental health promotion. Those working collaboratively need to:

- — Build on existing activity in sectors, settings and organisations.
- — Create different partnerships for different purposes, at varying levels.
- — Create collaborative action "horizontally" within government departments and organisations, and between those expert in policy, practice, and research.

The need for collaborative practice in mental health promotion is firmly established by the sociopolitical and economic determinants of health. That is, influencing the determinants of health, such as enhancing social connectedness, ensuring freedom from discrimination and violence, and workplace and physical environmental change, will not be achieved by health sector action alone but rather through an inter sectoral approach. The multidisciplinary approach involving research, policy, and practice in employment, education, justice, welfare, the arts, sports, and the built environment aims to improve mental health through increased participation and social connectedness.

The settings for this practice can include schools, workplaces, and community arts or sports. Population groups include students, employees, employers, older people, low income communities, young people, and people from immigrant or minority groups. A diversity of strategies are used in these settings policy development; organisational change; theatre, narrative and consultative processes; community development and engagement; and changing the physical and social environment. The nature of collaboration will vary in settings and sectors and across different levels. Good outcomes almost always require shared planning and ownership across the sectors involved.

Collaboration and partnership take time and a commitment to ensuring shared goals and outcomes, however. The challenges include vertical funding within sectors, diverse professional backgrounds and views, competing priorities, various and often inequitable funding models, population group models of health, and complex decision-making processes. The most significant components of an inter sectoral approach to achieve better health outcomes include:

— The adoption of a unifying language with which to work across sectors.

— A partnerships approach to allocation and sharing of resources.

— A strengthening of capacity across the individual, organisational, and community dimensions.

Models of health that stem from indigenous paradigms are now seen to be models of good practice for all. Samoan communities have a "fonofale" model of health, for example, that is based on the traditional house or "fale". The roof represents cultural values and beliefs; the foundation is the family, nuclear and extended; and the four posts represent "physical biological", "spiritual", "mental and emotional", and "other" well-being (which includes variables such as gender, sexual orientation, age, and social class). Indigenous Australians, like Samoan and Maori communities, do not recognise a mental/physical divide. The interaction of elements is crucial in establishing well-being. This view of mental health necessitates the formation of partnerships with communities to develop mental health promotion that is culturally sensitive. International collaboration and the role of WHO.

It is clear that mental health promotion depends on inter sectoral collaboration and that most of the interventions may actually be the responsibility of sectors outside traditional mental health. There is also a clear need for advocacy, since mental health issues are often implicit rather than explicit and hidden rather than in the open. The need for international collaboration, hence, is crucial.

WHO, as the lead international agency responsible for health, has recognised the value of mental health and its promotion. Its activities emanate from the core conceptualisation of health as "a state of complete physical, mental and social well-being and not merely the absence of diseases or infirmity" given earlier. The WHO Constitution also stipulates some core functions. These include:

— "To foster activities in the field of mental health, especially those affecting the harmony of human relations".

— "To assist in developing an informed public opinion among all peoples on matters of health".

Numerous World Health Assembly (WHA) Resolutions related to mental health promotion have urged Member States to take steps to prevent mental illness and to promote mental health, and requested the Director-General to undertake steps to provide information and guidance regarding suitable strategies. In 2002, a resolution was adopted urging WHO to "facilitate effective development of policies and programmes to strengthen and protect mental health". It called for "coalition building with civil society and key actions in order to enhance global awareness-raising and advocacy campaigns on mental health". The role of WHO in mental health promotion can be briefly summarised as follows.

— To generate, review, compile, and update evidence on strategies for mental health promotion, especially from low and middle-income countries

Though there are numerous published studies on mental health promotion and, from time to time, efforts have been made to assimilate them, a comprehensive review of literature related to evidence-based research in this area has not been available. Promoting Mental Health: Concepts, Emerging Evidence, Practice and the accompanying work on prevention of mental disorders are an attempt to fill this gap. The evidence for effectiveness of mental health promotion is least available in areas that have the maximum need, such as in low and middle-income countries and conflict areas where mental health is especially compromised. More efforts are needed to generate evidence from these settings. Attention also needs to be paid to strategies that have been found to be ineffective or inappropriate on the basis of all kinds of evidence. Information on these is useful in order to prevent wastage of precious resources.

— To develop appropriate strategies and programmes.

WHO can assist countries in developing appropriate strategies and programmes for implementation. Some of the factors to be considered are :

— Evidence of effectiveness.

— The principle of prudence.

— Cultural appropriateness and acceptability.

— Financial and personnel requirements.

— Level of technological sophistication and infrastructure requirements.

— Overall yield and benefit.
— Potential for large-scale application..
— To facilitate partnerships and collaboration.

Mental health promotion requires the collective efforts of all organisations with responsibility for sectors that may have a direct or indirect impact on mental health. At the international level, these include professional associations, other international organisations, national governments, nongovernmental organisations, the health industry, and prospective donors. WHO is well positioned to forge strategic links with all these bodies and to develop effective programmes for mental health promotion. International organisations with which WHO regularly collaborates in this area are the International Labour Office (ILO), the United Nations Children's Fund (UNICEF), the Office of the United Nations High Commissioner for Refugees (UNHCR), and the World Bank.

References

Arboleda-Florez, J.E. and Stuart H.L.2001. "A public health perspective on violent offenses among persons with mental illness." *Psychiatric services* 52 . 654-9.

Bachman, K. 2002. "Health promotion programs at work a frivolous cost or a sound investment." *Conference Board of Canada.*

Durlak, J.A. 1998. "Why program implementation is important." *Journal of Prevention and Intervention in the Community 17* : 5-18.

Health Canada. 2000. "Best Advice on Stress Risk Management in the Workplace." Ottawa: Health Canada.

Keyes, Corey. "Complete mental health: An agenda for the 21st century." 2003. Quoted in C. Keyes & J. Haidt, *Flourishing. Positive psychology and the life well-lived.* Washington: American Psychological Association.

10

Social Work for Social Change

Changes in the distribution of power and authority are characteristic of the processes we call globalisation. The erosion of state sovereignty and the weakening of workers' rights are two obvious examples, but globalising capitalism also reshapes relations between women and men, adults and children, people of different cultures, and those with varying levels of technological competence.

This is not just a "power shift" from public to private interests, as Jessica Mathews has claimed, but a deeper and more complex process in which large numbers of people see their position systematically eroded by economic, social and political forces which work to the benefit of a small proportion of the world's population. Left unchecked, these forces will create an unprecedented degree of inequality and insecurity within and between societies, which will never be sustainable. NGOs who wish to promote "sustainable development" must therefore decide how they are going to address this situation.

At one level, the answers to this question are already apparent: those who are marginalised by global processes must have a "fairer deal" in economics, politics and social policy. However, at another level this is clearly insufficient without much deeper changes which encourage people to conserve scarce resources, share their wealth and opportunities, protect each-others' rights, and co-operate to advance the "common good" the long term health and welfare of the planet and its social fabric on which all our futures depend.

Making people "more competitive" and increasing their voice on the political stage will not promote the changes we seek unless we all learn to use the power we gain in less selfish and self-centred ways. The individualism and materialism that characterise globalising capitalism make this exceptionally difficult, for they undermine the co-operative solidarities and institutions we will need to confront the collective problems that will shape the 21st century transboundary pollution, global trade and capital flows, conflict and the mass movement of refugees and displaced persons. It is one of the paradoxes of globalisation that the more we succeed as individuals in the global marketplace, the more we may fail in other areas of our lives and our relationships with others, a failure which destroys the possibilities of similar success for millions of people now and many more in generations still to come. We cannot compete ourselves to a co-operative future, and if the future of the world depends on co-operation then clearly we must try something different.

10.1. Perspective of Change

From the perspective of change, all social systems rest on three bases: a set of principles that form an axiomatic basis of ethics and values; a set of processes the functioning mechanisms and institutions that under gird the system; and the subjective states that constitute our inner being our personal feelings and intuitions in the deepest sense. The first of these bases of change describes how we understand and rationalise the workings of the social order, while the third describes how we understand ourselves.

Some of this understanding revolves around our own place in the social order, but it also concerns the deeper questions we ask ourselves about the meaning of human existence and the nature of reality. When we explore any episode of historical change, we can identify how these three bases of change have worked together to produce a particular set of power relations. For example, the evolution of capitalism was built on the axiomatic basis that individual self-interest leads - by and large - to collective welfare. Its institutional structures are rooted in private property and market based incentives. And the subjective state of being most compatible with capitalism is a commitment to individual advancement and competitive behaviour.

The interaction of these three bases of change determines how different forms of power are exercised in society. Economic power is expressed in the distribution of productive assets and the workings of markets and firms; social power is expressed in the status and position awarded to different social groups; and political power defines each person's voice in decision-making in both the private sphere and public affairs. These systems of power combine to produce a "social order", and transforming this social order is the task of social change.

The social order that is emerging under globalising capitalism is one which excludes or oppresses certain groups of people, especially those already on the margins, women in labour-rich economies, and those with less access to skills and education wherever they live. However, the linkages that develop between these different bases of change are not immutable. Considerable room-to-manoeuvre exists to alter the ways in which they interact, in order to produce a different framework of power relations, a better set of outcomes, and a new social order.

It is this room-to manoeuvre that NGOs are trying to exploit in their work, they rarely do so consciously. For example, people may rebel against the subjective state that is promoted by a particular set of social transformations, as they have always done in relation to capitalism and the selfish values it breeds. Or, working from a different subjective or axiomatic base, they may experiment with new processes and institutions that try to produce the same economic outcomes with fewer social and political costs much as NGOs are doing today in their work with multinational corporations and corporate codes of conduct. The point about these experiments is not that they generate ready-made answers to questions of economic and social life, but that they consolidate a new bottom line of values, principles and/or personal behaviour from which better models may evolve in different ways in different contexts. Any relationship that is truly principled will lead towards a more fulfilling conclusion, even though we can never be sure what it will look like at any level of detail.

Social change requires a recognition and conscious integration of all three bases of change, and each of these systems of power. The problem is that few theoretical systems acknowledge this, and even fewer institutions use it as a framework to guide their practice. For example, social theories generally emphasise the axiomatic and institutional aspects of change, assuming that the related subjective states are simply universal descriptions of human nature, or that changes in subjective states follow automatically from changes in institutions and incentives. At the opposite extreme, many of the world's religions focus on the subjective states of persons and their transformation, and attach less importance to the institutional basis of social change.

Of course, not all religions are identical in this regard. Some assign more importance to outer behaviour; others to the inner motivation that lie behind it. But the tendency to privilege one category over another remains, condemning both social theories and religious teachings to a partial approach that downgrades the links between social change and personal transformation. A fresh look at the links between value systems, institutional processes, and subjective states is therefore essential, especially at a time when the processes of globalisation are altering each of these things and their relationships with each other.

10.2. Importance of Integration

Against this background, it is clear that social change requires us to adopt an integrated approach that looks for positive synergies between different bases of change and different systems of power. When change in one area supports change in another, there is more of a chance that the outcome will be sustainable, as when ethics of co-operation are matched by institutions through which they can be expressed, and the deeper personal commitment required to put those ethics into practice. Such self-reinforcing cycles of cooperation, sharing and stewardship are the key to a social order that enables all people to meet their basic needs for security, voice and equality of rights, with less of a risk that in doing so they will deny others the same opportunities for a fulfilling life.

It is important to recognise that integration is an exercise in re-balancing, not the wholesale replacement of one rationality by another. Not all competition generates overweening selfishness, nor do markets always exploit the poor or powerless. There are many examples that show how well-regulated markets and open trade can benefit the poor, and how economic growth can contribute to poverty eradication, the improved provision of social goods, and the conservation of natural and social capital. If it is unrealistic to focus on economic systems to the exclusion of personal change, it is equally unacceptable to call for inner transformation unless we can show how material needs will be met in less damaging ways.

However, the general point we wish to make remains valid: the emergence of a new social order requires those who gain power to make room for those with less; and all to use the power they gain in more responsible ways - not submerging their own self-interest entirely, but modulating it so that individual advancement is not bought at the cost of the broader conditions required for a secure and prosperous world.

History offers us at least some examples of such an integrated approach to social change, notably the Indian nationalist movement under Mahatma Gandhi. There, a powerful underpinning of personal belief in the power of universal love and nonviolence energised and sustained large numbers of ordinary Indians in the movement's tumultuous struggle for political independence. The testimony of those who participated in this movement suggests that ordinary people not only behaved and believed differently, but that they were different in a more fundamental sense. The failure of Indian politics and society to sustain these transformations in the post Independence era suggests that the process of integration was far from complete, but it does not invalidate the basic principles involved. Indeed, there are many more examples of incomplete integration which show why social change is so hard to achieve even when many of its component parts are in place.

We have chosen the example of "development-as empowerment" because such strategies are central to current NGO practice. By doing so we are not suggesting that NGOs are worse offenders in this respect than other institutions merely that even the socially-committed will be unsuccessful if they ignore the inner basis of change. Democratising the ownership of productive assets, capacities and opportunities continues to be a priority under globalisation, even if the nature of these things is changing. NGOs have been enthusiastic advocates of this form of empowerment for a decade and more, yet rarely do they question how people use the power they gain.

The assumption is that greater material security, organisational capacity and political voice will be used to promote the common interest as well as the advancement of those individuals who benefit directly. Is this true? In industrial societies, we know that rising wealth and democratic strength tend to produce a "culture of contentment", or the ebbing away of the "habits of the heart". In these circumstances, rising incomes may act as a block against more fundamental changes which are necessary for the rest of the population to attain the same level of satisfaction of their basic needs.

The same pattern is evident from many Third World communities, though it is often mediated by cultures which do encourage sharing and co-operation, especially in times of crisis. All over the world, broader economic participation breeds selfish and competitive behaviour unless it is accompanied by a deeper shift in values, and by new institutions which allow those values to be expressed in collective action. This is especially true in a world of integrated markets where the temptation to cut costs and "race each other to the bottom" is particularly strong.

Even when successful, economic empowerment may leave the structures of social power untouched, or even reinforce them, especially discrimination based on gender and age. Equally, social advancement may be unsustainable unless political power is also redistributed to the benefit of those who have less voice. Rarely do empowerment strategies make the links that could generate shifts in inner values strong enough to ensure that improvements in one area are not bought at the cost of damage done elsewhere.

10.3. Personal Change

Generalising from a theoretical situation like this is clearly dangerous, but the problem it describes is familiar: change at the subjective level is exceptionally difficult to achieve. It is rarely possible to generate sustainable changes in human behaviour simply by altering the rules and institutions that govern our lives. The missing ingredient is personal change, which acts as the wellspring of change in all other areas. Why?

A common lesson of experience is that processes of social change can easily lose touch with the values and principles that originally motivated and sustained them in the rough and tumble of the struggle. As a result, attempts to generate a new social order can unwittingly be poisoned by the "thieves of the heart" the negative feelings of personal ego, jealousy and fear that destroy one's inner tranquillity. If people are not caring and compassionate in their personal behaviour they are unlikely to work effectively for a caring and compassionate society.

Resisting these feelings, and developing the inner security required for a lifetime of co-operative endeavour, requires a disciplined process of self-reflection and contemplation about the values and purposes of our lives, and the desire and willingness to change ourselves. Undertaking this inner journey with courage can reward one with inner peace, greater energy and more effectiveness in one's actions, an expansive compassion in our attitudes towards others, and a tenderness of the heart that, on a mass scale, can have profound social implications.

We are not so native as to believe that a simple recognition of such things will change people's behaviour. But acknowledging the fact that the absence of personal change can impede the social transformations we are searching for can be salutary in the search for a more integrated approach. Nor are we speaking of social indoctrination under duress, exemplified by the Chinese Cultural Revolution or Maoist self-criticism sessions. Inner change cannot be forced by the self-righteous; when hearts and minds are brutalised into submission or silence there will be little energy left for social engagement. Our vision is a positive one: the energies unleashed by serious and deep-rooted personal transformation can fuel the search for more humane social and economic systems as little else can.

What kind of personal changes could energise the move towards an economic order which re-balances competitive and co-operative rationalities, a politics of dialogue rather than unrepresentative democracy, and a social policy that works against marginalisation and values the care and nurture of all human beings? The first principles for such change lie at the heart of the teachings of all the great religions "Love thy neighbour as thyself" in the Judaeo-Christian tradition, "See God in each other" in Sanskrit It is fascinating to recognise that the core of religious teaching concerns our feelings towards each other a deeply social statement as much as it is profoundly personal.

But to love our neighbours as ourselves, we must come to understand our own inner being to recognise that in our deepest essence we are compassionate, capable of giving love, and worthy of receiving it. Even when imperfectly established in this positive self-knowledge, we can identify more easily with the same inner being in other people - what the Hindu Vedanta calls "unityconsciousness." It then becomes easier to empathise with what it means to be the "other" from whom we usually distance ourselves in subtle or overt ways.

That shift is crucial because it provides the foundation for personal behaviour which is more expansive and less damaging to others for why would we damage the life chances of someone who is as much a part of our Selves? The irony of today's globalised world is that, as knowledge about each other grows, so do the criteria of "otherness" that breed selfishness, greed, anger and hatred the fault-lines of race, ethnicity, gender, sexual orientation, caste, class, nationality, region, and economic blocs. We will return to this theme when we come to the role of NGOs in constituency-building.

One question that often comes up in this context is whether more attention to inner transformation will divert one's energy away from social change. A related question is whether greater personal tranquillity will sap the angry energy needed to struggle against injustice. Anger is certainly a powerful form of energy that can be harnessed, particularly in the struggles of the socially oppressed. But over time it can be corrosive of those who use it, becoming a deadly and increasingly-uncontrolled weapon. Inner centredness, on the other hand, can take more controllable but no less powerful forms. Those who have espoused nonviolence, in India, South Africa, the USA and elsewhere, have not been weak.

Their courage and energy have often been startling, and their example has sometimes and unexpectedly catalysed a process of transformation in their opponents. Inner-centredness can release enormous energy for the struggle against social injustice without having to draw upon the destructive legacy of anger or hatred. Are there other dangers in the call to link social to personal change? Throughout the ages, organised religions have often spawned fundamentalist bigotry and a narrowing of the realm of personal beliefs to accord with what is considered by some to be "moral" conduct. Our own age shows us the dangers that religious fundamentalism brings to social institutions when it spills over from the private to the public realm.

Social conservatism is rarely more dangerous than when it cloaks itself in religious garb that cannot adequately be challenged by rationalist arguments for social justice because it assumes an other-worldly authority. The rising tide of religious bigotry across the world in recent decades is one of the reasons why space for serious discussion of the links between social and personal change has been so narrow. The other is a woolly-headed and self-indulgent "new egoism" that confuses material detachment with a wholesale retreat from social engagement.

However, disciplined self-enquiry of the kind we have described provides a way out of this impasse, by constantly exposing attitudes and behaviours that masquerade as compassionate or detached. Paradoxically, the expansive compassion and tenderness of heart of which we speak calls for all the toughness of mind, courage and flexibility that are also required in the outer struggle for social change.

10.3.1. Role of NGOs in Personal Change

NGOs are unlikely vehicles for the direct transformation of the individual, though the best traditions of the sector - like selfless service among volunteers and the courage to undertake the seemingly impossible sometimes generate experiences that come close to the spiritual realm. However, the model of social change we have described makes it clear that there are many indirect ways to encourage the transformation of people's subjective states, so long as our approach to processes and institutions is properly-integrated in other words, that the goal of personal change is a conscious and explicit element in all that we do.

Most of us know that our true Self is loving and compassionate, but feel we must disguise it in the street fighting of everyday life. However, when we consciously create more institutional spaces for inner transformation, we can begin to exercise our economic, social and political responsibilities in ways which both draw from and encourage the personal changes we are looking for. It may sound romantic to call for an economics or politics that is loving and compassionate, but this is exactly what we can shape through conscious action.

We want to look briefly at three areas in which NGOs have a crucial role to play in fostering these integrated changes: their programme activities (the work they support in the field, directly or through others); their fund-raising and constituency building work; and their own organisational praxis the ways in which values are expressed in structures, systems and management.

10.3.2. Programme Activities

The overriding challenge for NGOs in the 21st century will be to help re-balance the competitive and co-operative forces that motivate each one of us, whether in economics, politics or social life. They can do this by regulating - and ultimately reconstructing all systems of power in ways which achieve three things: a more equal distribution of what they deliver, less costly ways of producing it, and more co-operative values and behaviour among those involved as producers or consumers. When we talk of "costs", we explicitly include damage done to ourselves, the social fabric that sustains us as fully-human beings, and the environment we all depend on for our future.

Although NGOs rarely see their work in this way, there are plenty of experiments already underway which show how such integrated transformations might work at a much larger scale:

— In economics for example, new forms of enterprise are competing effectively in open markets but distributing work and profits with a social purpose, backed up by codes of conduct to level up working conditions and supported by a growing movement for "ethical consumption." The links that are developing between peasant production systems in Latin America and supermarket campaigns in industrialised countries provide a good example of this wave of the future. The best NGO credit schemes provide another.

— In politics, Latin American municipalities are inventing new forms of "dialogic democracy" in which representatives from civil society and business share in decisionmaking with local government. Similar experiments are underway in other parts of the world like India's "Panchayati Raj" system of decentralised governance and around Agenda planning, post-conflict reconstruction, and the elaboration of national development strategies. These innovations give everyone a voice in decisionmaking and reduce the dangers of "elected dictatorships" which favour the interests of the rich. At the same time, they build new capacities for dialogue and co-operation across old institutional boundaries.

— In the area of social policy, organisations like SEWA in India and the Grameen Bank in Bangladesh are promoting different ways of sharing the costs and responsibilities of childcare so that women can increase their incomes and assets without sacrificing their own health and welfare to the interests of their children. These innovations achieve a better set of trade-off between social and economic outcomes, challenging the structures of social power in the process and building the material security people need to participate in dialogic politics.

Although personal change is rarely an explicit element in these experiments, there is a clear linkage between the processes and institutions they foster, and the subjective states they grow from and reinforce. Ethical production systems are not viable without ethical consumers, for example; equitable social policies are impossible if men and women are unwilling to share the burden of paid and unpaid work. Such experiments can consolidate their gains by making personal change a more explicit part of their agenda, so that new, more co-operative institutions can be backed up by corresponding innovations in values and behaviour.

Mainstreaming these experiences will require pioneers in all walks of life, but government and business are unlikely to spearhead moves for radical changes which involve reduced consumption or the ceding of authority to non-state actors. The major pressure must come from those parts of civil society who are committed to new social and economic models. It is NGOs and other civic groups that are already lobbying corporations to be more responsible, organising collective approaches to welfare, and acting as a counterweight to vested interests in decentralised politics. We believe that these activities will dominate civic action in the next fifty years.

10.3.3. Constituency-Building

Although there are many interesting experiments like these to report on, they do not add up to much when compared to the forces that really drive change in the contemporary world. What are missing are scale, depth and sustainability - to make these innovations the norm rather than the exception. Achieving those goals requires a mass base to support radical change, and that in turn requires an inner transformation on a scale not realised in any period in history. Motivating large numbers of people to shift to more co19 operative behaviour and persuade those in power to create more inclusive institutions goes against the heart of the current socioeconomic order. Without personal change towards more caring and compassionate ways of being and dealing with each other, it will be very hard to generate the momentum to bring about such a shift.

At first sight this might appear to be the job of the churches and other faith based groups in civil society, not of development NGOs. It is no accident that dissatisfaction with current models of development and foreign aid has coincided with a resurgence of interest in the developmental role of the Faiths, even in such non-spiritual organisations as the World Bank. However, there are a number of reasons for thinking that development NGOs also have a crucial role to play, not least because the established religions so often fail to live up to their theology. More broadly, it is the secular world of environmental and social activism that forms at least as powerful a connection in most people's lives between the "personal and the political."

We no longer reserve our moral expressions for church on Sunday; indeed, the increasing diffusion of moral action through civil society and beyond is one of the most heartening developments of the late-20th century. Development NGOs have been an important part of this expanding moral space, but they have never fulfilled their potential as constituency-builders on the wider stage. In contrast to environmental NGOs, they rarely use their high levels of public trust and extended fund-raising networks as channels for personal transformation and lifestyle change, and their membership of civil 20 society (both domestic and international) is increasingly called into question.

Consequently, we still lack institutional expression for the exercise of conscience on the scale that would be necessary to resolve world poverty or intervene against fundamental abuses of human rights. Without such mass-based institutional pressure, there will be another Rwanda, and then another.

The decline of foreign aid provides a window of opportunity to advance a transformation agenda, by refocusing attention on international co-operation and the values that make co-operation work. There won't be a constituency for international co-operation unless there is a commitment to co-operative living generally, for why should people cooperate with distant strangers if they do not do so with their neighbours? Global regimes impose clear limitations on personal autonomy, so it won't be the United Nations that will solve global warming, but you and us by reducing the energy we use in our homes, cars and factories. Co-operation requires the constant exercise of co-operative values, rather than the peddling of stereotypes about other people who need a "sponsor" to "save" them. This implies relationships among equals, and the acceptance of responsibility to put our own house in order. And at root, that is always a matter of personal change.

10.3.4. Organisational Praxis

The claim that development NGOs are explicitly "values-based" organisations is something of an article of faith these days. There is less evidence that NGOs put these values into practice in their organisational structures and behaviour, or even that they are clear what their core values are. This is a major weakness, because it is the link between values and actions that is crucial in generating legitimacy when arguing the case for change. Institutions must be seen to implement values as the bottom line in their own practice if they are to build a coalition in support of those values on the wider stage. The best way NGOs can help to foster the mass movement that has been missing from the field of international development since the end of the Cold War is for them to be exemplars of the society they want to create - to show that it is possible to be an effective organisation which values its employees as it does its partners, fights discrimination, practices 22 internal democracy, and always uses the organisational power it has in liberating ways.Unfortunately, few development NGOs have done this. For one thing, high levels of dependence on foreign aid and the limitations of contractual relationships make it very difficult to expand into real values-based action there are simply too many compromises that have to be made. For another, NGOs are not immune to class, race, and gender problems, nor the oppression and sexual exploitation they breed. Behind the screen of progressive attitudes toward social change in the world outside, the world inside the organisation can be an ethical morass. Such organisations cannot be the basis of far-reaching social change.

Fortunately, this point is beginning to be taken to heart in many NGOs. The link between personal change and organisational effectiveness is increasingly being recognised, even though its practical application remains weak. These pioneers stress that is certainly possible to help others effectively, but only if we realise that in doing so they help us to grow to a fuller, more independent knowledge of ourselves closing the circle once more between personal change and change in the wider world. If our own practice is autocratic, closed, and chauvinist it is unlikely that we will be able to encourage others to be democratic, open and egalitarian.

What remains is for NGOs to experiment more seriously with management practices, organisational structures, and personnel policies that create the feedback loops we are looking for between personal change, institutional performance, and wider impact. A start has been made in this direction, but a huge area remains unexplored. Perhaps a revisioning of NGO strategy around values-based action in programme work, constituency building and organisational praxis would be a useful place to start.

10.4. Community-Based Policy Practice

Although there is not complete agreement on what constitutes policy practice, there is general agreement that social workers must assume policy roles and learn to perceive policy practice as among the skills of a practising social worker, not the purview of a policy expert. Bruce Jansson first developed the concept of policy practice for social workers in the mid-1980s as a specific intervention designed to make changes in the political arena. Wyers and Figueira McDonough began calling for an increased recognition of policy practice interventions as a necessary continuum of skills for social workers to help clients at larger systems levels.

There are many ways that authors have conceptualised the various components of policy practice; as political social work, class advocacy, political advocacy, community practice, social action, and legislative advocacy, to copy righted material name a few. In 1991, Wyers attempted to integrate some of the micro and macro approaches to policy practice by defining a model that included a continuum of policy practice skills, including

— A policy expert one who conducts policy analysis and provides expert knowledge and skills pertaining to the policy arena.

— The social worker as a change agent working in an external environment, meaning that she or he works outside of her or his organisation advocating for legislative initiatives, working in policy development, or working for change in services.

— Working for change in his or her own agency.

Being a policy conduit for change, meaning being an expert in an area and providing education on needed changes to policymakers. Wyers concluded by stating that "all social workers need to participate in the modification of social policy that is harmful to clients and the elimination of policy deficits by working for new policy". McInnis Dittrich agreed that the meaning of professional social work, by definition, means integrating social welfare policy and social work practice.

However, most definitions of policy practice are largely defined by interventions designed to change policies in legislative, agency, or community settings from a largely macro practice perspective. Figueira- McDonough defines policy practice as the formal process of influencing both legislative and judicial decision making, as well as constituency- based patterns of influence in communities and organisations.

She outlines four methods of policy practice in these arenas: legislative advocacy, reform through litigation, social action, and policy analysis. Jansson defines policy practice as efforts to change policies in legislative, agency, and community settings. He further differentiates policy advocacy from policy practice by stating that policy advocacy focuses on performing policy practice methods with powerless groups, to improve their resources and opportunities. However, he admits that he uses the terms interchangeably throughout much of his discussion.

A related term, which has been used repeatedly in the literature is, political social work. Political social work has been defined differently depending on the author. In a discussion of these differing definitions, Fisher suggested that "policy implementation, electoral activity, community organising macro methods were what most people in the profession understood as political social work". This approach to political social work focuses largely on a more traditional sense of politics, such as "legislation, the executive branch, interest groups, lobbying, working with the media, and running for office".

Contrary to this approach is a more integrated approach that sees all social work as political social work, regardless of what level of practice, micro or macro, one focuses her or his interventions. For this integrated approach, political social work is seen as social work based on a politicised understanding of social welfare, and methods of practice are integrated. Thus, the goal is to train politicised social workers who see issues of power and justice as central to understanding and addressing social problems, as well as confronting client needs.

Many authors have used the term advocacy in their definition of what we consider policy practice skills. Advocacy related to policy practice must be distinguished from case advocacy because of the systemic nature of the change. For example, if a social worker has a client who experiences a problem manoeuvring through the maze of social programs and we assist her or him in gaining resources, then we are performing case advocacy. But if we see client after client having the same problem, then it becomes a waste of valuable time and resources to individually advocate for each client. That is when policy practice comes into play. We want to advocate making a policy change so that all of the clients can receive these services, and we do not have the time to advocate for each one of them individually. It is time to perform policy practice.

But even within the description of class advocacy, there is a rather complex array of definitions of various attributes of advocacy.

For example, Schneider and Lesser differentiate in great detail their definition of advocacy as the "mutual representation of a client or clients or a cause in a forum, attempting to systematically influence decision making in an unjust or unresponsive systems" from other forms of social work practice.

For example, they suggest that advocacy is a form of social action, incorporating many of the concepts of system level change and influence, but it is specifically responsible to a client or client system in a forum within an exclusive and mutual relationship. Distinguishing their definition from community organising (CO), they state that CO is primarily an organising and capacity- building function with emphasis on collective support through education and participation to address common concerns.

Ezell created a typology of different forms of advocacy, indicating that there was actually little variation in their meaning, although scholars have seemed to have a preference for one or the other on a theoretical level. He includes class advocacy, an intervention on behalf of a group of clients who share the same problem; systems advocacy, changing policies and practices affecting all persons in a certain group; policy advocacy, efforts to influence those who work with laws, public programs, or court decisions; political advocacy, which appears the same as class, policy, and systems advocacy; legislative advocacy, promoting and influencing legislation; and community advocacy, organising and educating on behalf of communities who have similar problems or needs but may not be known to each other.

Federalism is a system of government that divides responsibilities of governing among various levels of government. In the United States, responsibilities have traditionally been divided horizontally across the executive, legislative, and judicial branches, but also vertically among the federal, state, and local levels of government. In his historical account of federalism in this country, Linhorst explains that prior to the Great Depression U.S. Federalism was characterised by dual federalism, where clear roles were assigned to the federal and state governments, with states holding considerable power. Cooperative federalism developed after the Depression, however, because state governments needed assistance in response to adverse economic conditions. Federal power and control over programs increased drastically during this time. Throughout the 1960s cooperative dualism existed in this country, until the current state of federalism was initiated by President Nixon. Believing that the federal government had grown too large, he provided block grants and general revenue- sharing dollars to local governments, increased uniformity in the food stamp program across states, and initiated supplemental security income.

This state of federalism was dubbed "New" federalism. It did not decrease revenues to the state. but gave them more flexibility to create programs that were locally appropriate. But President Reagan took the concept of new federalism to another level, by supporting less government at all levels, devolving federal power to the states, and at the same time cutting federal social programs and reducing funds originally targeted to state and local governments. The 104th Congress took devolution even further by seeking to eliminate federal entitlement programs, reducing overall federal spending even further, and cutting taxes at the same time. Although most of the responsibility for implementing social programs has now shifted to the states, the federal government continues to be the primary funder.

Much of the decisionmaking authority now rests with state and local governments, making it easier for agencies to create their own rules and regulations based on local mandates. Thus, the decision-making authority is much closer to home. The social work literature is replete with research on how the way devolution has been handled has hurt the poor, decreased protection of oppressed populations, and increased the inequities in social protection between the states.

However, devolution also had the consequence of bringing much of the power base and decision making back to state and local governments. Whereas in the past, policy practitioners spent much of their time working at the federal level of government, the changing nature of federalism requires social workers to adapt their policy practice to the state and local levels. One of the consequences of the new federalism is that although few initiatives have been enacted by the federal government that have helped our constituents, considerable gains have been made at the state level. Unfortunately, the research does not indicate that the new federalism has helped promote social equity or justice at the local levels, yet federal oversight is still needed to ensure that local communities meet the needs of their citizens.

With the state of new federalism, it is unlikely that the federal government is willing to provide much oversight for citizen protection. However, because many problems are community based, meaning that the problems and often the solutions—can be found in our own communities, social workers are in a unique position to hold local communities responsible as well.

What social workers need is the knowledge and skills to be able to identify problems, seek out alternative solutions, and make changes that can assist as many community members as possible. Although interventions at the federal level are still important, it is an opportune time to turn our attention to state and local policies because they now have much of the decision- making authority. They are closer to home, are easier to communicate with, have a better understanding of the local problems that we encounter, and have an increased likelihood of successful policy interventions at a more local level.

Social workers should engage in social and political action that seeks to ensure that all people have equal access to the resources, employment, services, and opportunities they require to meet their basic human needs and to develop fully. Social workers should be aware of the impact of the political arena on practice and should advocate for changes in policy and legislation to improve social conditions in order to meet basic human needs and promote social justice. There are six principles in the code of ethics from which the standards derive.

If a problem is affecting a large number of people, then something is amiss. Either a community is having economic problems of some sort that are affecting a large number of people, a policy that is supposed to support families is not working properly, or an agency that is supposed to supply a certain service is not functioning effectively. All of these issues point to a target system that needs an intervention of some sort. This is policy practice.

The goal of social justice as part of both the social work code of ethics and our profession's person- in- environment perspective has been a challenge for social workers. Although social work as a profession has made a commitment to social justice for the families we work with, social workers are often challenged because they lack skills in the strategies and techniques of policy practice needed to realise policy change.

As Gordon points out, by not taking a leadership role in the formulation and implementation of the policies that affect our clients, the profession's person in environment perspective is largely missing from programs and services. Learning policy practice methods and skills is seen as a "necessary means to the implementation of the neglected goal of social justice". The integration of policy practice methods emphasising social and organisational change with direct practice content is a challenge. But this integration is essential to broad enter influence that social service workers have to promote positive impacts in our clients' lives.

References

Brierley, D. 2003. *Growing Community: Making Groups Work with Young People*, Carlisle: Authentic Lifestyle.

Cooke, I. and Shaw, M. 1997. *Radical Community Work. Perspectives from practice*, Edinburgh: Moray House.

Elsdon, K. T. 1991. *Adult Learning in Voluntary Organizations. Volume 1: case studies 1 and 2*, Nottingham: University of Nottingham Department of Adult Education.

Francis, D. and Henderson, P. 1992. *Working with Rural Communities*, London: Macmillan.

Gilchrist, A. 1995. *Community Development and Networking*, London: Community Development Foundation.

Henderson, P., Jones, D. and Thomas. D. N. eds. *The Boundaries of Change in Community Work*, London: George Allen and Unwin.

Bibliography

Arboleda-Florez, J.E. and Stuart H.L.2001. "A public health perspective on violent offenses among persons with mental illness." *Psychiatric services* 52 . 654-9.

Bachman, K. 2002. "Health promotion programs at work a frivolous cost or a sound investment." *Conference Board of Canada*.

Batten, T. R. and Batten M. 1967. *The Non-Directive Approach in Group and Community Work*, London: Oxford University Press.

Brierley, D. 2003. *Growing Community: Making Groups Work with Young People*, Carlisle: Authentic Lifestyle.

Butcher, H., Glen, A., Henderson, P. and Smith, J. eds. 1993. *Community and Public Policy*, London: Pluto Press.

Calouste Gulbenkian Foundation. 1968. *Community Work and Social Change. A report on training*, London: Longman. 171 + xiii pages.

Calouste Gulbenkian Foundation. 1973. *Current Issues in Community Work. A Study by the Community Work Group*, London: Routledge and Kegan Paul.

Cannan, C., Berry, L. and Lyons, K. 1992. *Socicl Work and Europe*, London: Macmillan.

Cooke, I. and Shaw, M. 1997. *Radical Community Work. Perspectives from practice*, Edinburgh: Moray House.

Curno, P. ed. 1978. *Political Issues and Community Work. Community Work 4,* London: Routledge and Kegan Paul.

David N. Thomas. 1983. *The Making of Community Work*, London: George Allen and Unwin. 3

Durlak, J.A. 1998. "Why program implementation is important." *Journal of Prevention and Intervention in the Community 17* : 5-18.

Elsdon, K. T. 1991. *Adult Learning in Voluntary Organizations. Volume 1: case studies 1 and 2*, Nottingham: University of Nottingham Department of Adult Education.

Francis, D. and Henderson, P. 1992. *Working with Rural Communities*, London: Macmillan.

Gilchrist, A. 1995. *Community Development and Networking*, London: Community Development Foundation.

Hardcastle, D. A. and Powers, P. R. 2004. *Community Practice: Theories and Skills for Social Workers* 2e, New York: Oxford University Press.

Harrris, V. ed. 1994. *Community Work Skills Manual* 2e, Newcastle: Association of Community Workers.

Health Canada. 2000. "Best Advice on Stress Risk Management in the Workplace." Ottawa: Health Canada.

Henderson, P. and Thomas, D. N. eds. 1981. *Readings in Community Work*. George Allen and Unwin.

Henderson, P., Jones, D. and Thomas. D. N. eds. *The Boundaries of Change in Community Work*, London: George Allen and Unwin.

Hoggett, P. ed. 1997. *Contested Communities: experiences, struggles, policies*, Bristol: Policy Press.

Jacobs, S. and Popple, K. eds. 1994. *Community Work in the 1990s*, Nottingham: Spokesman. 177 pages.

Jones, D. 1977. 'Community Work in the UK' in H. Specht and A. Vickery. eds. *Integrating Social Work Methods*, London: George Allen and Unwin.

Jones, D. and Mayo, M. eds. 1974. *Community Work One*, London: Routledge and Kegan Paul.

Kelly, T. 1970. *A History of Adult Education in Great Britain. From the Middle Ages to the Twentieth Century*, Liverpool: Liverpool University Press.

Keyes, Corey. "Complete mental health: An agenda for the 21st century." 2003. Quoted in C. Keyes & J. Haidt, *Flourishing. Positive psychology and the life well-lived.* Washington: American Psychological Association.

Kuenstler, P. ed. 1961. *Community Organization in Great Britain*, London: Faber and Faber.

Leaper, R. A. B. 1968. *Community Work. Common ground explored in an experimental course*, London: National Council of Social Service.

Loney, M. 1983. *Community Against Government. The British Community Development Project 1968-78: a study of government incompetence*. Heinemann.

Lupton, R. D. 2005. *Renewing the City: Reflections on Community Development and Urban Renewal*, London: InterVarsity Press. 240 pages.

Mayo, M. 1975. 'Community development: a radical alternative?' in R. Bailey and M. Brake. eds. *Radical Social Work*, London: Edward Arnold.

McDonald, D. and Tungatt, M. 1992. *Community Development and Sport*, London: Community Development Foundation. 42 + x pages.

Midgley, J. et al. 1986. *Community Participation, Social Development and the State*, London: Methuen.

Ministry of Education. 1944; 1946. *Community Centres*, London: HMSO.

Ministry of Housing and Local Government. 1969. *People and Planning. Report of the Committee on Public Participation in Planning*,. 'The Skeffington Report'), London: HMSO.

National Institute of Social Work. 1982. *Social Workers. Their Role and Tasks*. The Barclay Report). Bedford Square Press.

Office of the Deputy Prime Minister. 2002. *Tenants Managing: Evaluation of tenant management organizations in England*, London: Office of the Deputy Prime Minister.

Ohri, A., Manning, B. and Curno, P. eds. 1982. *Community Work and Racism. Community Work 7,* London: Routledge and Kegan Paul.

Pearse, M. and Smith, J. 1990. *Community Groups Handbook*, Nottingham: Journeyman.

Pierson, John. 2007). *Going Local: Working in Communities and Neighbourhoods*. London: Routledge

Popple, K. 1995. *Analysing Community Work. Its theory and practice*, Buckingham: Open University Press.

Principal Community Education Officers, Scotland. 1992. *Community Development in the Community Education Service*, Edinburgh: Scottish Community Education Council.

Putnam, R. D. 2000. *Bowling Alone. The collapse and revival of American community*, New York: Simon and Schuster.

Reynolds, J. *et al.* 1993. *A Town in Action: Voluntary networks in Retford. Volume 4 of Adult Learning in Voluntary Organizations*, Nottingham: University of Nottingham Department of Adult Education.

Robertson, C. and Shaw, J. 1997. *Participatory Video. A practical approach to using video creativity in group development*, London: Routledge.

Ross, M. 1955. *Community Organization. Theory, Principle and Practice*. 1967 edn.), New York: Harper & Row.

Scottish Executive. 2003. *Working and learning together to build stronger communities. Working draft Community Learning and Development Guidance, Edinburgh*: Scottish Executive.

Smith, J. 1991. *Community Development and Tenant Action*, London: Community Development Foundation. 42 + x pages.

Smith, L. and Jones, D. eds. 1981. *Deprivation, Participation and Community Action. Community Work 6,* London: Routledge and Kegan Paul.

Stewart, S., Reynolds, J. and Elsdon, K. T. 1992. *Adult Learning in Voluntary Organizations. Volume 2: case studies 3 - 15*, Nottingham: University of Nottingham Department of Adult Education.

Taylor, M. 1991. *Signposts to Community Development*, London: Community Development Foundation.

Twelvetrees, A. 1982; 1991; 2001. *Community Work*, London: Palgrave Macmillan.

Van Rees, W. *et al.* 1991. *A Survey of Contemporary Community Development in Europe*, The Hague: 7 Opbouwteksten. Alinsky, S. D. 1946. *Reveille for Radicals*. 1969 edn.), New York: Random House.

Willmott, P. 1963. *The Evolution of a Community. A study of Dagenham after forty years*, London: Routledge & Kegan Paul.

Young, A. F. and Ashton, E. T.1956. *British Social Work in the Nineteenth Century*, London: Routledge and Kegan Paul.

Younghusband, E. L. 1959 *Report of the Working Party on Social Workers in the Local Authority Health and Welfare Services*, London: HMSO.

Index